A critical history of ESOL in the UK, 1870–2006

Sheila K. Rosenberg

promoting adult learning

© 2007 National Institute of Adult Continuing Education
(England and Wales)

21 De Montfort Street
Leicester LE1 7GE

Company registration no. 2603322
Charity registration no. 1002775

NIACE has a broad remit to promote lifelong learning opportunities for
adults. NIACE works to develop increased participation in education and
training, particularly for those who do not have easy access because of class,
gender, age, race, language and culture, learning difficulties or disabilities, or
insufficient financial resources.

For a full catalogue of all NIACE's publications visit
www.niace.org.uk/publications

Cataloguing in Publications Data
A CIP record for this title is available from the British Library

ISBN 978-1-86201-268-4

Cover design by Creative by Design Limited, Paisley
Designed and typeset by Avon DataSet, Bidford-on-Avon, Warwickshire
Printed and bound by Ashford Colour Press, Gosport

Contents

Contents

A reader for ESOL students published by the National Extension College in 1979 and drawn from Amrit Wilson's *Finding a Voice*, Virago 1978

A history of Neighbourhood English classes, established by Ruth Hayman in 1969 to provide ESOL tuition across north London. As a charity it attracted its own funding but it also worked with local LEAs to increase and improve provision.

Volume 2. Published by Longman in 1942 to help the thousands of Allied service personnel stationed in the UK to learn English for the war effort.

Published jointly by the Home Office and National Extension College in 1980 to provide background information and teaching notes for teachers all over the UK who were supporting the 'boat people'.

FOREWORD

Sheila Rosenberg's work, for the first time, describes how a series of migrations created the need for the teaching of English to speakers of other languages (ESOL) in the UK from the 1870s onwards. Like all migrations, these were sometimes driven by the need to escape persecution and the ravages of war, sometimes by the desire for better-paid work and a new life, sometimes by the necessity to support the wider family left at home; and/or by various combinations of all of these. Secondary migration – the continuing chain – brought spouses and family members, sometimes more and sometimes less prepared for living in a new land. Why particular groups of people have come to the UK rather than somewhere else has been the product of history, geography and politics. Some major reasons have been the Empire, being in transit to the United States, joining groups already settled here, the displacement of millions of people in the two European wars and, most recently, the expansion of the European Union. Sometimes the reason has simply been the long British tradition of offering a home to refugees. This book analyses how official policy towards teaching ESOL has been shaped by the politics of these migrations and how policy has oscillated accordingly.

These many factors behind migration explain the enormous diversity of the people who have settled over the last 140 years in terms of their cultures, religions, languages, education and skills and their expectations about Britain. This diversity, certainly in the last 40 years, has presented ESOL teachers in many parts of the country with perhaps the defining characteristic of their work – heterogeneity of motivation to learn and of previous educational cultures and levels. This heterogeneity is radically different from the context in which foreign language teaching generally has developed in Europe and the teaching of English, in particular, has developed worldwide.

But it must also be remembered that by no means all migrants to Britain have been speakers of other languages. The Irish were much the largest group in this period. And the politics of immigration has seldom recognised that during much of this period as many British-born people were leaving the UK to settle elsewhere as settled here.

Migration to Britain over this period was only a very small part of the massive growth in migration throughout the world. This growth has been driven by the appetite for labour created by the unprecedented economic change and expansion reflected in growing urbanisation worldwide. At the same time, populations have been destabilised by brutal wars and internal conflicts and have had access to progressively cheaper transport and communications. It appears that economies have been unable to develop and grow without migration from pools of cheap labour. And when a cheap labour pool is not available or acceptable nearby, migration takes place across thousands of miles. Sheila Rosenberg's accounts of policy discussions show again and again how little global awareness was brought to these discussions and how often politicians and officials insisted Britain was not a country of inward migration and ESOL needs were temporary and minor.

How countries across the developed world have reacted to inward migration reflects their histories, political values and systems and their sense of national identity. New settler nations such as the United States, Australia and Canada have been more likely to welcome certain categories of migrants as citizens, and allow some bicultural identities a degree of latitude, because growth in population has been seen at times as desirable and even essential. In these same countries, the economic exploitation of migrants may be quite uncontroversial and seen as the way the country works. Autocracies, on the other hand, such as China and parts of the Arab Gulf, may grant internal and external migrants very few rights and control and confine their movements simply in terms of the labour market. European nation states, which are liberal demo-cracies, such as the United Kingdom, have found migrants create a civic dilemma. On the one hand, it is difficult to fit migrants into their historical view of national identity; on the other hand, it is difficult to reconcile the economic exploitation and considerable social exclusion of some minorities with society's growing national commitment over the past fifty years to equality and human rights.

In Britain, the most desirable, if largely unspoken, solution to immigration over the period covered in this history has been to hope for a degree of assimilation leading to a level of 'invisibility' which does not cause 'problems'. This solution does not easily happen when there are differences of language and/or religion and/or skin colour side by side with poverty. Legislation against racial discrimination has been consistent and progressively firmer since 1967. But clear and consistent policy over many other practical needs in relation to immigration has never been addressed by successive UK governments, who have characterised such needs as 'temporary'. This failure is richly illustrated by the case of teaching and learning English as a second or other language. This categorisation of the learners as 'temporary' has prevented a consistent approach to solutions and made it difficult if not impossible to learn from past experience. Sheila Rosenberg's research brings out clearly the lack of continuity and of quality of thinking about adult ESOL at many official levels. For example, ESOL for adults has at different times during the period covered by this book been the responsibility of the immigrant communities themselves, voluntary philanthropic organisations, the Home Office, the Department of Employment and the Department of Education. So practitioners have had to struggle to build consistent expertise for ESOL and government departments have played pass the parcel with responsibility for policy and funding.

Overall, immigrants have been valued a lot more for their immediate economic contribution and a lot less for the broader economic, cultural and social contribution they may make in the longer term, which is so richly illustrated by some minority communities now well established in Britain. The first generation of settlers may have been willing to accept less than a full entitlement to citizenship, at least for a time, but many of their children are not. It is their children, therefore, who may at times, as a consequence, be perceived as a much greater threat to national identity and social cohesion than their parents. There has been a lack of official analysis and recognition that there is a connection between how parents have fared in Britain and how their children feel about Britain as a consequence. The needs of first generation adults have been pushed down the policy and spending agenda. This process of thinking is vividly illustrated in the low priority and short-term support given over the years to ESOL programmes.

ESOL teaching has been a difficult and complex task in itself and it has often been criticised as not very effective. Professionally, it has grown out of the teaching of English as a foreign language (EFL), though affected also, especially in the earlier period, by theories of teaching

English to native speakers. This book traces the interaction with EFL theory and practice as well as second language acquisition theory down the decades. But the academic background and pedagogy of EFL, like all foreign language teaching, has been developed within the context of academic learning. Adult immigrant learners have challenged this for obvious practical reasons and teachers have responded in ways this book describes. ESOL teachers have also always tried to take into account the backgrounds of their students. But the sheer heterogeneity of ESOL classes in terms of the students' experience and concepts of second language learning and of learning culture generally, as well as the very varied ages and experience of students, raises major questions about psychology and learning which have never been adequately explored.

Another very important factor has been that most ESOL students have not had learning English per se as their primary motivation in attending classes. Their motivation has tended to be either very specific, for example to acquire more English for a particular job or particular further education course; or much more general, for example to make social contact and be able to get around. These different motivations create hugely different needs and require very different approaches to meeting them. In addition, there is often little opportunity for such learners to use their new English at all. Sheila Rosenberg describes some of the most successful radically different approaches to provision: most notably, the work of the Industrial Language Training Service developed in workplaces and public services in the 1970s and the development of ESOL provision embedded in vocational and academic courses in some colleges in the 1980s. The essence of these approaches was to invest time in analysing why and how English is needed in order to inform curriculum design and also to draw in other English speakers – such as fellow workers or supervisors, patients in hospitals and vocational teachers in colleges – so ensuring learners have the opportunity to use their English skills as they acquire them. Drawing the wider community into the language learning process in this way also afforded opportunities to tackle some of the attitudinal barriers to communication across ethnic groups, which are often as major an obstacle to communication as language itself. Such approaches required a much broader approach from teachers and very different funding arrangements. Unfortunately knowledge of this approach, which should have been nurtured and encouraged in the new commitment to ESOL from 1993 and then1997 onwards, was largely lost. Such approaches were ignored in the influential reports of FEFC and Ofsted inspectors from 1993 onwards, as they increasingly addressed the effectiveness of ESOL provision. There are recent signs, however, of the rediscovery of these approaches; for example, in the roles of union learning reps in providing ESOL in a few workplaces and in recent research into 'embedded' vocational programmes in colleges, which has demonstrated much better results.

The mainstreaming of ESOL funding for dedicated classes and for additional learning support within colleges of further education in 1993. led to considerable expansion and many improvements in quality, particularly after the Skills for Life initiative of 2000. However, as a result, ESOL became another subject within a qualification-led funding system and an inspection-led improvement system, neither of which were informed by models of provision based on practical analysis of the diverse needs of learners or how different groups can learn most effectively. This approach was reinforced as ESOL became a subset of Skills for Life policy and practice. ESOL had imposed upon it the goals of success in graded tests derived conceptually from the primary school reading strategy via adult literacy and numeracy planning. Adult literacy has contributed an approach based upon tackling the experience of failure at school and of quite specific individual learning needs and difficulties. No clear connection has been established between these approaches and the most effective ways of providing ESOL for its heterogeneous and diverse student body.

There is certainly some outstanding ESOL provision and many successful learners within the Skills for Life model of provision. But the wider goals around workplace communications and access to training and to public services will have only limited success this way. Sheila Rosenberg explores the persistent criticisms of the quality and effectiveness of ESOL made over recent years. The major conclusion is that weaknesses arise from inadequate provision of teacher education and, no doubt, this is very important. But equally, this book shows how the questions of how really effective teaching and learning can be provided in conventionally organised programmes for diverse groups of adult migrant learners have never been settled. Such knowledge, in so far as it has existed, has often been ignored because it did not fit within the wider policy framework and targets, or has been rapidly lost in the context of discontinuous policies, funding arrangements and responsibilities.

This book is an impressively comprehensive and detailed account of the contexts and policies for ESOL down the decades and of how teachers and teacher training have laboured to provide ESOL programmes in response. At the time of writing, adult ESOL policy and provision is a matter of great controversy and uncertainty. This book can make a most valuable contribution to the urgently needed consideration of an overall strategy for ESOL now and into the future in the context of the near-certain continuation of migration into this country. This strategy needs to be positioned within the wider debates now taking place about workplace learning, about social cohesion, about learning English and access to citizenship and about the stringent rationing of public funding for personal adult education.

Tom Jupp
August 2007

ACKNOWLEDGEMENTS

This book would have been impossible to complete without the support of a great many people. I thank my family for their forbearance and help with reading proofs.

I thank Pamela Frame, Hilda Schiff, Margaret Siudek, Judith Smith and Helen Sunderland for reading the many drafts. And I thank all those who scoured their memories, ransacked their bookshelves and attics and added immeasurably to my knowledge and understanding:

Adele Attwood
Rakesh Bhanot
Dick Booth
Clarice Brierely
Jean Brown
Helen Casey
Celine Castelino
Peter Clyne
Andrea da Silva
June Derrick
Sheila Dunman
Pamela Frame
Derek Grover
Madeline Held
Elizabeth Hoadley-Maidment
Ursula Howard
Carol Irvine
Ann Janssen
Tom Jupp

Elizabeth Knight
Robert Leach
Jenny Lo
Ann Morgan-Thomas
Marianne Moselle
Lynette Murphy-O'Dwyer
Sandra Nicholls
Martin Norfield
Hazel Orchard
Celia Roberts
Greta Sealey
Mary Simpson
Margaret Siudek
Judith Smith
Marina Spiegel
Helen Sunderland
Alan Tuckett
Frances Weinreich
Joan Weir

INTRODUCTION

All history is work in progress. This one is no exception. While writing it I have been very conscious of the many others – including learners themselves – who have much to contribute to an understanding of the complex issues surrounding ESOL in the UK.

This account starts in 1870, but there were many incomers to Britain before that. The first refugees to be identified as such were the Huguenots in the sixteenth and seventeenth centuries, describing themselves as 'refugiate in a strange country' (Howatt and Widdowson, 2004, p. 18), giving us the term, 'refugee' that we use today. The Huguenots were followed by many more refugees, including, in the nineteenth century, Victor Hugo, Giuseppe Mazzini and Karl Marx.

Newcomers included George I (who never became comfortable in the language of his new subjects), and George Frederick Handel, who was naturalized through an Act of Parliament, became 'Master of Music for His Majesty's Chappel Royal' and was buried in Westminster Abbey.[1] There were, of course, more modest settlers – traders and students, and those who married Britons.

Most of this account relates to England. The focus is often on London and the South-East, which is where the greatest numbers of ESOL learners have always been found. However, newcomers have also always settled in other areas of England and, indeed, across all the countries of the United Kingdom. I have therefore tried to reflect this and to indicate something of the different positions in Scotland, Wales and Northern Ireland.

So why start in 1870? That date marked the beginning of state-funded education in England and Wales (and in 1872 in Scotland) and this opened the way to municipal adult education. The 1880s then saw the arrival of the first of the new waves of refugees.

The canvas for this history is necessarily broad because it has to take

1

account of the many factors which have influenced those who have come to settle in the UK. These factors fall into general categories, which become the themes which run through the following chapters, changing in emphasis and importance from decade to decade, but always there, if only in the background.

Immigration, racism and citizenship

I note briefly the patterns of immigration across the period and the UK government responses to these, starting with first Act to restrict immigration in 1905. After the Second World War similar Acts of Parliament were matched by formal legislation and voluntary action to ameliorate the conditions of those already here, nearly all of whom faced xenophobic hostility. From the late 1990s onwards there was a growing Home Office view that knowing English contributed to social cohesion and responsible citizenship, and as a result ESOL teaching and learning, which had always had a political dimension, became even more politicised.

Government provision for settlers

Governments throughout the period were sensitive to the negative attitudes of the public towards immigrants. This meant that the policies of successive administrations could often be characterised as 'doing good by stealth', with the funding channelled through voluntary organisations, resettlement boards and refugee committees, through local government legislation or in tandem with provision for adult basic education as a whole. Much of the funding was short-term, on the principle that the problem would soon go away. At times there was even the irritable denial: '[T]here's no need; we are not a country of immigrants.' So the funding was generally inadequate.

The needs of the economy

Another theme, from the 1870 Education Act onwards, was the government's concern to develop a higher level of basic skills in the population. The adult literacy movement played a significant role in this. Although for many years ESOL was not funded in the same way as adult literacy provision, it was influenced by it. From 1993 onwards, when there *was* similar funding for ESOL, the demand increased; there were still too few classes and too many aspiring learners, and this led to the proposal from the Learning and Skills Council (DfES) in 2006 to uncouple ESOL from other basic skills provision and end automatic fee remission. At the same time, other government departments dealing with employment were calling for the language skills of ethnic minority groups to be increased.

Conflicting demands of different government departments

Only occasionally was there a unified government response to ESOL learners. This absence of clarity was particularly significant at the beginning of the twenty-first century. It resulted in a conflict between the principles of learner entitlement, equality of access and the needs of the economy and society on the one hand, and, on the other had, the question of who should pay for English language tuition.

Employers' responses

This history notes the – often frustrated – attempts of successive admin-istrations to involve employers in the language training of their workers. These started with the Ministry of Education Pamphlet in 1963, and continued to 2007. In this context, the contribution of industrial language training was all the more remarkable.

Influences on ESOL pedagogy

The three main influences on the development of an ESOL pedagogy are traced. These were the new theories and practice of foreign language teaching; the growth of adult education; and the changing approaches to teaching English as the mother tongue to both schoolchildren and adults.

ESOL teachers, dealing with different language needs, often resorted to a plethora of acronyms – EFL, ESL, ESOL, EAP, ESP – and I have tried to disentangle these. I believe that the now commonly accepted 'English for Speakers of Other Languages' (ESOL) is the most accurate general description of the field, since it is a value-free description of the learners, and does not pre-empt any view of what they need English for. However, this history deals with meeting the language needs of adults resident in the UK, and not of overseas learners of English.

Because English language tuition for residents was habitually under-funded, it relied for much of the period on an army of volunteers and part-time teachers. Though their commitment was admirable, it meant that the workforce was generally under-trained and under-qualified, and the quality of the teaching and learning often suffered.

English as a lingua franca

A major factor which is noted, albeit briefly, was the growth of English as a powerful lingua franca. Championed by Winston Churchill in the Second World War, the international status which English subsequently had acquired by the beginning of the twenty-first century, and the wish of so many people to learn it, presented new and considerable challenges to the government.

The ESOL learners

This history also recognises that most ESOL learners are members of communities and usually live in families, so that the experience of adults is inevitably coloured by that of their children in school. Those children, in turn, often have to assume responsibilities beyond their years because their English is more fluent than that of their parents. The changing of intergenerational roles can affect the motivation and responses of adult learners. This role reversal, on the other hand, is often counterbalanced by the maintenance of the mother tongue in the domain of the home, which can strengthen and reinforce the cultural, linguistic and religious identity of the incomers. The wish to sustain this identity may also influence the attitudes of the adult learner towards the acquisition of English. There was no space in the course of this history to do more than cite some evidence along the way that learning the language of the country in which you have settled as an adult is almost never a simple act.

CHAPTER ONE

1870–1930: The new era

The period 1870–1930 saw the arrival in the UK of the largest groups of second-language speakers since the Huguenots, and these, too, were refugees: first, from the 1880s onwards, Jewish refugees from eastern Europe, and then, in 1914–15, Belgian refugees fleeing the German invasion. This period also saw major changes in the teaching of English, both as a foreign language and to native speakers, which affected the provision made for the newcomers to learn English.

The newcomers' experience was affected by the social, political and economic situation they faced and by the hostility they often met. This included the first pieces of legislation to restrict immigration.

Jewish refugees from eastern Europe

Howatt and Widdowson, in their account of the position of the Huguenot refugees in the sixteenth and seventeenth centuries, show how the newcomers met hostility and fear, and describe how learning English helped to counter this (Howatt and Widdowson, 2004, p. 20). The newly-arrived Jewish refugees at the end of the nineteenth century faced the same pressures. It is interesting to note that the dual-language dialogues that were published to help the Huguenots 'Refugiate in a strange country' (p. 18), i.e. to settle and survive, were remarkably similar to those that were produced within the Jewish community over two hundred years later (below).

There were, of course, Jewish communities already established in the UK, especially in London. When more Jews had arrived from Holland in the 1850s and 1860s, the existing community had set up the Jewish Board of Guardians in 1859 to help the newcomers settle (Lipman, 1954, p. 10).

The Board of Guardians was therefore already in place to help the thousands of Jewish refugees who fled from the poverty and the pogroms in Russia in the 1880s and 1890s. Many passed through the UK on their way west, but many others stayed here, and the resources of the existing Anglo-Jewish community were stretched to the full.

The refugees were forced to settle in areas that were already the poorest. The conditions in the East End of London in particular aroused the concern of humanitarians like Charles Booth. However, the newcomers faced not only poverty and overcrowding, but considerable hostility. The respectable *Nineteenth Century Magazine* observed that 'their standard of manners and living can only be compared to that of a not very particular pig', and *Country Life* believed they 'bring with them not only filth and poverty but crime' (Bermant, 1969, pp. 26–7).

Hostility to the newcomers grew, and led directly to the first piece of legislation in the UK to control immigration in peacetime.

The Immigration Acts

The 1905 Immigration Act was the result of a protracted anti-aliens campaign, the main target of which were East European Jews (Winder, 2004, p. 254). By 1905, 100,000 Jews were living in London's East End alone. However, other groups, such as the Chinese and Italians, were also affected. The Act allowed Britain to refuse entry to any immigrant with no visible means of financial support or means of making a living. It also excluded criminals, those carrying infectious diseases and those classed as insane. The restrictions were enforced by the on-board inspection of steerage passengers on vessels arriving in British ports. It was followed by further restrictive Acts in 1914, 1919, 1920 and 1925.[1] However, if the 1905 Act established a precedent for the many future acts to limit immigration, and created a bureaucratic structure to enforce them, it also had one far-reaching and positive consequence. It affirmed the right of asylum for those fleeing persecution.

In effect, the 1905 Act did not result in fewer new arrivals. This was because the original minimum number of steerage passengers needed for a ship to qualify for inspection was raised from 10 to 20. The shipping companies made sure they limited their passenger lists so that they did not fall into the category which required inspection.

Meanwhile, those who had arrived had to settle into a new life, search for accommodation, find work and tackle the language.

Learning English and sustaining a bilingual tradition

In tracing something of the experiences of these settlers of learning English, emphasis in this account is often on London – where in 1880 they formed 70 per cent of the national Anglo-Jewish population (Lipman, 1954, p. 82). However, similar communities were established in Manchester, Bradford, Hull, Leeds, Glasgow and Edinburgh. What all the new adult arrivals shared was that they learned English – or not – in the context of speaking Yiddish and, in many cases, reading and under-standing Hebrew (and reading Yiddish texts that were written using Hebrew characters). Many incomers also had access to a number of European languages – especially German, Russian and Polish.

It was a central aim of all those living alongside, or working with, the new settlers that they should learn English. This was true of both the assimilated members of Anglo Jewry (Livshin, 1989, p. 85) and the idealistic volunteers at Toynbee Hall (Briggs, 1984, p. 50). It was also an aim of the community groups – often centred on synagogues – established by the refugees themselves. This was all an integral part of a powerful move towards 'Anglicisation' (Lipman, 1954, pp. 144–9).

However, running parallel to this was an often passionate concern among the newcomers to retain the culture, religion and language traditions that they had brought with them. Hebrew classes were mandatory on the young. For the older generation there were clubs and other cultural centres to provide reading material in Hebrew, Yiddish, German and Russian, and there were many locally published Yiddish newspapers (Lipman, 1954, pp. 131–2). Those seeking to maintain their other languages could turn to the School Board for London's provision of German and Russian classes in its Evening Continuation programme, alongside French, Spanish, Portuguese and Latin (below). After its form-ation in 1904, the London County Council went on to add evening class tuition in Yiddish as well as Irish and Welsh (LCC, 1912, p. 99) (below).

Sustaining two traditions and languages
The sustaining of two traditions and cultures – English and Yiddish/Hebrew – has been seen by some modern scholars as a successful early example of 'syncretism'[2] (Gregory and Williams, 2000, p. 13). Accounts from within the earlier Jewish community present a very positive view that maintaining the two languages and cultural traditions even contributed to academic success. On the other hand,

7

there were whole families who discouraged the use of Yiddish in the home, and schools that discouraged its use in the playground.

The clearest and most positive accounts of the linguistic richness of the new communities – not only in London but also in Manchester and other areas of settlement – come through the reminiscences of people interviewed in their older years. They remember how as children Hebrew and Yiddish were used in the home, how fathers read Yiddish newspapers and mothers normally used Yiddish to speak to the children (Gregory and Williams, 2000, p. 83) and in the market. Children were also told fairy stories in Yiddish (*ibid.*). Yiddish was used to help the new families settle in and familiarise themselves with the new systems. There was a Yiddish manual in the common lodging houses (White, 2003, p. 7). The Board of Deputies produced a Yiddish version of the 1891 census form (BL). Yiddish interpreters were employed in the Police Courts (Board of Deputies Annual Report for 1900). Children were almost universally sent to Hebrew school. One of them argued very strongly that learning the grammar of Hebrew made the learning of English grammar very much easier when she came to it at school (Gregory and Williams, 2000, p. 6).

This sustaining of Yiddish and Hebrew was supported by a thriving commercial publisher, printer and stationer called R Mazin. Based at 141 Whitechapel Road, Mazin was a publisher of Yiddish music, a stationer and a prolific language publisher. His languages list is impressive. In addition to books for teaching and learning English, Hebrew and Yiddish, he published works in and on Arabic, Burmese, Hindustani, Japanese, Tamil and Turkish, alongside materials in all the major European languages.

There was an obvious market for instruction in Hebrew, especially among the second generations of immigrants, and Mazin published a number of works. These included two by Philip Blackman, an LCC schoolteacher who produced some of the early dual language books for learning English (below). Blackburn published *Hebrew Self-Taught: A Manual of Conversation* in 1924 and *The Beginner's Hebrew Self-Taught* in 1935. An examination of this last shows that by 1935 he had developed considerably in his thinking about language teaching and learning since the publication of his *English in Yiddish* in 1915 (below). By 1935 the emphasis was on the spoken language and complete utterances, and the work would seem to reflect Blackman's growing understanding of modern theories of good language teaching.[3] However, this increased

8

understanding came too late for it to influence the textbook he produced for learning English.

There was also a market for learning Yiddish.[4] Whether this was again among the younger generation of immigrants schooled in the English system, or among workers and volunteers who wanted to communicate with the older members of the community, is not clear.

Learning English: community-based and municipal provision

Children

In the last two decades of the nineteenth century, a large number of pupils in many Stepney schools came from homes in which English was not the first language – and, indeed, where many children knew no English at all when they started school. In 1891, 40 per cent of the boys in Standard 1 in Commercial Street School knew no English (White, 2003, p. 166). Provision had to be made for such pupils. There were Yiddish-speaking teachers (p. 167), Philip Blackman among them (below). One woman remembered the use of realia to learn the names of common objects such as cup, fork, etc, and the relief she felt at finally learning the English alphabet (Gregory and Williams, 2000, p. 91). Some remembered teaching each other as children. One child agreed to teach Yiddish to a Sephardic child who, since her family had not come from eastern Europe, did not speak it, in return for being taught English (White, 2003, p. 82). Another remembered using Yiddish to teach English to a newly arrived immigrant (p. 167).

There is overwhelming evidence that, however they learned it, in the ordinary School Board for London (SBL) and London County Council (LCC) schools, or at the newly established Jewish Free School, the children acquired English quickly. They especially won the approval of the School Board for London and its East End headmasters. Mr Joseph Rawden, headmaster of the Deal Street School where Philip Blackman taught, gave a verdict that was echoed by others of his colleagues:

> *Jewish boys soon become anglicised and cease to be foreigners. My first classes contained 175 boys; of these 108 were born in England and 67 were born abroad. The parents of 170 of these lads were born abroad, so that practically all of these children are of foreign parentage. Notwithstanding this fact, the lads have become thoroughly English. They have acquired our language. They take a keen and intelligent interest in all that concerns the welfare of our country*

9

> *… They enter heartily into English games . . . I am firmly convinced that the*
> *Jewish lads who pass through our schools will grow up to be intelligent,*
> *industrious, temperate and law-abiding citizens and, I think, will add to the*
> *wealth and stability of the British Empire.* (Lipman 1954, p. 145)

Similarly, in Manchester the children picked up English very quickly (Livshin, 1989, p. 86).

Adults

The position of their parents – and, indeed, of all who arrived after school-leaving age – is less well documented. First of all, the picture is much more varied than it is for the children. Some never acquired much English at all: 'My mother spoke English in 26 different languages' (White, 2003, p. 82). Another refused to use English in order 'to preserve Yiddish' (p. 82). One devout Hasidic father in Manchester refused to allow English books in the house, and if he found one threw it into the fire (Livshin, 1989, p. 86).

However, there were strong pressures on adults to acquire English (Gartner, 2001, p. 239 and passim), and it happened in different ways. Some learned English from their children (Livshin, 1989, p. 87). Some attended evening classes – in Manchester the 'Derby Street Night School (p. 87). Others had private tuition (Gregory and Williams, 2000, pp. 83–8). Some used self study; one father read the English newspapers with the aid of an English–Yiddish dictionary, drawing on a life-long tradition of Hebrew studies to transliterate the English words into Hebrew characters to help with the pronunciation (p. 84).

Such evidence of individual study of English is perhaps unsurprising in a literate community that valued learning, including learning that continued beyond schooldays.

Self-study materials

There were a number of publications to help the home student. Philip Blackman, the teacher at the Deal Street School and author of the Hebrew textbooks (above), produced two publications for learning English.

His first work, *A Textbook of the English Language for Yiddish Students* (Blackman, 1915) was published by R Mazin. This went into a second, enlarged edition in 1915.[5] It was on its title page that the author identified himself as belonging to the Deal Street LCC School.

This textbook had a very heavy focus on grammar. The first chapter dealt with the English alphabet and its pronunciation using the Hebrew characters used for writing Yiddish. The succeeding chapters moved through the article (one chapter), nouns (six chapters), adjectives (one chapter) and a final section containing passages for reading. The explanations and translations were in Yiddish. The English language in the sentences illustrating points of grammar was formal and often stilted. The limited number of verbs used in the final reading passages is unsurprising, considering the lack of any tuition in verbs at all.

Blackman's second work, which appeared quite late in 1919, was part of a series of 'Self Taught' books published by Marlborough & Co of 51 Old Bailey, London, and joined a list of self-study manuals on topics ranging from Norwegian to phonetics.

Blackman entitled this work *English in Yiddish*. It was less grammar-based than the textbook he had published with Mazin. It selected vocabulary according to situations and usage and tackled the spoken language. The preface said in Yiddish:

> The manual is aimed at those who want to teach themselves English without spending a lot of time and effort learning grammar. Those words which are most useful in ordinary life have been selected, divided into classes, together with a vocabulary for commercial, military and travel use. There are useful phrases for verbal communication. The main rules of English grammar are given. The vocabulary and phrases are precisely translated so that 'even a child will not make a mistake'. The phonetic transcriptions [into Yiddish] should help the student to learn the correct pronunciation of English, but it is obvious that a teacher would be of great help in this. By the end of the book the student should be able to have a conversation with English people and be ready for more advanced study of the English language.[6]

The first chapter dealt with the alphabet, explored the mysteries of English orthography (including letter combinations such as *gh*) and introduced a systematic attempt at a phonetic transliteration of the sounds in Yiddish. The next chapters dealt with vocabulary – mainly nouns – by collocational groupings, starting with 'The World' and going through 'Minerals and Metals' via 'Animals', 'The Human Body', 'Food and Drink' and 'Laundry List'. Each word was given first in Yiddish, then in English using the English alphabet, then by a transliteration of the English word into the Hebrew characters.

11

Later chapters introduced complete utterances, and there was the beginning of what we would today recognise as functional language. Under 'Making Inquiries', students were given pattern sentences: 'Do you understand me?' 'Which is the way to … ?' Under 'Notices' they were offered 'Bedroom to let', 'No admission' and 'Free Library'. In a restaurant they were offered the questionable models of 'Give me the salt' and 'Show me the bill of fare'. More emollient examples were given with 'How are you?' but the student was put in confrontational mode with the dressmaker – 'It is too short-waisted' – and the laundress – 'You have scorched my dress' and 'This is not my handkerchief'. Only towards the end of the volume was attention paid to what we today would see as vital topics: times of the day, days of the week, money, measures, weight and capacity.

However, it is easy to see that this little manual, despite its deficiencies, would have been useful to the home student. It would have supplemented Yiddish–English dictionary for the father (above).

These early dual-language texts of Blackman showed little influence of the newly developing theories of language teaching (below), but another text developed by the Russo-Jewish Committee was somewhat different.

Community-based English classes and materials

A philanthropic Russo-Jewish Committee was set up in 1881 to cater for the many welfare needs of the new settlers. It was in this context that they established free English evening classes. There appears to have been some initial reluctance among the new settlers to attend such classes, but by 1897 the Russo-Jewish Committee was able to report that 'a certain prejudice which was experienced to a limited extent when the classes were first started has now entirely passed away, and any illusory ideas as to any possible religious decadence … from the preliminary step of learning English … are no longer entertained' (Gartner, 2001, p. 239; Russo-Jewish Committee Annual Report for 1897). These classes were started in 1892,[7] in order 'to impart a knowledge of the English language, habits and usages to adult Russian Jews and Jewesses resident in London'.

The evening classes followed a course of study that lasted two years. At its conclusion, it was reported that the students would be able to 'read/understand, say, an average newspaper article' (Gartner, 2001, p. 239; Russo-Jewish Committee Annual Report, 1894). The classes were held in School Board for London (SBL) day school rooms, usually each Monday, Tuesday and Wednesday evening from 7.30 to 9.30, with an average nightly attendance of 500–600 people. The focus was on reading and writing, and it was reported that specific instruction in speaking was only incidental.[8] Three-eighths of the group were women. (Gartner, 2001, p. 240). The judgement that these classes did little to develop the spoken word is counterbalanced by the manual that the Russo-Jewish Committee commissioned from Joseph Jacobs and Herman Landau (below).

The Board of Deputies' Annual Report for 1892 gave a very favourable account of the Russo-Jewish Committee English classes in London and their contribution to the assimilation of the new arrivals. It wished

> . . . to extend it to provincial centres of Jewish population. The Board recognized the vital importance not only to our unfortunate Russian co-religionists, but to the entire Anglo-Jewish community, of inducing the former to assimilate themselves as far as possible to the English people in all matters outside their religion. Animated by this feeling, the Board gladly acceded to Mr Cohen's request, and it addressed the Wardens of Provincial Congregations in which Russo-Jews were supposed to be resident, urging them to establish adult evening classes for their instruction on the lines of those so well initiated by Mr Cohen. A responsive movement in the Provinces resulted from the excellent example set in London.
>
> It is believed that classes have been established at Liverpool, Hull, Cardiff, Edinburgh and other places. A Yeddish [sic]–English manual for the instruction of Russo-Jews was compiled for the Classes Committee by Messrs Joseph Jacobs and Herman Landau, and gratis copies were forwarded to the above-named towns.[9]

These compilers of this Yiddish–English manual were eminent members of the Anglo-Jewish community. Joseph Jacobs was a historian and folklorist, and Hermann Landau was the banker and philanthropist who had set up Temporary Shelter for Poor Jews.

The Yiddish–English Manual compiled for the English Evening Classes Committee in connection with the Russo-Jewish Community[10] (Jacobs and Landau, 1893) was based on a work originally in Polish which had been effectively adapted to help the new settlers learn the English they needed in order to live in the UK. The introduction to the manual (in English) is interesting in itself, revealing a not-inconsiderable understanding of the problems of translation and transliteration, as well as the language needs of the new learners:

> *In compiling this Manual at the request of our colleagues on the English Evening Classes Committee, we have made much use of the most practical work on the subject with which we are acquainted, VANEL's Englisher Tolmetch ... We have, however, corrected the English, largely supplemented the dialogues and added reading lessons and glossary. We have also adopted an entirely different system of transliteration, which will, we trust, be found to be both more practical and more accurate than VANEL's or the other manuals that we have in part consulted and in part utilised.* (Jacobs and Landau, 1893)

Using the dual-language approach, this textbook started in the same way as the Blackman publication, with the alphabet and sound system; but, unlike Blackman's later book, it immediately put sounds, vocabulary and grammar into complete utterances. The approach was not so very different from the French Huguenot manuals (Howatt and Widdowson, 2004). The set of situational dialogues gave a clear insight into the lives of the new settlers. They ranged from polite requests and refusals, e.g.

'Take a cup of tea if you please'
'I thank you, I never drink tea' (p. 26)

to reflecting on immediate experience and understanding:
'New York is bigger than Moscow'

to adapting to life in the new country:
'At home he was a shoemaker' (p. 34)
'Our neighbour's wife is a seamstress' (p. 34)
'My father is a baker but he thinks of taking a boarding house.' (p. 37)

There were also clear reflections of the hardship and heartache facing the new settlers:
'We shall be glad to have some work' (p. 32)
'My condition is bad but the condition of my brother is still worse' (p. 31)
'The poor woman who came with us by the same steamer' (p. 37)

'She has to feed a great family' (p. 30)
'He has nothing but his hands' (p. 30)

But there were also celebrations:
'Tomorrow my son's bride will come' (p. 79)
'I came here a bachelor and I am now, thank God, the father of six children' (p. 81)

The manual was arranged by topic but followed a pattern of increasing linguistic complexity. So the polite invitation to 'Take cup of tea' was later developed into 'Good day, sir. I should like to buy a good knife but at a moderate price' (p. 95). And the section on asking for and receiving directions presents a range of quite detailed options (p. 94). Similar exercises developed by ESOL teachers some seventy years later would serve the same purpose and would equally reveal the challenges facing the new settlers. The second part of the *Yiddish–English Manual* consisted of reading passages drawn from folklore and fables, such as the tale of the wolf and the lamb (p. 160).

If this manual had indeed been used by teachers in the evening classes, it would have been impossible for the students to avoid listening to spoken – though admittedly literary – language, and even to avoid speaking, albeit in a perhaps mighty chorus.

Comparison with the American experience: the focus on citizenship
A comparison between these English textbooks and those produced in the United States at the same time shows similarities but also an interesting differences. One American textbook would seem to have been very successful (Goldwasser and Jablonower, 1916). As with its English counterparts, there was a focus on grammar and sentences were translated into Yiddish. The immigrant experience was again powerfully reflected: 'The father will leave but the family must stay in Russia.' It developed a lively situational approach, built on the experiences of a fictional Mr Cohen as he negotiated life in the new country. The difference between this American course book and the English ones was the explicit American emphasis on preparation for citizenship, with passages on Thanksgiving Day and Lincoln Day: 'To live in a land like America makes a man feel happy' (p. 74).

However, there was an interest in education for citizenship in the UK at the time, and the School Board for London was developing citizenship classes in its continuation classes (below), though these were not aimed at immigrants.

Opportunities to learn in municipal adult education classes

The new learners arrived in the UK just as municipal adult education began to develop. There is evidence that they took advantage of the opportunities that this offered.

The 1870 Elementary Education Act in England and Wales authorised the setting up of locally elected school boards across the country, charged with the responsibility of implementing the requirements of the Act. Initially neither 'elementary education' nor the age of the 'child' was defined in the Act, and there was no rule on when schools should be open or how old the students should be (Devereux, 1982, p. 21). This enabled some boards to try set up evening continuation classes. However, the picture was not clear – not even the curriculum to be offered – and there was no specific funding. A succession of Codes and Acts then followed which combined to clarify the situation. Finally in 1893 there was the Education Code, for Evening Continuation Schools allowing greater flexibility and a wider choice of subjects for adult students (Devereux, 1989, p. 29). From these beginnings grew the modern adult education movement.

Provision made by the School Board for London and the London County Council

The development of adult education provision in London was, and continued to be, so important for the new settlers that it warrants special consideration.

Once it was set up to implement the 1870 Act, the School Board for London (SBL) almost immediately began to plan for evening schools (Devereux, 1989, p. 21). These initial attempts were to set up classes that not only followed the Elementary School Curriculum but also offered others, fee-paying, in the arts and sciences. They failed. (Devereux, 1989, pp. 21–2). But in 1882 – in time for the majority of the new arrivals into the East End to take advantage of them – a new resolution was passed to provide

> *...elementary education under the Code. Instruction in subjects recognised by the Science and Art Departments and by the City and Guilds of London*

Institute and in such special subjects that the Board may from time to time approve (advanced classes). (Devereux, 1989, p. 24)

The 'Code' was the 1881 Elementary Education Act, which would also have a significant influence on the education in English offered for adults (below).

The overall curriculum offered by the School Board for London for the 1883–4 session was extended to science and modern languages, but for a fee (Bray, 1900, p. 258). A major change came with 1890 Education Act, which released the education of adults from the strictures of the elementary school curriculum. At the same time German, along with bookkeeping and shorthand, no longer attracted fees (p. 259). Then the National Code of 1893 offered still greater flexibility, with an extended programme in modern foreign languages (p. 260) and tests by inspectors were replaced by examination results. In the 1894–5 session classes in citizenship were added (p. 260), and in 1898 fees were abolished and commercial schools established (p. 260). All these developments increased educational opportunities for the new settlers.

As the programmes developed, so the average age of the students increased. The original curriculum for the SBL evening continuation classes was aimed at providing opportunities for young school-leavers to complete their elementary education. So the expectations were that the students would be 13, 14 and 15-year-olds. However, as the provision extended and diversified it attracted many older – even much older – students.[11]

At the same time as the curriculum expanded to meet the wider needs of its learners, the number of 'specialist schools' increased. The 1900 School Board for London Report (Spalding, 1900) noted that there were three schools for special instruction in commercial subjects, two specialising in commerce, science and art, and five specialising in science and art. The commercial schools were more likely to teach languages – including ESOL – and their development both increased the number of classes available and directly influenced the production of successful textbooks for teaching English to second language speakers (see below, p. 000).

The advantages for the new settlers that arose from all these developments were threefold: (i) they had the opportunity to learn English; (ii) they had the opportunity to maintain and develop their modern foreign languages (below); (iii) they had the opportunity to develop craft skills, including skills like cap-making (School Board for London 1904, p. 292), a staple of the East End clothes trade. These opportunities were complemented by the Technical Education Board, which the London County Council established in 1893.

Influence of the mainstream English and modern foreign languages curricula

The English curriculum

The English curriculum for native speakers of English, and the mainstream textbooks that were produced for them, heavily influenced the provision for ESOL learners at this period. This influence continued well into the twentieth century, particularly in the role given to literature. It is important therefore briefly to review this curriculum.

In the early stages, the Continuation Classes curriculum in English placed considerable emphasis on the national 1881 Elementary School Curriculum, or Code, in which pupils were assessed by Her Majesty's Inspectorate at levels from Standards I to VII. The emphasis in English was on reading and writing, and the curriculum was very narrow, with some minimal attention to literature. Writing skills were taught at a fairly low level and paid little attention to expressing individual needs or developing personal creativity. Accuracy in spelling and punctuation were paramount, and regular dictation exercises tested the students' mastery of these.

At this stage the even older students in evening continuation classes were tested in these skills by Her Majesty's Inspectorate, alongside the 'scholars' in the day classes of the schools in whose buildings the classes were held.

Clearly, any newly arrived immigrants who found themselves in evening classes in English that were aimed at native speakers would have struggled. They would have been following the same curriculum as their children at school during the day, and alongside older children who had arrived later in their school careers and had not completed the full programme. And there is no evidence that the Continuation Classes programme covered the teaching of basic reading.

When the Education Act of 1890 released evening continuation classes from the requirement to follow the Elementary Schools Curriculum (Devereux, 1982, p. 28), more latitude was allowed in the teaching of English' (Bray, 1900, p. 259). By the time S E Bray was writing in 1900, the 1893 National Code for Evening Continuation Schools had been passed to allow for even greater flexibility. The literature curriculum had been expanded, and specialist lecturers appointed to teach it (Bray, 1900, p. 265).

The effect of these changes on the curriculum is demonstrated in the English requisition list approved by SBL Evening Continuation Classes subcommittee for 1900 (London Metropolitan Archives). This shows that there was nothing that could be identified as 'literacy', or indeed of any very early primers that might have been used in the infant classes of elementary schools. The assumption is that the students had already acquired basic skills in reading.

The list of standard grammar and composition books included a number of works by the prolific and influential J C Nesfield. John Collinson Nesfield is an interesting case study in the development of English language teaching. Like Michael West (p. 40), he was an education officer in India, having been the Director of Public Instruction in the United Province of Agra and Oudh. He was also an Orientalist and a linguistician.[12] However, despite his wealth of experience, and unlike Michael West in Bengal, Nesfield did not draw on his skills and knowledge to develop a theory of second language teaching and produce appropriate materials. He preferred, rather, to engage in a bad-tempered controversy[13] over his idiosyncratic theories of grammar.

Nesfield's *Manual of English Grammar and Composition* (1898), included in the requisition list, is particularly interesting. It dealt with grammar (parsing, and clause analysis), the development of vocabulary, and what he called 'diction'. This turns out to be what today we might describe as discourse analysis and genre. But he also included a section on prose and poetry and the history of the language.

This inclusion of literature in a grammar book is typical of the time. It was in line with current thinking, in which language and literature were fused, and which identified an ability to read with a familiarity with the canon of English literature and saw English literature as a means to acquire reading and writing skills.

The same SBL requisition list also shows which literature texts, all based on the classics, were being used in the evening continuation English classes. These were in three categories: (i) readers based on simplified versions of the classics; (ii) the classics themselves; (iii) literature. The difference between categories (ii) and (iii) are not always clear, but the answer perhaps lies in the SBL's wish to extend the curriculum in terms of literature by employing not just day school teachers, but 'advanced' teachers.

Nesfield thus illustrates clearly how, at the turn of the century, English literature was being used to develop students' language and promote their skills in reading and writing (below). This approach would affect the materials produced for all learners of 'English' (including ESOL students) for the next 30 to 40 years, and would strongly influence the Cambridge Certificate of Proficiency in English when it was established in 1913 (see p. 31).

Foreign language learning

The 1900 SBL report provides an interesting insight into the teaching of foreign languages and the way in which the new theories of language teaching were being adopted. Here, unhampered by the requirements of a national code, the Board's inspectors sought to encourage the new methodologies:

> *Modern languages form an important part of the curricula of these schools. It is only of quite recent years that a really rational and effective system of teaching this subject has been adopted – a system mainly based on education by the ear, and on conversational practice by the student. Many systems are still being used in the evening schools, each with its own exclusive name, but all really based on the above-mentioned method. French, German, Spanish and Portuguese are thus taught in these schools.*
> (Bray, 1900, p. 266)

Specific provision for learners of English as a second or other language

The 1900 report also included a clear and very important acknow-ledgement of the difficulties facing the new arrivals who needed to learn English. S E Bray, the farsighted inspector writing the report, expressed his satisfaction that special provision has been made for them in the evening continuation classes.

> *There is no test of nationality for newly arrived Russians, Germans, Poles, French, Spanish, and many others of foreign extraction and birth are to be found in East End schools, struggling with praiseworthy zeal, and with the aid of Yiddish speaking teachers, to master the elements of the English tongue.* (Bray, 1900, p. 264)

It may come as a surprise to the modern reader that mother tongue teachers were employed to teach the adults, as well as the children in elementary school. However, there is no further precise information on the methodology or textbooks being used in the adult classes.

In 1904 the School Board for London published its final report (School Board for London (SBL), 1904), providing an evaluation of the whole curriculum. There was trenchant criticism of the curriculum and teaching of English in schools: English as a class subject was 'meagre, mechanical and unpopular'(SBL, 1904, p. 102). Since the evening classes in basic English were generally taught by tired day school teachers, probably using the same approaches in the evening as they had during the day to children, it might be assumed that these classes too were unsatisfactory (p. 262).

On the other hand, the teaching of modern foreign languages in the continuation classes – especially in French – was again seen as very effective. The use of new methods, especially Gouin (below), was commended. The provision was also praised for the emphasis on oral communication and for the fact that the teachers had been specifically chosen and trained for the purpose, including in the use of phonetics. The broadening of the language offer to include French, German, Italian, Latin, Portuguese, Russian and Spanish (SBL, 1904, pp. 299–300) was also seen as a matter for congratulation, along with the fact that Russian, which had been taught by a volunteer, was now being taught by paid teachers.[14]

The Report noted that plans to open a class in Gaelic had been shelved (SBL, 1904, pp. 292–3), but this indicated a sensitivity to the wishes of the capital's different language communities. The Report also listed the results in the Society of Arts (now the Royal Society of Arts and Sciences, RSA) examination in English, French, German, Italian, Portuguese, Russian and Spanish.

There is further information in this Final Report on the curriculum for 'The Life and Duties of the Citizen',[15] but there is no indication that there was any focus here on the needs of the new settlers as there would be at the beginning of the twenty-first century (Chapter 7).

The London County Council

When the School Board for London was abolished, the responsibility for education was taken over by the London County Council (LCC). The LCC continued to support adult education with the same energy and enthusiasm as its predecessor. A detailed report in 1912, *Eight Years of Technical Education and Continuation Schools* (LCC, 1912), gives a valuable insight into the widening curriculum, alongside some thoughtful and often trenchant evaluations of the quality of the teaching. It reported that there were classes 'in English for aliens' (p. 50), but gave no details of the curriculum. In a further recognition of the language backgrounds of London's different communities, the modern foreign language offer had been extended to include Welsh, Irish and Yiddish (pp. 50, 99).

The teaching of English literature came in for some criticism (LCC, 1912, p. 92), and there was a concern that ordinary students in commercial and technical education might have insufficient knowledge of their mother-tongue language and *literature* [my italics], and that this was needed not only for their technical and commercial education, but 'as a qualification for citizenship in the fullest sense of the word' (p. 93).[15]

Modern foreign language teaching

Once again, the teaching of modern foreign languages, including Welsh and Yiddish, was seen as effective. The inspector, Cloudesley Brereton, reported that the teachers were assessed for their competence. They were encouraged in the use of 'the principles and methods of the new reform movement in modern languages'(LCC, 1912, p. 97) (below) and to learn phonetics (p. 97). Teaching oral skills was encouraged (p. 98). Learning foreign language was seen in the context of evening commercial work (p. 96), and the approach was utilitarian, with a recognition that students' needs differed – post office workers required different skills from those engaged in commerce and trade. However, the importance of teaching a richer appreciation and understanding of the culture associated with the particular language was also encouraged (p. 98). This would find an echo in Harold Palmer's distinction between the two approaches to language teaching and learning (below).

Brereton's report did not identify ESOL separately, but it seems clear he always included it in his brief and believed that effective ESOL teaching had much in common with effective modern foreign language teaching. He referred to ESOL specifically in his *Modern Language*

Teaching in Day and Evening Institutes (Brereton, 1938), recommending the teaching of phonetics in ESOL classes and advocating separate classes for the speakers of 'Nordic' tongues and those of 'Latin tongues'.

Reorganisation of LCC adult education and the development of commercial institutes

Another important development at this stage in adult education in the LCC came in 1913, with its 'Reorganisation of Evening Schools'. This envisaged evening education as more than an extension of the day school provision. It aimed 'to lift evening education to another plane', and, recognizing the substantial increase in the number of adult students, to 'infuse freshness and attractiveness into the system' (Devereux, 1989, p. 67). The 'schools' would be renamed 'institutes', and would be divided into vocational and non-vocational, and men's and women's institutes.

By 1912 the number of commercial centres (including those teaching science, art and commercials subjects) had risen to 31 (LCC, 1912, p. 10). Most of these taught languages as did many of the general institutes. After the reorganisation they were divided into 'commercial' and junior commercial institutes, developing into 'one peak of the evening continuation school system' (Myers and Ramsay, 1936, p. 8). Teachers in these schools and institutes would produce some of the new ESOL textbooks (see Marshall and Schaap, 1914 and Thorley, 1910 and others below).

However, it was not just in London that important developments were taking place in the teaching of languages in adult classes. The Tenth Annual Report (1911–12) of the evening schools in the City of Manchester shows that its Municipal Evening School of Commerce was offering French, German, Spanish, Italian, Portuguese, Danish, Russian, Greek, Dutch, Japanese, Arabic, Hindustani, Swedish, Latin, Greek and commercial English.

The new immigrants from eastern Europe arrived, therefore, at a time of expanding municipal adult education provision, and this accelerated in the first two decades of the new century. In London in particular, there were many classes for learning English, particularly in the commercial institutes. At the same time, textbooks drawn from within the community itself were developed to help the newcomers to learn English.

In the second decade of the twentieth century new groups of refugees would arrive, many for only a temporary stay, and these would present a different challenge to local and central government and charitable organisations.

Belgian refugees, 1915

Following the German invasion of Belgium in August 1914, a quarter of a million Belgian refugees fled to Britain, constituting the largest refugee movement in British history. Perhaps for many people today, the only echo of this upheaval remains in Agatha Christie's fictitious Hercule Poirot. However, at the time the German invasion provoked an international outcry because it broke the Treaty of London, which was supposed to guarantee Belgium's neutrality. The subsequent ill-treatment of Belgian civilians created further outrage, and this was particularly strong in the UK.

The official government policy under Prime Ministers Asquith and Lloyd George was to welcome the refugees, and ensure they be given temporary shelter and support. This policy applied to Belgian refugees alone. The government response to requests for help for Dutch refugees – Holland was theoretically neutral – was to refuse admittance but to offer money (Cahalan, 1982, pp. 119–23). This is perhaps unsurprising in light of the mood of the time. A general xenophobia, often aimed at the Jews of the East End (p. 105), had been fuelled by a national spy hysteria at the outbreak of the First World War (p. 104). This had led to the Aliens Restriction Act and Aliens Registration Order of 1914.

Even the Belgians, plucky little allies, met hostility. In September 1915 there were riots in Fulham against the newcomers, who were seen as receiving special treatments (below). In fact, they were living in the squalid conditions of 'absolute piggery'(Cahalan, 1982, p. 350).

This great influx demanded major organisation. At the outset the government adopted a policy of dispersal, and refugees were sent across England, Scotland and Wales. However, as would happen with similar policies of dispersal for the refugees from Uganda and Vietnam later in the century, there was an immediate secondary migration, especially back to London, where the incomers could find jobs (Cahalan, 1982, p. 200).

To manage the nationwide programme for the refugees, the government set up a War Refugee Committee (WRC) in the Aldwych in London and allocated financial support. However, this assistance had to be indirect, so that no allegation could be made that the government was supporting aliens above its own citizens. The WRC's task was to co-ordinate the programme nationwide, and the support itself was managed through a national network of local committees (Cahalan, 1982, pp. 142–57). These grew to number 2000 (p. 171). It was these committees that dealt with matters of billeting, subsistence, relief and education, and also drew on voluntary contributions and support. There was a good deal of such voluntary support – from local communities, Catholic organisations and the Jews' Temporary Shelter in London.

The Local Government Board issued guidelines to local authority leaders across the UK. This noted that '[t]he refugees are largely of the peasant and tradesman class, and very few can speak but French or Flemish, and many of them only Flemish' (Ministry of Health, 1920, p. 92). The guidelines stated that children should be admitted to local schools and as many people as possible should be found work. For this the refugees were divided into three categories: (i) those with skills the UK needed, (ii) those with skills who needed work, and (iii) the professionals (p. 12).

The British volunteers recruited to help the refugees originally expected them to be mainly rural Walloons who spoke French, and they were disappointed to find that two-thirds of the refugees were urban Flemish speakers (Cahalan, 1982, pp. 179–82; Kushner, 1999, p. 4). The British volunteers could not communicate with them therefore, and there was difficulty in finding sufficient Flemish speakers to act as interpreters and to teach the children.

At the same time, there was a disproportionate number of professional and well educated people among the refugees (Kushner, 1999, p. 4), and this influenced the programmes that were set up to find them appropriate work and education.

Education and learning English

Children
Originally the children went to local schools. They seemed to have done well and learned English quickly (Cahalan, 1982, p. 342). In Edinburgh a civic meeting in 1915 to raise funds for the National Relief Fund reported with satisfaction that the children were in school in Glasgow (*Scotland's Debt to Belgium*, 1915). Such efforts were repeated across the UK. In November 1914 the Director of Education for Pembrokeshire sought a Flemish-speaking teacher for the 60–80 children of fishing

families from Ostend who had arrived in Haverfordwest. There were also 100 children in Milford Haven who needed a Belgian teacher, who (it was hoped) might be recruited from teachers among the refugees.[16] The Director of Education was also keen to ensure the Belgian children had Catholic instruction.[17] In London the LCC's commitment went beyond elementary schooling. It admitted 21 refugees to central schools and waived fees for secondary schooling (Education Minutes, 10 March 1915).

However, as it became clear that the war would not end quickly, there was a powerful movement to maintain the children in their own religious, linguistic and educational traditions (Cahalan, 1982, pp. 342–8), and Belgian schools were set up across the country. In Milford Haven effort was transferred from providing help in local schools to setting up a Belgian school.[18] The LCC set up two schools for 270 children in Fulham (Education Committee Minutes, 6 December 1916). This was particularly important as a considerable number of Flemish speakers had settled there. The area was already poor, and it was there, in May 1916, that riots had broken out against the settlers (Cahalan, 1982, pp. 349–56).

The LCC also set up a 'vacation play centre' for the children at the Poland Street Belgian school. (Education minutes, 7 July 1915). By the end of the war there were over 100 primary schools, 13 écoles moyennes and 2 écoles normales, for Belgian children across the country (Cahalan, 1982, p. 347).

There is considerable evidence that the children continued to acquire English quickly (Ministry of Health, 1920, pp. 52–8), even learning it in the Belgian schools where they were taught in French or Flemish (Varlez, 1917, p. 119).

Adults

There is less information on how the adults fared. Some refugees wanted to continue their studies, others to pursue their professions, and still others to find work according to their technical and craft skills. Many encountered great difficulty in finding employment (Cahalan, 1982, pp. 204–26). However, efforts were made on their behalf. The LCC, at the request of the National Union of Teachers, agreed to employ suitably qualified teachers, as long as they were not eligible for military service (Education Committee minutes, 17 March 1915), and they appointed two Belgian teachers to the Camberwell School of Art (Education

Committee minutes, 7 July 1915). The LCC also admitted a student to Furzedown Training College, free of charge (Education Committee minutes, 28 April 1915) and waived, or reduced, the fees for Belgian refugees to study in 'the Council's technical institutes, schools of art and day trade schools' (Education Committee minutes, 3 February 1915).

Oxford and Cambridge admitted students who were at an appropriate stage in their studies, and these gained a 'certificate' rather than a 'diploma', which was recognised in the Belgian system (Varlez, 1917, p. 119). Particular efforts were made to place refugees from the professions, though this seems to have been easier for the medical profession than others (p. 91).

Knowledge of English and English tuition

However, in the accounts of the period there is generally little specific reference to any language difficulties faced by adults. The reference to problems faced by young women trying to find clerical posts if they did not have fluent English (Cahalan, 1982, p. 293) is unusual. Perhaps one reason for this apparent lack of concern is that the professional classes would have known French and some might have known English; those with craft qualifications – Varlez mentions needlewomen (p. 122) – might need only a little English if they found work, as would those in domestic service. In addition, and perhaps most important, many refugees were pressed into war work in French- or Flemish-speaking munitions factories, or else were conscripted into the army.

This may be why there are equally few references to the steps taken for adults to learn English. The memorandum sent by the Local government Board to local committees for the care of Belgian refugees on 12 November 1914 noted:

> *Many of the adults will welcome opportunities of being instructed in English.*
> *In such cases, also the Inspector of the Board of Education should be informed.* (Ministry of Health, 1920, p. 93)

I have found very little evidence of this happening. Volunteers were pressed into service in Bristol, where '[the] University came to the aid of the adults by starting classes to teach English, which have been much appreciated' (*Belgian Refugees in Bristol*, 1915, p. 6). Maybe such university classes were appreciated by 'the better class of refugees' who, the Report says, had been allocated lodgings separately. (Making such distinctions among the classes of the refugees was universal throughout the programme.) The Jewish refugees being looked after at the Poor Jews Temporary Shelter in London for their part would certainly have had access to the textbooks and manuals described earlier in this chapter. And there were the LCC classes in commercial English for aliens (below). But I have found no specific reference to Belgian refugees taking advantage of such provision.

The Belgian refugee programme was predicated on the government's assumption that it was making temporary provision and that the refugees would return to Belgium once the war was over. By and large, this is what happened.[19]

Refugees after 1915

Britain accepted only 200 Armenian refugees from the massacre in 1915 (Kushner and Knox, 2001, p. 71). Ukrainian and Russian refugees began arriving after 1917, fleeing further pogroms. Most were housed in trans-migrancy centres, such as the Atlantic Park hostel in Eastleigh, Hampshire, hoping to get onto the quota list to be accepted for entry into the United States. These did want to learn English. One complaint about them was that they wanted books in Hebrew and Russian as well as English (Kushner, 2000, p. 46). The educational provision for adults warrants some further exploration. The children had their own schools and also went to local schools in Eastleigh. For a detailed account of the very unsatisfactory general conditions, see Kushner and Knox (2001, pp. 79–88).

Resident aliens

While the new groups of immigrants and refugees were still arriving, there were other ESOL learners, already living in the UK, who wanted another kind of English class. These were the increasing numbers of students who enrolled in classes in English for commerce and trade. It was for them that the main commercial publishers, for the first time, began to be interested in producing ESOL textbooks. Some of these works showed the influence of the new theories of language teaching and learning, which had already had an impact on modern foreign language teaching in the SBL and LCC classes (above).

It is, therefore, important to summarise how far the thinking about language teaching had developed by the first two decades of the twentieth century.

Early theories of language teaching and learning

A standard history of English language teaching and learning (Howatt and Widdowson, 2004) traces in some detail the different theories of language teaching that were being developed in the second half of the nineteenth century and the way they were put into practice. For the purpose of this study, it is sufficient only to state that the fruitful collaboration of Henry Sweet in England, Otto Jesperson in Denmark, Wilhelm Vietor in Germany and Paul Edouard Passy in France led to the Reform Movement. The main principles of the Movement were 'the primacy of speech, the centrality of the connected text as the kernel of the teaching-learning process, and the absolute priority of an oral classroom methodology' (Howatt and Widdowson, 2004, p. 189).

There was one other practitioner whose name occurred frequently in discussions about language at the time. This was François Gouin, already cited in the LCC report, above. He too focused on the oral approach and the systematic learning of complete utterances, drawing on his (by today's standards, limited) understanding of how children acquire language. He set up schools in London, and influenced Daniel Jones who in the early twentieth century began his work on phonetics at the University of London (Howatt and Widdowson, 2004, p. 185). However, Gouin's influence was short-lived and his 'Series' theory fell into disfavour with academics until a recent rehabilitation by J T Roberts (1999).

Outside this academic world was the influential figure of Maximilian Berlitz. Berlitz seems to have fallen upon his own method of language teaching almost by accident, in Boston in 1875, when he employed as a French teacher a native speaker of the language who knew no English. Berlitz developed the methods used by this teacher into a well-organised commercial system, using an oral approach and employing the target language in the classroom at all times. This approach was a prototype of what came to be called the 'Direct Method'. By 1900 there were Berlitz schools in London, Leeds, Bradford, Manchester and Newcastle-on-Tyne (Howatt and Widdowson, 2004, p. 224), all major commercial centres. Berlitz's schools probably provided the best-known examples at the time of not only the development of 'natural language teaching' (pp. 210–28), but also of acquiring a language for immediate, utilitarian ends.

Harold Palmer started his long and influential career in the first decades of the twentieth century.[20] In his *Oral Method of Language Teaching* (Palmer, 1921), he summed up the ideals of the Reform Movement and its relationship to what he called the 'utilitarian' methods of language teaching, typified by Berlitz. Both were 'modern reactions against antiquated methods' (p. 10). Both employed oral approaches. But there were significant differences, and his analysis of these is of interest to the ESOL teacher today. The Reform Movement was identified with the province of the 'educationalist', and the utilitarian approach with the province of the 'linguist':

> *The linguist is aiming at language mastery because a language is useful for all sorts of immediate and ultimate purposes; the educationalist is aiming at language mastery because a language is an instrument of culture.* (Palmer, 1921, p. 8)

Palmer gave as a pointed illustration:

> *The missionary does not learn Pekingese or Tamil in order to have access to the best thoughts contained in the literature of North China or South India.* (p. 9)

A purely oral approach, with no recourse to the written word, is similarly limiting, because it cuts the learner off from the full range of the culture and experience of the native speakers of that language.

Palmer therefore summarised the dichotomy between acquiring limited – but essential – language for immediate and specific use, and the developing of generic skills, knowledge and understanding on which to grow and build in a language and culture. Maintaining a balance between these two aims would always present a challenge to ESOL teachers, whether their students were working in shipping offices after the First World War or were Allied service personnel in the Second World War, mill workers in Bradford in the 1960s or Polish builders in 2005. Government funding for ESOL would sometimes have a narrow 'utility' focus and sometimes a wider 'culture' focus, depending on whether it was supporting the development of language skills for immediate economic ends or for education, citizenship and social cohesion.

The Direct Method

Both Berlitz and Gouin advocated the use of the 'Direct Method', which entails using the target language at all times, including as the medium of instruction, and with no recourse to translation or interpreting. They also advocated using native speakers of the language as teachers.

The Direct Method is clearly a useful way to teach multilingual classes. It avoids the difficulties associated with the fact that so often there are no direct equivalences between one language and another. However, there has always been a case to be made for the judicious use of the learners' mother tongue in teaching another language. I have already described the bilingual manuals produced for Yiddish-speaking refugees which were of some use at the time. I have also noted the informal use of translation and interpreting that happens naturally–children interpreting for each other and for their families, for example. As the ESOL provision developed through the twentieth century, it became apparent that there were formal situations in which the learners' own language could be used, for example in the programmes developed by the BBC (below) or in classes of monolingual learners with a teacher who spoke the same language. It also has many uses in multilingual classes.

Translation was, of course, always used for phrase books, dictionaries and vocabulary lists. However, the textbooks reviewed below revealed that there were pitfalls here too, and that the choice of which words to translate could be bizarre and even contentious.

Finally, the strict rule that the teacher must always be a native speaker of the language would also be challenged as ESOL provision was developed to help the different communities of immigrants and refugees settle in the UK.

New course books and examinations, 1910–1930

The rest of this chapter is devoted to a consideration of the courses and textbooks that began to appear in the opening decades of the twentieth century under the imprint of mainstream commercial publishers. It will evaluate how far these were influenced by the new developments in language teaching on the one hand, and by the English curriculum for native speakers on the other. Similar influences were apparent in the English language examinations, too.

The Cambridge Certificate of Proficiency in English (CPE), established in 1913, was influenced to some degree by the Reform Movement, but, as the standard history of the examination testifies, also by the schools English curriculum for native speakers. This examination, taken in the beginning in Great Britain only,

> *was academic in orientation and initially modelled on the traditional, essay-based native speaker language syllabus including an English literature paper, an essay, and also a compulsory phonetics paper with a grammar section, and translation from and into French and German. There was also an oral component with dictation, reading aloud and conversation . . . The examination closely matched the contents of Henry Sweet's 'The Practical Study of Languages' . . . In all, the candidates spent 12 hours on an extremely demanding test of their abilities in English.* (Weir and Milanovic, 2003, p. 2)

The CPE's original focus on French and German speakers was replicated in many of the textbooks that the mainstream publishers now began to publish, although the languages for translation in the CPE were increased in 1926 to include Spanish and Italian. Who took the examination at this point and where they studied is not clear.

English for commerce

As a knowledge of commercial English – along with a similar knowledge of the languages of the other major trading economies – became increasingly important in the first two decades of the twentieth century, the publishing houses began to be interested in developing materials for this new market. Their major English textbooks were produced by practising teachers and were all written on the basis that the intended learners were living in the UK and were fairly well educated. These works are invaluable for what they tell us about the curriculum being followed and the methodology being used in class, and therefore repay some attention.

The two early entrants into the field of 'English for foreigners', and aiming at students in commercial schools and institutes, were Macmillan and Hachette.

Macmillan

Macmillan's main author was Wilfrid C Thorley. Thorley was a prolific poet, and a whimsical children's and fairytale writer; but he had also spent ten years teaching abroad and had a clear view of the needs of students who were going into positions in offices and trade. He brought all these experiences together in his textbooks. His works assumed that his students were living in the UK, were learning in council-run commercial institutes and had access to French and German. His textbooks were influenced by the schools curriculum in English, but also showed an awareness of the latest theories of language teaching.

A Primer of English for Foreign Students, Thorley's first textbook (1910), 'is intended for the use of students in commercial schools'. Many of these would have been in London, but the fact that the course book was used outside London is seen in the reference to student exchanges between Southport and Lille (Thorley, 1910, pp. 131–3).

Thorley believed that, though students might need the language of commerce, they also needed to have at their command 'a vocabulary concerned with the commoner interests of life' (p. xi). His experience had also taught him that learning technical vocabulary out of context usually meant that it was quickly forgotten. And in any case, students' specific occupations could change (p. xi). His initial emphasis was on generic language, leaving the more technical language to a later stage. This foreshadowed something of the dichotomy identified by Palmer, as well as debates later in the century on the balance between general ESOL and language related to particular vocations or areas of academic study.

In this rather endearing illustrated primer Thorley advocated the Direct Method, emphasised the importance of developing oral skills before reading and writing, gave many examples of idiomatic speech (using contracted forms) and enlivened the lessons with games, puzzles and rhymes – the latter somewhat undermined by rhyming 'food' and 'good' (p. 7). He believed in 'learning by doing' and was up-to-date enough to include lessons on how to make telephone calls. The influence of the standard school curriculum in English is clear in exercises such as those on direct and reported speech and on antonyms and homonyms and in the use of literature. The book carried advertisements for Nesfield's publications (see p. 19) and J H Fowler's *English Literature for Secondary Schools.*

Thorley's next book, *Examples and Exercises in English for Foreign Students,* was published, again by Macmillan, in 1912. Again the emphasis was on oral skills, and there were whimsical mnemonic rhymes – 'Knees are for kneeling, fists are for knocking/Fires are for burning, keys are for locking' (pp. 11–12). There were gap-fill exercises on *Vanity Fair, Ivanhoe* and *David Copperfield.* The second part of the book concentrated on the serious business of business, with passages on companies, the law, rubber and municipal rule. There was an assumption that the students would know French. However, Thorley's lively approach was undermined by examination questions asking students to 'Write a composition using regular verbs in the past definite tense.'

His third publication, *Colloquial and Business English for Foreign Students*, again with Macmillan but this time written with Robert T Lewis, appeared in 1921. Lewis was identified on the title page as 'Associate of Kings College, London and Assistant Master at Westminster City School', indicating that he might be contributing his practical experience of teaching native speakers of English. The tone of this work was generally more earnest than Thorley's earlier ones. However, the philosophy was the same, and the preface noted that 'the aim throughout has been linguistic rather than technical, and as far as possible a middle course has been steered between literary purism and the mere jargon of trade ...' (p. vii). The first part had some 30 pages of exercises in grammar and usage, which included some of the rhymes from *Examples and Exercises for Foreign Students* but also included exercises to replace Saxon words with words of Latin or French origin. (The modern reader is left to wonder whether the intended learners had become even more highly educated.) This first part was followed by 50 pages of general interest passages with question-and-answer exercises. The last part addressed matters of business covering passages on the Stock Exchange, Bank of England, Royal Mint, marine insurance, coal, cotton, and so on.

In their emphasis on literature, Thorley's textbooks were influenced by the schools curriculum in English; but, as has already been noted, there was an equal emphasis on the importance of literature in the thinking of the Reform Movement, which Thorley also followed.

Hachette

Hachette's two authors drew directly on their experience of teaching 'English for Foreigners' at the LCC Barnsbury Park Commercial Institute. They made some of the same assumptions about the ESOL learners and their needs as Thorley did, but they hoped their textbook would be useful for speakers of English as a mother tongue, too.

These authors were E C Marshall and E Schaap, whose *Manual of English for Foreign Students* was published by Hachette in 1914. This manual was clearly very successful.[21] As late as 1955, the authors published *A Concise Manual of English for Foreign Students*, a revised and condensed version of the 1914 book (Marshall and Schaap, 1955). As will often be seen in this history, such longevity is not remarkable; furthermore, as ESOL practitioners and students testify, textbooks frequently continued in use long after their last publication date.

The *Manual* of 1914 was long, detailed and thorough. The preface assumed the students were resident in the UK:

> *Most foreigners resident in this country are engaged in commercial pursuits and are anxious to get a working knowledge of the language as quickly as possible.* (Marshall and Schaap, 1914, p. v)

The *Manual* endorsed the Direct Method, and from the very first edition included a detailed syllabus and scheme of work which paid considerable attention to oral work, including teaching the International Phonetic Alphabet (IPA) and intonation and stress. Grammar was taught systematically. Unusual at the time – and perhaps even since – students' own work was often used in the earlier stages of learning as models for composition. The more advanced students were given passages from writers such as Ruskin, Tennyson and George Meredith as models for their written work. The practice in dictation and translation was aimed to prepare students for a range of examinations, including those offered by the National Union of Teachers – but not the Cambridge Proficiency test.

The authors hoped the work would also be useful to older pupils in secondary schools, doubtless endorsed by Hachette's wish to increase sales:

> *Although this manual has been especially written for the use of foreign students, it will be found suitable in parts for the English student. General teaching experience proves beyond doubt that educational devices framed from the abnormal – in this case the foreigner – are in nearly every case of great help in the earlier stages of the education of the normal – here the English Student in the Upper Forms of a Secondary School.* (Marshall and Schaap, 1914, p. vi)

Such duality of purpose was not unique. It would occur again with *A Modern English Reader with English, French and German Annotations*, which Schaap produced in 1935, this time with E L Paul.[22] This reader aimed to meet the language learning needs of native speakers of English, French and German equally. The vocabulary at the foot of each page gave not only the French and German translations, but also synonyms in English for the English-speaking student. It is obvious that the publisher, this time Macmillan, hoped to capture the widest possible audience with this rather ill-judged venture.

This wish to develop materials that would meet the needs of several groups of learners, and so widen the market, would continue to characterise provision for ESOL learners resident in the UK. This included the production of textbooks and BBC programmes (below).

Publications in the 1920s

The period following the end of the First World War saw an increasing interest in course books to teach English to foreigners. In 1920 Hachette again drew on the work of a teacher in an LCC adult institute when it published R W Douglas's *English for Foreigners: An Elementary Manual* (1920). Douglas himself was identified as a 'Lecturer in English for foreigners at LCC Marylebone Commercial Institute, and at the Marlborough Institute, Sloane Square'. The subtitle to this work, 'An Elementary Manual Equally Adapted for Evening Classes, Schools, Private Students, and Correspondence Courses', illustrates once again publishers' interest in meeting the needs of several markets.

The title page of this book offered the learner '[a] novel vowel-sound method for learning pronunciation, etc'. This turned out to entail giving the approximately similar sound in the student's own language, and the first choice for this approach was French. However, the IPA symbols were also used. The work was grammar-based but also contained 'topics' such as the human body and weights and measures. Anecdotes and riddles were introduced to enliven the learning. Later sections of the book dealt with writing business letters and speaking on the telephone.

The section for the home student on developing oral skills contradicted what was already being accepted as good practice in language teaching and ran counter to the theories that would soon be published by Harold Palmer:

> *The key to Conversation is opportunity for practice. Each lesson in the book contains a 'Drill', which should be repeated again and again by the pupil to himself to acquire fluency of expression.* (Douglas, 1920, p. vi)

However, the dialogues that were offered for practice contained no contractions or short answers.

In the introduction to the book, Douglas did acknowledge that it was easier to acquire language skills with a teacher and, in a piece of free advertisement, offered himself, via his home address in Battersea, as an adviser on the readers' writing (Douglas, 1920, p. vi). The unsatisfactory nature of this book came again, at least in part, from trying to meet the needs of too many different categories of learners.

The next major commercial publishers to begin publishing ESOL textbooks were Pitman and Longman. In their different ways, they would both have an important influence on ESOL learners.

Pitman

Sir Isaac Pitman seems to have entered the ESOL publishing market relatively late. This is surprising. Pitman had been publishing English textbooks for commercial students since before the end of the nineteenth century. Furthermore, even before the end of the First World War, the importance for world trade and commerce of being able to communicate across language barriers was unquestioned.[23]

Pitman did extend his English list in 1918 to include F F Potter's *English for Technical Students*. The preface noted disapprovingly that:

> the weakest point in the general education of the average student is his lack of command of his mother tongue and his inability to express himself in the plain language of educated people. (Potter, 1918)

But the book was little more than an adaptation of the standard English curriculum, plus what were felt to be suitable reading passages on coal, cotton and wool.

It was not until 1927 that Pitman introduced a textbook in English for foreign students. For this he turned to Simeon Potter, who would become Professor of English Language and Literature at Liverpool University 1945–65 and is probably today best remembered for his later general works on language.[24] Potter produced his *Everyday English for Foreign Students* in 1927, aimed at more advanced learners. This went through eight subsequent editions and reprints until its last edition, 40 years later, in 1967. This may be a striking example of textbook longevity, but it is not a testament to the usefulness of a work, which showed too little awareness of modern developments in how to teach languages.

Everyday English consisted of a series of reading passages of increasing complexity, followed by exercises to test comprehension and develop vocabulary. It also contained injunctions to students to learn passages of dialogue by heart. The work claimed to be suitable for students 'who, having mastered the elements of English, wish to become acquainted with the living language in everyday life' (p. v); but this claim about the language of everyday life was misleading. Some of the passages did contain some dialogue, but there was little direct emphasis on speaking skills – apart from injunctions to learn by heart (above). The author – who himself had been a teacher in Czechoslovakia – left that to the classroom teacher (p. v). If, however, the question-and-answer exercises at the end of each chapter were used, the teachers were instructed that the students' answers 'should consist of complete sentences always, pronounced as distinctly and quickly as possible' (p. vi). No short answers were acceptable, and the student had to reformulate the entire question before giving the answer.

This directly contradicted the increasingly accepted views on the importance of teaching idiomatic oral language.

The claim about British life was also misleading. There were reading passages devoted to British life and literature – British houses and meals, education, British cities – but there were also passages on other cities, as well as matters of general interest

There were few changes in *Everyday English* over the next 40 years, the replacement of the crystal set by the valve radio in the chapter on the 'wireless' (4th edition) and the updating of some of the photographs being the most notable.

Potter's books were heavily influenced by the work of Professor William Alexander Craigie, eminent linguist, philologist and lexicographer, and contributor to Oxford University Press's *New English Dictionary*. Potter drew particularly on Craigie's *Pronunciation of English* (1917), aimed at native speakers and paid tribute to Craigie in the prefaces to all his works. Pitman regularly publicised Potter's books as using the Craigie punctuation or diacritrical marks. Craigie used this series of diacritics above or below the letters to identify the pronunciation of vowels and consonants and indicate the place of stress within the words. It was consistent within its own criteria and was aligned with the International Phonetic Alphabet.

However, the system took no account at all of the difficulties faced by students whose first language was not English, since it provided no guidance 'when the pronunciation is quite normal' (p. ix), however that may be interpreted. It assumed that the learner already knew about the 'silent "e"' and the short vowel after a double consonant, and so on. Furthermore, as a reviewer of the sixth edition in 1947 noted, the fact that the system was totally different from the International Phonetic

Alphabet could only confuse students from Europe who had mastered the IPA.[25]

In addition to the *Everyday English* course book, Potter went on to produce a succession of other works. In 1932 he published, also with Pitman, *An English Vocabulary* for *Foreign Students*. This was most notable for the assumption, once again, that the learners knew French and German. This led to a most idiosyncratic selection of the words which Potter felt should be included in the vocabulary list:

> *Words of Romance origin and their derivatives have been largely omitted where the meaning and pronunciation present no difficulties to a person having some knowledge of French. . . . On the other hand, space has been found for all the most important commercial expressions.* (p. v)

It was assumed that the course book would cater for German speakers too, since a selection of common nouns such as 'match' were translated into both French and German.

By the time Pitman published his *English Grammar for Foreign Students* in 1932, Potter had recognised that there had been recent important developments in the theory and practice of language teaching. His bibliography cited standard works by Daniel Jones on phonetics and by Henry Sweet on grammar. It also cited Harold Palmer's *Grammar of Spoken English on a Strictly Phonetic Basis* (1924). However, a comparison of Potter's slim volume and Palmer's detailed and illuminating examination of the spoken language (illustrating the dual functions of grammar and semantics, and dealing with stress and intonation) shows just how little of Palmer's teaching Potter had really absorbed.

Because Pitman's colleges and publications played an important role in ESOL teaching and learning from the 1920s onwards, and were particularly important for the refugees in the 1930s who sought to learn English with their help, this weakness in their main course book was not negligible.

Theories of English language teaching in the 1920s

In his *English Grammar for Foreign Students* (1932), Potter signalled that important developments in thinking about language teaching had taken place during the 1920s. These would influence the major new ESOL course books and materials to appear in the 1930s. The two main areas of new thinking were on teaching the spoken language, and the criteria to be used in the selection of vocabulary.

Earlier work on the spoken language by phoneticians like Daniel Jones was carried further in the 1920s by Harold Palmer. Building on his *The Oral Method of Language Teaching* (1921) Palmer published in 1922 his *Everyday Sentences in Spoken English*. In this he underlined the importance of intonation and stress, identified the main features of the spoken language – including the use of contractions and short answers – and emphasised the importance of helping students to understand register. Then in 1924 his major contribution, *A Grammar of Spoken English, On a Strictly Phonetic Basis*, appeared (p. 39). Palmer's influence on the next stages in the development of ESOL courses and materials would be considerable.

Developments in teaching the spoken language were paralleled by equally important explorations of the issues involved in vocabulary selection. The Imperial Education Conference in 1923 analysed the inadequate teaching and learning of English as a second language in the Empire, and called for research on how to improve it.

Drawing on his experience in the Indian Education Service, Michael West wrote a report entitled *Bilingualism with Special Reference to Bengal* (1926), supporting bilingual approaches to learning and advocating courses that concentrated on pupils' reading skills. He drew on his experience in Bengal to argue that most people working at the level of clerks, for instance, would rarely if ever need to speak English, but would need to be able to read and write it. His major contribution lay in his advocacy of a system of graded vocabulary, with new words introduced and practised systematically. His 'New Method Readers', published by Longmans, Green and Co., started appearing from 1927 onwards. These established a model for reading schemes and books that would be followed for the rest of the century, and for both second language and mother-tongue learners – from *Janet and John* to *Ladybird* and onwards.

West's books are interesting also for the practical advice he gave to teachers and his advocacy of clear, uncluttered spoken instructions in English. Harold Palmer himself joined West as a collaborator and colleague, publishing his *A New Method Grammar* (Palmer, 1938).

It was not until 1953 that the culmination of West's work appeared with the publication by Longmans Green of his important and influential *General Service List of English Words* (West, 1953). However, his work was immediately influential, affecting the approach to ESOL teaching and the production of textbooks in the 1930s (p. 44).

Conclusion

The experience of the speakers of ESOL who arrived in the UK between 1880 and 1930 in many ways foreshadowed that of the many groups which would follow.

Provision was made for them both from within the community and through the newly-established municipal adult education classes. The course books and programmes of study available were conditioned to some extent by current theories of teaching and learning foreign languages, but also by the English curriculum for native speakers of the language. These influences would continue.

The newcomers at the end of the nineteenth century met considerable racist hostility, and the government responded in 1905 with an Act to limit immigration. However, this same legislation also affirmed the policy of offering asylum to those facing persecution. In the case of the Belgians, the government also responded positively by setting up special settlement programmes, though these had to be managed covertly through other organisations. Similar programmes would be set up for other groups.

The two main groups of learners – the East European Jews fleeing pogroms and the Belgian refugees at the outbreak of the First World War – responded differently to their experience here. The Jewish refugees saw their stay as long-term, and the host community reluctantly accepted this. The Belgian refugees regarded themselves, and were regarded by the government, as temporary residents who would require only temporary support. These two responses affected the incomers' attitudes to learning English. Within the Jewish community there was a powerful movement towards Anglicisation and assimilation, because they were here to stay. Learning English was part of this assimilation. The Belgians, on the other hand, knew that their stay was temporary, and felt that learning English was less important than sustaining their Flemish and French, especially for their children. Within both communities there was the same concern to maintain and sustain their own language, traditions and culture. This foreshadowed the tension, experienced by most settlers, between adapting to a new life and remaining true to an old one – a tension that could even lead to a feeling that learning English was in some way a betrayal. There is time in this history to note only briefly the evidence for this as it emerges.

Provision for the Jewish and Belgian children demonstrated how local and central government responded to new communities by first fulfilling their legal responsibilities to them. The children learned English quickly but, in the case of the Jewish children, in doing so they influenced the perceptions and motivations of the adults and affected intergenerational relationships. Future groups would experience similar tensions.

There was one aspect of the situation facing these early newcomers that would, however, gradually change. That was the unquestioned acceptability in official and polite circles of an open and virulent racism.[26]

What had yet to emerge by 1930 was the influence of an official government view of English as a world language, and its relationship to the international role of the UK. This would come with the establishment of the British Council in 1935, with Churchill's support for Basic English, and with the allocation of considerable resources to support the educational needs of Allied service personnel in the Second World War.

CHAPTER TWO

The 1930s and 1940s:
Refugees and Allied armies

The next major demand for ESOL came in the 1930s and 1940s, with the arrival of successive groups of refugees and the influx of Allied service personnel.

First in the 1930s came refugees from fascism in Germany and Spain, many of them children. The numbers were not large. After the outbreak of the war in 1939, these were followed by many more refugees and by the tens of thousands of men and women who made their way to the UK to fight with the Allies. Most needed some training, and for this they needed to learn English.

The belief and hope, shared by the government, the British Council, the many voluntary organisations involved and the incomers themselves, was that they were here as temporary residents. Once war had broken out, the government allocated considerable resources for their support,[1] but on the assumption that they would return to their own countries when the war was won. In the event, many could not, or did not want to. The vast majority of Jewish refugees from Germany and Austria did not wish to return and were in any case stateless. And, following the establishment of the Soviet-backed regime in Poland, very many Polish servicemen and women (and refugees) chose not to return.

The programmes of study for these new incomers were influenced by further developments in language teaching but also by the extent to which the writers of course books were able to respond to entirely new needs. The language used by a Spitfire pilot in the Battle of Britain was very different from that required by a clerk in a shipping office. To meet the needs of these new learners the publishing houses and the armed forces themselves had a part to play, while the government made a significant contribution through the newly-established British Council.[1]

The attitudes of the new learners themselves to the task of acquiring English varied widely.

English language teaching in the 1930s

Vocabulary: selecting the right words

There were major developments in the 1930s in establishing the criteria for the selection of vocabulary. In 1934 E L Thorndike, the American expert on statistical word frequency, met Harold Palmer, Michael West and Lawrence Faucett in New York to discuss these matters. As a result a project was set up, financed by the Carnegie Corporation, which in 1936 produced *The Interim Report on Vocabulary Selection*. This listed some 2,000 words, whose inclusion depended on:

- word frequency
- structural value (all structure words [were] included)
- universality (words likely to cause offence locally [were] excluded)
- subject range (no specialist items)
- definition words (for dictionary making, etc)
- word-building capability
- style ('colloquial' or slang words [were] omitted).

Although the culmination of this work came only in 1953, with Michael West's *General Service List of English Words* (noted above, p. 40), from the mid-1930s onwards everyone involved in language teaching had to tackle the issues involved in deciding what vocabulary to teach, and when. Various lists were drawn up, and once again Harold Palmer made an important contribution.[2]

At the same time, C K Ogden was beginning to publish works on his Basic English with Evans Brothers. For Ogden, 'Basic' did not indicate first level but was an acronym for 'British, American, Scientific, International, Commercial', and was based on a strict scheme for vocabulary selection (p. 72). The first work, *Basic English*, was published in 1930, and with its appearance began two decades of heated scholarly controversy. This not only involved personal disagreements between Ogden and Michael West, but led to debates in the British Council and culminated in the enthusiastic intervention of Winston Churchill himself (p. 73).

What Ogden, West and the other compilers of vocabulary lists had in common was the aim to be universal and generic, and so they did not include specialist terms. This approach on its own had only limited use in the training of aircraftsmen or soldiers. These new learners required a core of general language, plus a programme of English for specific purposes (ESP). These were not available in either the older course books or the new publications that began to appear in the 1930s, although the best of these new publications took full account of the current thinking about language teaching

New major course books

An examination of two major courses – Lawrence Faucett's *Oxford English Course*, begun in 1933 (Faucett, 1933–9) and C E Eckersley's *Essential English*, begun in 1938 (Eckersley, 1938–42) – shows how the writers confronted the challenge of vocabulary selection in particular. Their introductions are particularly interesting.

Faucett, writing before the Carnegie conference, drew on the existing work of Thorndike and E Horn to identify the most-used 1,500 words:

> *With few exceptions these are the words that are used in every kind of writing and speaking. They comprise about 85 per cent of the words occurring in straightforward modern English prose of a general nature. To these 1500 words were added 500 more of special usefulness in school days. The choice of the remaining 500 words was made to satisfy the needs and interests of pupils studying English overseas, as reflected in the reading matter'.* (Faucett, 1933, Book 1, 'Teachers Book', pp. 4–5)

The learners Faucett had in mind were reflected in his choice of reading passages, which, redolent of *Boys' Own*, concentrated on the martial, Imperial and heroic. This was of only limited use to newly-arrived refugees or service personnel. However, the course was thorough and systematic, and the instructions to teachers were clear, as befitted an experienced teacher trainer, lecturing at the London University Institute of Education. In 1939 Faucett produced an Alternative Course, which progressed at a slower rate.

C E Eckersley's books were more appropriate to adult learners living in the UK because they were based on his teaching at the Regent Street Polytechnic in the 1930s, where the students were older and were already living in an English-speaking environment. In the introduction to his first course, *An Everyday Course for Foreign Students*, published in 1937, he acknowledged the new developments in vocabulary selection and presented his own approach. This concentrated first on the language used in the classroom, then moved on to the 'wider fields of practical life', including everyday life in London, and paid close attention to the spoken language. 'The aim has been to make the book colloquial, to give the language of everyday as it is familiarly spoken by the man-in-the-street' (pp. v–vi).

Eckersley developed these views in much more detail in the introduction to his highly successful *Essential English: A Progressive Course for Foreign Students*, the first book of which was published by Longman in 1938. Harold Palmer had been appointed ELT consultant at Longman in 1936 and would certainly have been involved in this major venture. In his introduction to Book I, Eckersley noted that:

> *The last twelve to fifteen years has seen a completely new outlook on the problems of teaching foreign students English. This has been due to the research and experiments carried out in various parts of the world.* (p. vii)

He described the work of Thorndike at Columbia and Horn in Iowa, as well as the Carnegie Report and the more recent work by Lawrence Faucett, and paid tribute to their achievement and usefulness.

However, he also identified their limitations. He noted that in Thorndike's list words like 'button,' 'stocking' and 'grandmother' occurred only in the second 1,000 words, while 'bacon' occurred only in the fourth 1,000. (It did not appear at all in the Carnegie list, though 'grandmother' did.) Furthermore, in Thorndike's list such frequent words as 'cigarette', 'marmalade', 'taxi', 'aeroplane' and 'cinema' did not come even in the eighth 1,000 list (p. ix). Eckersley then described the 'distinctive character' of his *Essential English*:

> *... this course is designed to teach 'real' English. It is a starting point for an ever-increasing mastery of conventional and literary English. Its outlook is modern, adult and sophisticated, and so, though every word has been tested against the frequency lists, I have not hesitated to include in the first 500 such words as aeroplane and cinema, bus-conductor, marmalade, theatre and tennis-racket.* (Eckersley, 1938, p. xi)

Eckersley went on to describe how he introduced grammar and syntax as simply as possible, and he concluded with a statement that summed up the philosophy behind all his course books of the period:

I firmly believe that one of the first essentials of a book is interest. 'No profit grows from where no pleasure is taken,' and every effort has been made to cover the pill of learning with the jam of gaiety. (p. xi)

Eckersley located all the lessons in his *Essential English* with a fictitious group of multinational students and their wise, encouraging teacher, Mr Priestly. As they progressed through their mastery of English, the group considered sentence construction, sang songs, learned about letter-writing and told jokes, explored material about London and England and were tested in their grammar (p. xii).

An examination of the four successive course books, which appeared between 1938 and 1942, shows that Eckersley achieved a considerable measure of success with this structure. The text was broken up with woodcuts, line drawings and cartoons, and there were crosswords. He also kept up to date with what was happening in Britain. In Book III, which appeared in July 1941, the Polish student announced:

I am joining the Polish Air Force. There are several squadrons of them here in England – grand fellows who escaped from Poland and France and have been training with the RAF. My place is now with them – if they will take me. (Eckersley, 1941, p. 233)

Mr Priestly and the rest of the group wished him well. In Book IV, which appeared in April 1942, there was a great deal about the war. Mr Priestly gave an account of the Air Force and the presence in it of Allied forces from the Commonwealth and Occupied Europe, and 'Jan' returned to describe the role of Bomber Command. Other lessons were devoted to the army and navy, and Dunkirk was described. There were drawings to illustrate vocabulary items such as 'tank.' These books sold well, and British Council evidence suggested that Allied service personnel in the war were learning English from them (below).

Harold Palmer's *New Method Grammar* appeared in 1938. This work, with its slim, accompanying Teachers' Book, bore clear witness to the author's thinking. Although the emphasis was on grammar, both the course book and the teachers' book focused on oral skills as well; there was also guidance on vocabulary selection, and above all students were encouraged to use their own inductive powers to master language in use. The use of technical terminology was kept to a minimum:

> *In this book grammar is neither treated as a method of interpreting thought and reasoning by means of language, nor is it presented as a 'teaching subject': it is looked upon simply as a series of definite instructions as to how to build up English sentences in the manner of those who use English as their mother-tongue.* (Palmer, 1938, p. vi)

The text was clearly set out and illustrated with lively line drawings.

Other publishers and course books

Other courses of the time showed varying, and often limited, levels of awareness of the new theories and the changing needs of the learners.

Students who attended Pitman's College would discover the successive editions of Simeon Potter's *Everyday English*. In 1936 Pitman's added W O Vincent's *Textbook of English for Foreign Students* to its list. This was a rather old-fashioned course, even for the time, relying on the written word to teach both speaking and writing skills. It emphasised the importance of teaching and learning vocabulary in context, minimised the teaching of grammar and relied on dictation exercises and com-position to reinforce the students' acquisition of the language. The preface again suggested that the learners were interested in commercial English.

Dent had Walter Ripman, the eminent linguistics scholar and phonetician, as its adviser for its Modern Foreign Languages series. Ripman had himself published books for teaching English to children. In 1935 he produced his *English Course for Adult Foreigners* (Ripman, 1935). In his preface he cited the success of his books for boys and girls, first published in 1904, and reported that he had received many requests for a book for adults. He hoped the new volume would be as useful as the earlier ones had been for children. In fact, the work is rather disap-pointing, coming as it did from someone so committed to teaching the spoken language. Ripman taught the grammar systematically (but quite rapidly), ensured that the new structures and vocabulary were taught in context, and transcribed all the 52 lessons phonetically. However, although the reading passages contained dialogues, these were literary and contained no contractions or short forms. The questions on the passages were stilted and unidiomatic: 'With what do you write?' (p. 2). There was no apparent philosophy for the selection of vocabulary other than to explain the words in the folk stories and cautionary tales used as reading passages. This meant that the word 'vast' appeared as early as Lesson 11. None the less, the course seems to have survived.[3]

Much more useful was the work produced in 1938 by Ripman's wife, to which he contributed. *Let's Talk English: Everyday Conversation for the Use of Foreigners*, by Constance Ripman (1938), consisted of a series of dialogues of increasing complexity following the day-to-day life of a middle-class English family and describing the ordinary situations they found themselves in. This family was based on the Ripmans: the head of the household was a professor and education inspector. The dialogues were idiomatic, used contractions and short forms, and were all transliterated phonetically. There was even a passage describing the difficulties a foreign guest has in using weak forms, and his flawed attempts at speaking were transcribed phonetically.

In 1939 Dent published *English for Foreigners* by William Freeman, a lecturer at the City Literary Institute in London. Freeman's stated opposition to the use of phonetics — and his laboured attempts to substitute his own inappropriate system — must have caused Ripman considerable concern and suggested a weakening of editorial control. The work bore all the hallmarks of the author's experience as a teacher of journalism to native speakers. At its best, it was not very helpful to ESOL learners. At its worst, it was downright misleading, suggesting as it did that learners should pay no heed to English as it was normally spoken.

So the new learners arriving in the UK in the 1930s and early 1940s would have found a number of course books, some putting into effect the new theories about language teaching, others idiosyncratic or old-fashioned, and none exactly meeting their language needs.

Other major events of the period that had an impact on the new learners included the production by Longman in 1935 of the first English dictionary for foreign students and the first venture of the BBC into teaching English by radio in 1943 (Quinault, 1947).

The Cambridge Certificate of Proficiency in English

In 1931 the University of Cambridge Local Examinations Syndicate held the Proficiency Examination (see p. 31) overseas for the first time, and in 1939 it started the Lower Certificate in English. With the outbreak of war the number of overseas examinees for the Proficiency Examination inevitably fell, to be replaced by Allied service personnel and prisoners of war. In 1943:

> *The majority of the candidates in Britain [for the Proficiency examination]*
> *... were members of the Allied Forces, including Polish servicemen and*
> *Italian prisoners of war who made the most of an enforced stay in Britain.*
> (Weir and Milanovic, 2003, p. 7)

There seems some evidence that even English-speaking POWs took the examination to improve their skills and pass the time (p. 7).

The Proficiency Examination itself was changing. In 1939 candidates had a choice of papers between 'English Literature', 'General Economic and Commercial Knowledge' and 'English Life and Institutions'. The 'English Phonetics' paper had been dropped. Non-native speakers of English still had to take a translation paper (Weir and Milanovic, 2003), so examiners who were qualified in the languages of the new candidates would have to be found to set and mark the papers.

These Cambridge examinations were actively encouraged by the British Council (below) which had an official role in their management (Wyatt and Roach, 1947, pp. 125–6).

The British Council

The other major development that influenced ESOL provision was the creation of the British Council. Its role in organising ESOL tuition in the UK during the Second World War is described at some length below. It was able to fulfil this responsibility only because it was already firmly established by the time war broke out.

The Council was set up in 1934 as a voluntary association, officially inaugurated in 1935 by the Prince of Wales and granted a royal charter in 1940. Its original title was 'the British Council for Relations with Other Countries', but this was soon shortened to 'the British Council'. Its aim was to promote trade and improve the image of Britain overseas. In encouraging an understanding of the British way of life and culture, it sought to counter inimical propaganda, especially by the fascist regimes in Italy and Germany, which maintained that Britain was both brutally imperialist, and decadent and effete. From the outset, the teaching of English and the training of English teachers were part of a total programme of promoting books and cultural activities, and encouraging cultural exchanges. The fact that the Council was able to take on an additional role in 1940 and look homeward to the language-learning needs of thousands of Allied servicemen and women – who joined the refugees as 'resident foreigners' – was as significant as it was perhaps unexpected (below).

The new ESOL learners

The refugees

The 1930s again saw the arrival of refugees from Europe, but there was no repeat of the government's open-door policy which had welcomed the quarter of a million Belgian refugees in 1915 (p. 24).

Refugees from Nazi Germany began to arrive in Britain from 1933 onwards, and the numbers increased rapidly after the promulgation of the Nuremberg Laws in 1935. They were joined after the Anschluss in March 1938 by as many as could escape from Austria and would be accepted here. Though the majority were Jewish, there were also political refugees. The other refugees from fascism came from Spain, with the outbreak of the Spanish Civil War in 1936.

All these new arrivals came in relatively small numbers, most making their journeys through personal connections with professional organisations, individuals or charities, and sustained and maintained through them.

Two groups, however, were given specific permission to enter by the government, and both consisted of children separated from their families. In 1936 4,000 – mainly Basque – children came from Spain; then in 1938 and 1939 ten thousand *Kindertransport* children arrived, mainly from Germany and Austria. For both groups there had to be clear undertakings that the children would be no charge on the British taxpayer.

Educational provision for the new arrivals

Children

Provision for the two groups of refugee children varied. The Spanish children were mainly housed separately in 'colonies', where efforts were made to teach them some English. However, there is evidence that this was resisted:

> There were few interpreters, and of these none could understand the children who spoke only Basque. There were sporadic attempts to start classes in English, but they rarely continued beyond the third lesson. Enthusiasm waned since each lesson began with the verb 'to have'.

> The whole operation had been prepared as if it were some Scouts and
> Guides jamboree. But we Basque children were not Scouts and Guides:
> we had been in a war and separated from our parents unwillingly.
> Most had a political awareness uncommon in England even among adults.
> (Legarrata, 1984, p. 112)

In one smaller unit in Kingston, the children maintained their reading
and writing skills in Basque, but resisted learning English. One
interviewee is illuminating in the reasons he gives for this:

> ... there was a more or less passive, unconscious resistance. I believe that the
> same factors which made for happiness and cohesions in the home hampered
> that interest in the outside world which would have been the main incentive
> for learning a foreign language. (Legarrata, 1984, pp. 132–3)

Some children housed with foster parents did go to ordinary schools.
But in the main it seems the Basque children clung together, united by
their sad experiences and a powerful sense of national, linguistic and
cultural identity, as they looked forward to being reunited in their
homeland with their parents. In 1940 many did return, but some 400
had no one to return to so they remained to settle and even to fight in
the Second World War.

The *Kindertransport* children were fostered mainly with individual
families, though some were in homes such as the Dovercourt camp
near Harwich. There were some classes in English at Dovercourt
(Bentwich, 1956, p. 68), but many children were thrust straight into an
English-speaking context. Those under 14 went to ordinary
elementary schools, and there are many stories of how they adjusted
and learned English. Some went on to local grammar schools
(Whitworth, 2003, *passim*). The initial view that theirs might be a
short, temporary stay in the UK was soon seen to be unrealistic, and in
1943 the government took financial responsibility for them
(Whitworth, 2003, p. 71).

For most of these children there would be no return to their
homelands, and for many no reunification even with some members of
their families. The many testimonies, accounts and memoirs of the
Kindertransportees (Whitworth, 2003; Gershon, 1989; Benz, 2003) show
there was relatively little resistance to learning English, but there were
also expressions of regret at losing their mother tongue, and some took
up their German again later.

Adults

There was no centrally organised provision at all for the new adult refugees before 1939. There were English classes at the general reception camp in Richborough, a self-governing, self-financing organisation which originally aimed at being a transit camp for those Jewish refugees between the ages of 18 and 40 who had a definite prospect of emigration overseas. According to Norman Bentwich:

> *All received education in English for two hours a day. The language taught was partly by Linguaphone records played on a gramophone, partly by classes in 'basic English'. The camp leaders had the help of a voluntary band of one hundred English teachers, men and women from the neighbourhood, who gave their evenings to conduct classes, and befriend the men in their free hours at the weekend.* (Bentwich, 1956, p. 104)

The Linguaphone method, with its series of recorded dialogues, gave the learners a course that was carefully structured in terms of grammar and vocabulary, and the learners would hear native speakers; but the course was quite limited. What exactly was taught as 'basic English' is as unclear here as it is when the term was used by the Army. As with the Belgian refugees, volunteer teachers were again pressed into service. After war broke out, many of the Richborough camp inmates joined the Marquis of Reading's division of the Pioneer Corps (see p. 54).

On the whole, however, adult refugees made their own arrangements for learning English, many attending private language schools or council evening classes.

New learners' experiences

Evidence from interviewees and from biographies reveals a range of experiences. PB, who left Berlin with her mother in April 1939, had, at the insistence of her mother, attended English classes at the Berlitz Institute in Berlin in preparation. On reaching London, she discovered she could not understand a word that was being spoken in the London streets, so she took herself off to the City Literacy Institute for a course in English literature – on the surface an apparently idiosyncratic solution, but in the event an effective one.

Fred Jordan, who arrived on a *Kindertransport* but was too old to go to school, remembered being sent to a course for foreign students at Pitman's College. Lillian Herbert, a volunteer at Bloomsbury House, the administrative centre for the *Kindertransport* programme, paid Jordan's fees out of her own pocket. He recorded that he had no difficulty in keeping up with his multinational fellow students. On completion of his six-month course, he was confident his English was perfect! (Benz *et al.*, 2003, p. 241).

He was fortunate. Another respondent, GS, was 15 when she arrived on a *Kindertransport* from Vienna. She recalled wistfully that she would have very much liked to continue her education, but was kept busy helping in the milliner's shop run by her foster carers. The irony was that she lived very close to the Barnsbury Park Commercial Institute, which specialised in language teaching, and from where Marshall and Schaap had produced their *Manual* (see p. 34). Inge, another older *Kindertrans-portee*, was more fortunate, remembering going to evening classes to learn English (Gershon, 1989, p. 62).

One interviewee (MH) said that she already knew English when she came, having studied at Pitman's College and lived with an English family on a previous visit. Her husband, however, knew no English, and he went to three classes a day run by the LCC and (unspecified) Jewish organisations. MH emphasised the problem of speaking German in public at a time of heightened political awareness, and said that on buses with her family she preferred to speak broken Czech rather than her fluent German. Indeed, the refugees were specifically advised not to speak German.

This sensitivity was exacerbated at the outbreak of war, when all refugees of Austrian and German nationality over the age of 16 had to register and some were interned as possible enemy aliens. For a brief period between May and October 1940, following the fall of Holland and amid a national panic about Fifth Columnists, a great many more Austrian and German refugees were rounded up and sent to camps or even prisons – in the case of the women, to Holloway. The camp on the Isle of Man famously became the People's University, with English among the many subjects being taught by some inmates to others (Stevens, 1975, p. 198).

The internees were soon released, and many, eager to contribute to the war effort, joined the Marquis of Reading's Pioneer Corps. Here their situation was more akin to that of the Allied Forces, and there was some minimal instruction in English. Fred Pelican remembered:

> *I was very proud of myself, very excited and ready to submit to whatever was required of me. The 74th Company was divided into ten sections ... and an*

English sergeant was put in charge of each section. No time was wasted: six weeks of extensive training began, the usual square bashing, acquiring English words of command, daily inspections. (Pelican 1993, p. 43)

One group of adult refugees was especially vulnerable with regard to language, even when, as many did, they arrived as professionals and already knew some English. These were the writers. *Between Two Languages* (Abbey *et al.*, 1995) includes an article that looks at the experience of four refugee writers (Dove, 1995) and highlights the difficulties faced by even the most fluent, Hilda Spiel. Once in London, Hilda set about perfecting her already proficient English by writing her diary in English, devouring the Sunday papers and literary periodicals, and looking for role models in writers such as Cyril Connolly, James Agate and Philip Toynbee, whom she knew as members of the Pen Club. Her final decision to switch to English in her writing

... was precipitated by the outbreak of war, with its inevitable devaluation of German language and culture. (Dove, 1995, p. 106)

Spiel was writing a novel set in contemporary Austria. In her diary for 2 February 1942, she expressed her discomfort at writing about something so close to her heart in another language: 'Work on novel. I like it, but what will be said about it? It is basically outrageous to write the book in English.' She went on to translate it herself into German.

All four of the writers that Richard Dove deals with wrote in English while they were in the UK and then returned to Austria after the war and took up writing in German again. But their 'enforced migrations' between languages meant that they ended up in a professional and linguistic no-man's-land, and were read in neither country (Dove, 1995, pp. 114–15). Herein lay the central dilemma for Basque children and Austrian novelists alike – and, indeed, the dilemma of all refugees for whom language, identity and loss fuse so powerfully.

Newcomers after the outbreak of the war

More refugees

After the outbreak of war, the number of refugees from across Occupied Europe increased dramatically. One estimate is that at any one time during the war there were at least 114,000 in the UK, and many more would have been away with the armed forces (Proudfoot, 1957, p. 72).

The government set up a Central Refugee Programme and allocated funds which were augmented by contributions from individual volunteers and voluntary organisations. The refugee groups were now also able to join members of the Allied Forces in drawing on the increased resources provided by the British Council (below).

The Allied Forces

By the middle of 1940, the governments of Poland, Norway, Luxemburg, Holland and Belgium were in Britain, bringing with them fighting men, financial resources and three million tons of shipping (Taylor, 1975, p. 494). The setting-up of the Czech government in exile followed. At the same time, Charles de Gaulle was busy organising the Free French forces in the UK. These were very large numbers. By D-Day there were up to 270,000 Free French fighters in the UK. A study of Polish immigrants estimates that 249,000 Poles alone served under British command (Zubrycki, 1956, p. 57).

This influx of men and women from across Occupied Europe and beyond presented a very real challenge in terms of their training and learning English. The responses to this challenge varied.

Meeting the needs of refugees and service personnel after 1939

In-house solutions

First there were in-house solutions, most notably adopted by the French. The strength of two publications lay in the way that they ensured the selection of appropriate vocabulary. At the simplest level were the wordlists. In 1943 George Harrap published *An Aeronautical Dictionary in French and English compiled by Technicians of the Free French Air Force*, with de Gaulle's rousing June 1940 declaration, '*La France a perdu une bataille! Mais la France n'a pas perdu la guerre*', as the Preface. This was a thorough work, acknowledging that the task of choosing vocabulary is 'complex, extensive and difficult'. It listed not only relevant nouns and verbs, but also different ranks and their equivalents, printed metric–Imperial conversion tables and even such slang as 'tail-end Charlie'. There were some limited attempts at longer single utterances, such as 'we observed an aircraft stranded at...' What was missing was any suggestion of dialogue, and especially ground-to-air dialogues in flight, which might counter the nightmare communication problems painted by Andre Jubelin (p. 79). One hopes that learners had the opportunity for more directly useful oral practice.

A more general word list, also published in 1943, was produced by Albert Noblet. His *French–English Dictionary of Technical Military Terms* (Noblet, 1943) also had a glossary on military slang in both languages, listed equivalent ranks and grades in all the armed services, and included metric–Imperial conversion tables. There were no dialogues. The author was identified, among other things, as 'formerly Instructor at the Royal Military College, Sandhurst'.

Marcel de Chaumont's *I Want to Learn English* (de Chaumont, 1941), published in 1941 by Hachette as an Édition Réservée aux Forces Françaises Libres, was a more general course book. It was grammar-based, and the explanations were in French. It relied on exercises in sentence translation in which the language was hardly idiomatic: 'Have you two tongues?' (p. 36). It built up a controlled vocabulary, but this only rarely recognised the reality of using English in England and during wartime: 'My uniform is better than yours' (p. 38). There was an appendix on English customs which included passing the port in the correct direction!

Commercial ELT publishers

English for the Allies

The most directly relevant course books came from Longman, with C E Eckersley's *English for the Allies* (Eckersley, 1942, 1943), in which he drew on the considerable experience he had gained in writing his *Essential English* course.

The first book of *English for the Allies* was a fairly slim paper-bound volume. In the Foreword, Eckersley acknowledged the difficulties facing the Allied forces:

> *Many soldiers, sailors and airmen of our Allies are fighting two hard battles: one with us against the German aggressor, the other against the difficulties of the English language. I have tried in this book to help them master the second enemy (and so, indirectly, the first) as quickly and pleasantly as possible ... But in spite of its humour and lightness of tone of the book follows strictly the most modern research into methods of language teaching, and (except for 'specialised' words like aerodrome, hand-grenade, squadron, etc., which I felt*

were necessary in a book like this) is written entirely within the vocabulary of 'Essential English'. (Eckersley, 1942)

This first volume of *English for the Allies* did, indeed, cover basic grammatical structures and vocabulary; but the images were military, and the illustrative examples appropriate ('the Junkel is fast; the Heinkel is faster').There was humour, and the characters of Colonel Blimp, Private Dogsbody, Rosie Lee and Fanny Adams were introduced and would appear again in Book 2.

In his Preface to the second book, Eckersley stated that, since in Book 1 he 'covered the fundamentals of English grammar, vocabulary and usage', Book 2

> *... aims at mastering the more idiomatic and colloquial forms of the language and at widening the student's vocabulary, relating all, as far as possible, to the service background that is at present so large a portion of his life.* (Eckersley, 1943)

In this second, more substantial, hard-backed volume,[4] *English for the Allies* came into its own as a refreshing, if characteristically idiosyncratic, course. There was still the systematic teaching of grammar and a controlled, though wide-ranging, vocabulary, but the canvas broadened. The topics covered the family in wartime, with the father an ARP warden working in a munitions factory.The humour, again of the 1940s British Flying Officer Kite variety, may at times have been inaccessible to many a Czech and Pole. However, much of it was universal, with a dialogue between Colonel Blimp and Private Dogsbody relating their mishaps on guard duty.This was then followed by a passage on the use of prepositions. Exercises on direction and on left and right, and describing position, were illustrated with airplanes executing a right bank, ships in line abreast and map reading.There was also poetry and the illustrations included woodcuts of the English countryside – a recognition of the needs of the serviceman at leisure and on leave, and reminding us that Eckersley himself produced a series of works on England and the English.[5]

I have found no hard evidence of how widely *English for the Allies* was used, but the production of a second and more substantial, hard-backed volume so quickly after the first suggests some interest and take-up.

Teaching English to soldiers

Harold Palmer also produced a work for the troops. His *Teaching English to Soldiers* (Palmer, 1940) was written in collaboration with a soldier, Major H A Harman. Aimed initially at the King's Africa Rifle in Kenya, it was envisaged as being of use to other serving forces, including the Indian army. The book is still remarkably fresh in the way in which the language learning is directly related to the soldier's own experience in training and in the field. Its recognition that the learner would be more highly motivated when the learning was given practical applications chimes with modern experience of embedded learning. Particularly impressive is the way the guidance to the teachers acknowledged that the Army instructors would be serving commissioned and non-commissioned officers, with no knowledge of language teaching, and so the instructions they were given was in practical, non-technical language. Though not intended for use in the UK, this volume was a model of good practice for the time.

British Forces educational programmes

The armed forces themselves made some contribution to the teaching of English. The importance of education and training had been acknowledged just before the war began, when in 1939 the Central Advisory Council for Education in HM Armed Forces was set up (Hawkins and Brimble 1947, pp. 97–100). With representatives from the armed forces, the Board of Education, the universities, LEAs and voluntary organisations such as the YMCA and Pilgrim Trust, its aim was to mobilise their united resources. To this end it set up regional structures (p. 99). The national secretary was Basil Yeaxlee from the YMCA (p. 54; and see below).

The army itself, however, with a more established tradition of education, and with recent innovations of its own on which to draw, was going its own way and had set up its own Directorate for Army Education under F W D Bendall, who had been seconded from the Board of Education (Hawkins and Brimble, 1947, p. 101). The three original educational aims of the Army Education Directorate were, first, to support general education/liberal studies; second, to provide professional and technical education; and third, to teach hobbies and crafts, all of these activities drawing on a wide range of resources – librarians across the country were asked to trawl their stocks for suitable books (pp. 104–5). These educational initiatives were often greeted by the old guard within the army with outright hostility as 'newfangled nonsense' (p. 106) or, even more damaging, with apathy. However, a great deal of energy and commitment was invested in these new developments, which were soon followed by the British Way and Purpose (BWP) course – patriotic civic education for the troops (p. 138) – and by the development of more open-ended ABCA (Army Bureau of Current Affairs) general-discussion programmes.

Of particular importance for this history was the discovery that so many conscripts were functionally illiterate. This led to the development of a Basic Education programme (Hawkins and Brimble, 1947, chapter 14). However, initially there was no programme of ESOL teaching, and responsibility for providing this was delegated. The Central Advisory Council's first report, covering the period October 1940–March 1941, noted that the army had used its close relationship with civilian bodies to provide English language tuition: 'one regional committee had no fewer than 715 voluntary teachers conducting classes in English for Poles' (Hawkins and Brimble, 1947, p. 110).

The reason the army delegated this responsibility for ESOL was that, unlike the Indian army or the King's Africa Rifles, the British army at that time had no tradition of teaching English to troops who spoke it as a second or other language.

This was soon to change, as the army realised that (i) it had to deal with Commonwealth and Empire troops from the eastern end of the Mediterranean,[6] and (ii) it had to set up more systematic provision for Allied service personnel:

> *Considerable attention was given to the teaching of English … [to the Maltese, Cypriots and Greeks] … Later, in co-operation with the British Council, arrangements were made for providing instruction in English to Allied troops. A special establishment of teachers, at first chiefly civilians, was approved for this purpose. A year later some fifty-five ex-schoolmaster soldiers had been transferred to the Army Education Corps, trained in English teaching methods, supplied with books, and attached to units and formations of the Allied forces.* (Hawkins and Brimble, 1947, p. 243)

The passage went on to quote a contemporary comment which praised the – sometimes inappropriate – zeal of these teachers, and then added:

> *These soldier teachers are reinforced by locally employed civilians wherever they can be found. From the experiments going on continually it is clear that, whether classes are confined to an adaptation of basic English or given the freedom of the direct method, English can be taught by a skilled and enthusiastic teacher without his knowing a word of the students' language and without the existence of a common medium.* (Hawkins and Brimble, 1947, p. 243)

This somewhat unexpected evaluation of teaching methodologies does not make clear whether the basic English being described referred to C K Ogden's specific work or, as is more likely, just a general term. However, its endorsement of the Direct Method, and its conclusion that it was possible to teach multilingual classes effectively through the medium of English, are interesting. This counterbalanced the experience in other parts of the armed services, or in the national houses, where the groups tended to be monolingual (below).

The standard history of army education provides an interesting footnote to Fred Pelican's experience in the Marquis of Reading's division of the Pioneer Corps, largely made up of German and Austrian refugees (above):

> *Usage of the British language was made compulsory but it must be confessed that on occasion the resultant speech was barely recognizable by the residents in England's quiet countryside.* (Rhodes-Wood, 1960, p. 23)

However, Rhodes-Wood went on to record the commitment of the new recruits.[7]

Despite the endeavours of the individual services, however, it was the British Council that played the major role in providing the Allied service personnel and refugees with opportunities to learn English. All the armed services (including the army), plus the Ministry of Shipping and civilian organisations, drew heavily on its services.

The British Council's role and interventions, 1939–1950

A change in the role of the British Council occurred immediately war broke out. An official recognition of the new situation that the Council faced came in a memorandum of 2 October 1939 focusing on the needs of German, Austrian and Czech refugees, and the fact that their position since the outbreak of war has worsened and 'may become definitely unpleasant' (BW 2/228).

Entitled 'A Scheme for Promoting Social and Cultural Relations with the Peoples of Other Countries who are Resident in this Country during the War', the memorandum was submitted by the Council to the Aliens Department of the Home Office. It is clear that a main aim of the Council was to ensure that these refugees would return home after the war with positive images of Britain, but the memorandum also acknowledged that many would not want to return.

None the less, support would be not be for all refugees, and they were put into categories in terms of their suitability and possible future influence:

> It would not be practicable to regard all refugees as within its province. The limited resources of the Council, and the fact that its work is in any case primarily concerned with educated people, would make it necessary to limit any activity to effort on behalf of educated refugees. (BW 2/228)

Members of further national groups stranded in the UK could also participate. Organisations such as the Society for the Protection of Science and Learning, the Society of Friends and the National Union of Students would be approached to help provide appropriate educational and cultural programmes.

Resident Foreigners' Section

To put this limited and elitist programme into effect, a new section of the British Council, called the Resident Foreigners Section, was established, under the leadership of Nancy Parkinson from the NUS. This section was renamed the Home Division in December 1941 after its remit was widened to cater for service personnel from the Commonwealth and Empire (Donaldson, 1984, p. 113). The UK was divided into four regions: (i) London, East Anglia and the Home Counties; (ii) northern England and north Wales; (iii) southwest England and south Wales; and (iv) Scotland. Each region was required to report regularly on its activities. So by October 1939 a framework and structure were in place when the Allied service personnel began to make claims upon the Council's service.

As soon as war broke out, a fierce struggle erupted over responsibility for the British image abroad, and whether to incorporate the British Council into the Ministry of Information. In this conflict Lord Lloyd, the Council's new chair, had a doughty opponent in Lord Reith,

Minister of Information. Fortunately the Council had acquired some measure of protection when it was awarded its Royal Charter in 1940. At issue was the blurred dividing line between political and cultural propaganda. At one point Lloyd himself argued that 'the political effect of cultural propaganda increases in effectiveness in proportion to its detachment from political propaganda' (Donaldson, 1984, p. 74). In the end, the British Council maintained its independence in all cultural matters – including language teaching – and the Ministry of Information took control of political propaganda and films. The Council's Books and Periodicals Committee continued its work to promote the British way of life and values right through the war, with the focus of its activities moving from Occupied Europe to the Middle East, Egypt and South America.

This reaffirmation of the Council's broader educational responsibilities and its role to promote British culture, along with the reconfirmation of its independence, would have important implications for the education programmes it would now put on for 'Resident Foreigners'. First, English tuition continued to be viewed as part of a broader programme to promulgate the British way of life, culture and political traditions. Second, there was the assumption that the new learners were in the UK as temporary residents, and the official Foreign Office policy was that they must take back with them both the English language, culture and traditions, and a positive image of Britain (see below). This assumption of return had a secondary effect. It permitted the Council to encourage the various national organisations in the maintenance and development of the students' mother tongues and cultural traditions, and to support the wider educational aspirations of learners for their new lives after the war. Third, the Council's independence meant it could be neutral/non-aligned about English language teaching books, materials and methodologies. This independence allowed it to resist the most powerful pressure for the national adoption of Ogden's Basic English framework (below).

In the event, the British Council was often both pragmatic and diplomatic, and not only in the language teaching systems that it supported. After some initial difficulties (below), it seems to have managed to build and maintain effective working relationships with national groups, the War Office, the Ministry of Shipping, the Royal Air Force, the Admiralty, local authorities and voluntary groups.

Setting up the education provision

English language tuition for Allied service personnel began quite soon in 1940, after the invasion of Norway and the Low Countries and the fall of France. On 13 August 1940 the Finance and Agenda Committee agreed an allocation of £43 to meet the travel expenses of '40 teachers lent by Glasgow Corporation for the Polish troops'. It also agreed to provide financial help to the Institut Français (BW 2/228).

The British Council's response (29 August 1940) to an inquiry by the BBC tells us that, though these early programmes focused on English teaching, they were also broadly based and extended beyond provision for service personnel:

> *One of the most urgent problems that we hope to deal with is the teaching of English to the allied armies. This is being done on a large scale for the Polish army, and we have also been able to provide them with a Polish grammar. The other armies are being helped in a similar way, and both Polish and Czech armies are being taught by teachers provided by the Council. We are also supplying a large amount of reading material, both in English and the various foreign languages concerned, to the camps and in some places to civilian centres.* (BW 2/ 228)

However, there was some confusion over the funding and responsibilities of the different providers. This was resolved at an interdepartmental meeting at the Treasury on 28 August 1940, involving the Treasury, the British Council, all three armed services, the Ministry of Shipping, the Home Office and the Board of Education.

The resulting agreement was that the British Council should take responsibility for civilian refugees, internees in internment camps and Allied merchant seamen (the last at the direct insistence of the Ministry of Shipping (BW 2/228), and be allocated an augmented budget of £17,000 for this (Donaldson, 1984, p. 114). The three armed services would take responsibility for identifying their own needs and would then approach the British Council for help and advice on meeting them. In its turn, the Council would report on its findings and make the necessary provision if, and when, authorised to do so. It would then invoice the appropriate service department, which would be allocated an increased budget from the Treasury for the purpose.

The British Council's view that this created an unnecessary and complicated bureaucracy was supported by the Board of Education, which also shared the Council's view of the broader educational aims of the operation. The Education Board was as critical of the limited horizons of the armed forces as it was of the suspicious wariness of the Treasury:

> [T]he main criticism of the decision is that it disregards the nature of the task, which is not merely to teach a few foreigners a little English, but to take the whole body of foreigners and (a) relate them to British life and British hospitality and (b) give them the instruments (language, books and other cultural facilities) which will enable them to organise their own cultural activities.
>
> The ordinary government department has not the imagination to do this, but the British Council has been at it for some time. The problem is a single one and not a collection of spasmodic unrelated efforts.
>
> It is of great political importance, but each separate government department sees its own little bit as a rather troublesome little problem of teaching the minimum of English to those whose welfare has been forced upon them.
>
> I have little doubt that the Treasury do not understand what it is all about; and are chiefly anxious to avoid the allocation of a largish sum to a body like the BC which is engaged on admittedly experimental work. The Treasury do not like experiments. (BW 2/228, letter 2 September 1940)

However, the decision on this cumbersome administrative structure was irrevocable.

Given this structure, it was probably inevitable that problems would arise in the sharing of information. In February 1941 Ifor Evans of the British Council had to write to ask Basil Yeaxlee, secretary of the Central Advisory Council for Adult Education in HM Forces (above), for an account of its work with 'foreign troops'. Yeaxlee duly reported on a range of provision, which included talks and English classes for French troops in Bristol and French sailors in Exeter; English classes for Norwegians in Glasgow, and the irregular attendance of Polish troops in St Andrews (Report, 17 February 1941: BW 2/229).

A particular conflict emerged between the British Council and the more senior levels of the army. These arose from their different basic assumptions about the task. The British Council believed that it was responsible for a broad educational programme, in which English language tuition was included. The War Office at that point saw its responsibility to Allied troops as only to ensure minimal language competence. In a letter dated 28 January 1941 to the Foreign Office, A S Wood, Secretary-General of the British Council, complained:

> *It now appears that the War Office are not prepared to authorise cultural or educational work amongst the Allied armies on anything more than a trivial scale …* (BW 2/229)

and reported that the Allied governments in exile were complaining of less favourable treatment by the army than by the other services. The situation began to ease, however, and on 1 April 1941 a request came from the Director of Army Education for help from the British Council with 'British culture and way of life' (BW 2/229).

Finally, at a meeting 17 April 1941 between the British Council and the War Office, the new educational thinking that was already being developed in the army (above), seems to have prevailed, and Colonel Bendall, director of the Directorate for Army Education, could express his 'gratification that it is now possible to discuss the problems of educational and cultural work for the Allied units in a different atmosphere' (BW 2/229). It was agreed that the British Council would be given more freedom to work. Its officers

> *should survey and report to the Council on the educational and cultural needs of the Polish, Belgian, Dutch, Czechoslovak and Norwegian Armies and the Free French Forces.* (BW 2/229)

When the Council received these reports it would forward them to the War Office, 'indicating in what way their resources can usefully be employed'. For its part, the army would send to the Council the names of its own British Liaison Officers assigned to the Allied armies.

Challenges to the British Council presented by the new learners

An early challenge for the British Council came with its realisation that it would have to deal with learners well outside its traditional experience. Before the war its assumption, based on cultural exchanges and teaching overseas students, was that the students would be a quite highly educated elite. So there was dismay at the discovery that a group of Newfoundland foresters – English speakers – were functionally illiterate (BW 2/49).

Then the government's wartime responsibility extended beyond the UK to other – different – groups of foreigners. Groups of Polish women and children refugees had somehow made their way to eastern Africa. They were described as 'chiefly the better type of peasant', and it was decided that two Polish speakers would be better to teach the British way of life to 21,000 learners spread across Uganda, Tanganyika, Nyasaland and Northern Rhodesia (BW 7/3). Italian prisoners of war in Ethiopia were divided into three categories by educational background, with adherence to fascism being aligned with the lowest levels of education (BW 7/3). They too had to be taught English and the values of the British way of life.

A second challenge arose from the fact that the learners were located right across the UK and in very different situations. Some were serving in units alongside UK forces and/or being trained by English speakers; but many English language classes took place in national centres, on board ship, or within units in the forces, all of which dealt with one national group. This meant the learners were frequently in monolingual groups, and this in turn encouraged the adoption of translation methods of teaching and learning.

Finally, the Council had also to provide for the wider educational needs of the newcomers. There was a programme to train Poles to teach English in secondary schools in Poland after the war (BW 2/49), though in the event many of these could not return to the Poland of the communist bloc (below). Its brief was also extended to inquire into the 'continued university education of students serving in the armed units' (BW 2/229). Probably the most high-profile of these courses was the Polish medical school, under Professor Juracz, at Edinburgh University, but there were also Polish students at the Liverpool School of Architecture (Donaldson, 1984, p. 118). At a lower academic level, the further education needs of learners were also encouraged. Belgian candidates were entered for the London University matriculation examination (below), and there were professional programmes such as an Advanced Course in Civil Administration for Polish officers, involving input from the London County Council (BW 108/1).

Finally, the Council would also be involved in monitoring the provision of education for the children of resident foreigners (below).

Organisation of the programme

Committee structure

The Council therefore had to manage a very complex programme of work, and a Committee Structure was set up to oversee it. First there was the Home Division Executive Committee. This included representatives of the Home Office, Colonial Office, Foreign Office, Board of Education, Scottish Board of Education, the Institute of Education and Nottingham University, all under the chairmanship of Sir Herbert Emerson, High Commissioner for Refugees under the Protection of the League of Nations. There was also the Advisory Committee on Foreigners in Great Britain. This committee received regular reports from the Regional Committees and the National Houses (below).

The reports of these committees, along with others such as the Inter-departmental Committee on Basic English, the Books and Periodicals Committee and the Advisory Committee of English Overseas, which were outside the Home Division, plus a wealth of correspondence, provide a rich source of information on how the programmes progressed.

Day-to-day administration and financial organisation

These seem to have been a perpetual headache. The records bear ample testimony to the tireless work of Nancy Parkinson in particular, who was awarded an OBE for her services. In addition to very heavy administrative duties,[9] her office had to respond to endless requests from RAF camps and elsewhere for books – in French, in Polish, in Czech – as well as books for teaching English. Nancy Parkinson was responsible for approaching Evans Brothers with a proposal for a book on *Britain and her War Effort* in Czech, Polish and Dutch, though this does not seem to have materialised. There was also the large amount of correspondence on Basic English books to deal with (below).

Regional structures

Four regional officers were appointed to co-ordinate the range of complex activities across the four national regions. One insight into their work, and an account of the burgeoning provision of English language teaching, is provided in the unpublished memoir by H Harvey Wood, regional officer for Scotland. The focus is on the Poles, as the Polish army had re-formed in Scotland (Zubrycki, 1956, p. 64):

Teachers had to be found in very considerable numbers, to teach English to Polish troops, to Polish airmen and the crews of Polish warships. Many of these teachers had never taught English as a foreign language before, and some of the best of them had never taught English at all before, but had been modern language teachers, and were therefore familiar with the problems associated with teaching and learning a new tongue ... [all over Scotland] from the Borders to the extreme north. Some did their teaching aboard destroyers and submarines, and occasionally went to sea with their pupils, in order that the continuity of their studies should not be interrupted. The Poles were wonderful pupils, and rapidly acquired a command of English which, if not always faithful to idiomatic usage, was more vivid and picturesque than the original. (Donaldson, 1984, p. 120)

This may be a rather optimistic view of both learners and teachers, but the commitment, energy and enthusiasm are unquestionable. Harvey Wood sensibly recognised the value of having teachers experienced in teaching modern foreign languages.

National centres

National centres were soon set up all over the country, often characterised as national houses. In London there were the Polish Hearth, the Czechoslovak Institute, the Yugoslav 'Dom' and the Belgian, Netherlands and Norwegian Centres. In Liverpool there was a large Allied Centre, which was later bombed. There were smaller centres all over the country. Although their maintenance and the oversight of their day-to-day expenditure was the responsibility of the British Council, the centres could choose their programmes, and what they offered was wide and varied (below).

Wider educational objectives of the programmes in action

The detailed quarterly reports received by the Advisory Committee on Foreigners in Great Britain (above) provide a fascinating snapshot of the breadth and complexity of the programme nationally, and illustrate the British Council's aim to meet the widest adult and further educational wishes of the learners, to include the needs of children and to foster good public relations. The report for July–September 1943 is a good example (BW 2/49). ESOL practitioners today may note with some surprise the appointment of a Muslim teacher in Glasgow (below).

The London and South-Eastern Region reported on outings for Polish officers, an RAF reception for Indian officers, a luncheon for West Indian technicians, films shows for Gibraltarians, a concert for Danes at the YWCA and lectures on 'British Ideas of Citizenship' at the Belgian Institute, all in London. In Kent and Surrey there were 200 names on the register for English classes, and two candidates had gained the Certificate of Proficiency in English. In Cambridge there was a call for opportunities to develop other and/or peacetime skills from a Dutch meatpacker and a French naval expert interested in woodcarving.

Activities in the London Allied houses had been considerable. At the Belgian Institute nine students had sat the Proficiency exam; there was an advanced course in English for Belgian officers; and – very important for learners looking forward to their postwar education – classes 'are in preparation for the London Matriculation which the Belgian Board of Education will accept for entry to Belgian universities' (above). At the Czech Institute there were classes in Czech, Russian, English and short-hand; while at the Netherlands House, in addition to a concert by the pianist, Myra Joyce, there were classes in English, Dutch and commercial subjects, and correspondence courses were 'conducted' for children or adult language students. At the Polish Hearth four teachers were now employed for the teaching of English, and there were also Polish classes. At the Yugoslav Houses there were classes in English and Serbo-Croat.

In Scotland there had been a Belgian exhibition, and Jan Masaryk (a founder of Czechoslovakia and its first president) had visited the Czechoslovak House. There had been changes in ESOL teachers for the Polish army, while at the Polish Military Bureau in Edinburgh 'a series of courses for interpreters and staff officers continues with undiminished success'. There were English courses for both staff and patients at the Polish Military Hospital no 1. A special teacher had been teaching the merchant seamen on the Clyde, and a Muslim teacher had been appointed to teach in a Muslim Centre. Ways had been found to help 300 of the 1,500 Newfoundland foresters with their literacy problems, and 'pupils can now read and write simple English'. Courses to prepare Polish teachers of English in Poland after the war had received the approval of the Board of Education, the Polish Board of Education and the Scottish Board of Education. Books had been distributed to Canadians, Russians, French, Poles and Norwegians.

In the South-West, candidates had been entered for Cambridge Proficiency, matriculation and other examinations. Dual-language schools for children had been inspected, and there had been 'special shows for Allied children'. There had even been the teaching of French in a Brixham elementary school.

Such diversity characterised the work of the Home Division of the Council throughout the war.

The Books and Periodicals Committee

Although this committee was concerned mainly with its continuing overseas responsibilities, it also became involved with the situation of the Resident Foreigners. On 25 June 1940 it called for books to be sent to alien children interned on the Isle of Man; in July 1940 it authorised textbooks for the Polish army; in January 1941 the Committee was considering brochures (annotated lists) on 'British Life and Thought' for Resident Foreigners. In July 1941 there were moves for a 'Short History of England' to be translated into Allied Languages (all in BW 70/1). On 25 June 1942 it proposed sending vol 4 of Eckersley's *Essential English* to 'centres where the others are being used' (BW 2, p. 225).

A letter on behalf of the Committee dated 9 December 1940 recorded the Committee's involvement with Basic English. This involved not only supplying French, German, Poles and Czechs with Basic English textbooks (below), but also distributing works like *Arms and the Man* in Basic English (BW 2, p. 255).

The Advisory Committee on English Overseas

Within the broader programme offered to Resident Foreigners, the teaching of English was vital. No one methodology or course was promoted. Eckersley's books were certainly used, but by no means exclusively. In July 1940 the Home Division responded to requests from the various units of the Polish army in Scotland for Eckersley's *Basic English* ('well supplied and being appreciated') and also Linguaphone course books (BW 2/229). This eclecticism reflected the general policy of the Advisory Committee on English Overseas.

This rather august committee, under the chairmanship of Gilbert Murray, met regularly between 1941 and 1943. Its remit was broad. It was very concerned about the quality of teacher training, interested in the latest theories of language teaching and learning, and was represented on the joint committee with the Cambridge Syndicates 'for the general supervision of the Cambridge Certificate of Proficiency in English'.

71

In October 1942 the Committee was becoming anxious about the quality of English teaching for Resident Foreigners. Having learned – one wonders how – that Czech teachers to the Czech forces 'clearly knew little about teaching methods', the Committee cast around to find a writer for a 'brochure,' or what we would today call a handbook, of some 20–25 pages on teaching methods. Harold Palmer, a member of the Committee, was to be approached. He was also to be encouraged to prepare a course of English for adult foreign learners (BW 71/1). Nothing seems to have come of these ideas.

More significant for this study was the role the Advisory Committee saw for itself in investigating the various methods for teaching English. To this end, it invited presentations on various ELT programmes and methodologies: Michael West on his *New Method* publications, A S Hornby on his *Progressive English course*, C K Ogden on Basic English and Eckersley on his *Essential English*, as well as a speaker from Berlitz. Daniel Jones spoke on how to construct a gramophone course' and a Mr T Beach from Kilburn Polytechnic demonstrated the use of the gramophone in the classroom. Mr E H Paxton from the BBC gave a presentation.

Though the committee put its imprimatur on no one method or course, it was particularly opposed to the wholesale adoption of Basic English (BE). One of its own members reported a view that 'BE has a special value in that it teaches adults in the shortest possible time to move intelligently among ideas, emotions and facts' (BW 71/1, 24 February 1943) but this member herself believed the BE vocabulary was too limited. This Committee's general opposition to Basic English was in line with, and may have influenced, the British Council's overall hostility towards the promulgation of Basic English nationally and internationally (traced below).

Basic English

It is useful at this point to reiterate that 'Basic' is an acronym for 'British, American, Scientific, International, Commercial' and comprises the 850-word vocabulary devised by C K Ogden, which he believed was sufficient for a system of global communication. He is reported to have said that it would take seven years to learn English, seven months to learn Esperanto and seven weeks to learn Basic English.

The Basic English system

Some of the early criticisms of Basic English have remained. It is said that the system is constricting and that the circumlocutions necessary if the speaker/user is to remain within the restricted vocabulary can be clumsy. For second-language learners there is a further problem in the way the system can, in the wrong hands, encourage recourse to a number of idiomatic phrases which, though simple in terms of vocabulary, are difficult for the second-language learner to understand. There is continued debate over the actual choice of the 850 words, and criticisms of the restricted number of verbs and the use instead of 'operators', so that 'dined' would be 'had dinner'.

However, the system still has defenders of its strengths, particularly its clarity. In its promulgation of a controlled vocabulary and the systematic approach to acquiring language it was, and has remained, true to the mainstream of ELT thinking. Furthermore, one scholar has suggested that Ogden has not been properly accorded the credit he is due, and that his work on language stood 'at the "crossroads" where psychology, philosophy, linguistics and a host of other academic disciplines met' (Sargant and Anderson, 1977, p. 240).

Political importance of Basic English

International interest in Basic English grew throughout the 1930s, and centres to promote and teach it were set up across the world (Gordon, 1990). More and more works were reprinted in Basic English, and at one point the Basic English version of the New Testament was selling at 1,000 copies a day (Gordon, 1990, p. 39).

Political interest in the system increased, and Neville Chamberlain appointed a Committee of the Economic Council to investigate methods of teaching simplified English. The aim was to use the 850-word Basic English system as a basis for the development of English as the international lingua franca. However, war broke out and the Committee never met (Gordon, 1990, p. 49).

Basic English was then taken up and enthusiastically supported by Winston Churchill, who set up a Cabinet Committee on Basic English. In a report of 6 December 1940, this Committee recommended that 'definite encouragement should be given to the development of Basic English as an auxiliary international language and administrative language' (Gordon, 1990, p. 50). There followed a period of both enthusiasm and hostility. Churchill spoke publicly in its favour when he accepted an honorary degree from Harvard University on 6 September 1943, and then made the case eloquently in the House of Commons on 9 March 1944. He had this statement and the Atlantic Charter translated into Basic English.

It is not the business of this account to trace the detailed history of Basic English, with its attendant hostilities and conflicts and the Axis view that its promotion amounted to an English attempt to secure linguistic domination of the world (Gordon, 1990, p. 52). It is enough to note that never before had English language teaching received the attention of two prime ministers.

Such political interest would re-emerge at the beginning of the next century, but this time the position of English as the dominant world language would present a different challenge to central government (Chapter 7).

The British Council's role

The British Council became centrally and officially involved with C K Ogden and Basic English.[10] One involvement related to issuing course books to help in teaching English to Resident Foreigners. The second was the official task of encouraging the adoption of Basic English at a national level in order to promote it as an international language. The British Council acted on behalf of the government in 1946 when the copyright was assigned to the Crown.[11]

From the outset, members of the British Council were unconvinced of, if not absolutely hostile to, the wholesale appropriation of Ogden's Basic English system. The Books and Periodicals Committee opposed printing its brochures in Basic English (BW 70/1, 6 May 1941). On his side, Ogden expressed his pathological aversion to the British Council (Gordon, 1990, p. 51). None the less, the British Council set up its Interdepartmental Basic English Committee (BW 1/35).

Members of this Committee met the Chair of the Cabinet Basic English Committee on 10 September 1943 to discuss the report on the effectiveness of the Basic English system which the British Council was to present to the Cabinet Committee. The British Council had drawn its advice from reports from its centres across the world – though an examination of the archives themselves suggests perhaps that the favourable ones were not cited (BW 2/35).

In its criticisms of Basic English, the British Council pointed to the unidiomatic and distorted phrases that result from the use of 'operators' (above, p. 73), which could be ridiculed in an English-speaking context and had to be unlearned by the student. The Council used as illustration the fact that, as the system does not allow 'he loves'; the students must instead use 'he is loving', 'he makes love' and 'he has love of'. There were other criticisms over the actual choice of the 850 words, using as an illustration 'We will fight them on the beaches' would become 'on the edges of the land'. There was also criticism of the approach to stress and spelling.

Modern scholars point out that such attacks were frequent and often facile. Basic English was a foundation and, like all other systematic courses, did not preclude the learner from going on to acquire a full and detailed knowledge of the language.

Despite its reservations, however, the British Council was committed to supporting the development of Basic English course books, although, as has been seen, these were not promoted to the exclusion of other methods.

Basic English course books

C K Ogden's primary work on Basic English was developed between 1925 and 1927, and he set up his Orthological Institute in 1927 to promote it. He established the copyright to his work with four publications between 1930 and 1935: *Basic English; The Basic Vocabulary; Debabelization;* and *The Basic Words.* Following the publication in 1935 of *Basic Step by Step* (Ogden, 1935), he next produced a series of *Step by Step* ELT course books in various languages. An interesting development in his thinking came in a letter dated 16 April 1940 to Professor Routh, in which he says that he is now working on 'Basic English for the teaching of Science through English and English through Science' (BW 2/55), and in 1942 he published *Basic for Science.*

The 1935 *Step by Step* course was the one of immediate relevance to the learners in the Allied Forces. The 30 steps were followed systematically. The vocabulary for each step was divided into 'Things' – nouns – and 'Qualities' – adverbs and adjectives. The course started with 'The Body', so the 'Things' were 'hand, knee', etc and the 'Qualities' were 'right', 'left', 'straight', 'bent', 'opposite'. The course proceeded in this way through 'Food', 'Work', 'Weather', 'Family', 'Buildings' and so on. 'Time' was dealt with in Step 10. Step 16 was 'Amusement' and Step 17 was 'Education'. Each step had a reading passage of increasing length with no dialogue, and Step 18, 'Reading', contained a long piece of fiction. Each passage was followed by questions with prescribed answers. The reading passage for Step 26, 'Peace', reflected the recent memory of the First World War and its vocabulary – 'destruction', 'hospital', death', 'flag' and 'gun' would have been equally apposite for Allied soldiers in the Second World War. Step 29, 'government', with a vocabulary of nouns including 'agreement', 'control', 'trouble', 'war' and 'peace' and a passage on the role and duties of government, would have been equally apposite. Ogden was also aware of the need for oral practice, and his Introduction included a section on 'The Rhythm of English', which, while avoiding the terms themselves, dealt with word stress and sentence stress.

The publication of *Basic Step by Step* meant that the Basic English format was ready and open for adaptation and development. However, it was predicated on learners who were literate and who had had some level of education.

Next came the development of course books in various languages, building on the same format. *Le Basic English en 30 leçons graduées* was published in 1939. This followed the same pattern as the 1935 English book but had notes, lesson by lesson, in French, and there was a French–English vocabulary list. It also had illustrations, including a woodcut showing machinery and line drawings demonstrating prepositions of place.

Basic English and the Allied forces

At the outbreak of war there were *Basic English Step by Step* course books in French, German and Spanish, but there would clearly be a need for versions in other languages. On 28 June 1940 (BW 2/255), only six days after the fall of France, Ogden, writing to E Sykes, Secretary of the Books and Periodicals Committee of the British Council, reported that *Basic English in Polish* was already in proof and asked for a reprint of 1,800–2,000 copies of *Basic Step by Step* in French, at the cost of 2/– a copy, 'for refugees from France now in England'. He asked if the British Council could buy these up as there had already been a loss of £135 on books specially reprinted for the British Council (BW 2/255).

On 2 August 1940 fifty copies of 'Le Basic English Cours Gradue' [*sic*] were sent to a French unit in north Wales. More significantly, on 5 August 500 copies of the French version were sent to RAF Station Cosford, near Wolverhampton, for use with Czech airmen. They were clearly expected to learn English through French. There was therefore an obvious case for reprinting the Czech version of *Step by Step*, which had been published in Prague the previous year. Sykes noted in a memo of 2 August 1940 that there were 130,000 Czech nationals in the country, 'of whom the vast majority do not speak English', and urged the reprinting of 5,000 copies of the Prague version (BW 2/255).

New adaptations of the *Step by Step* series were soon commissioned and published under the general title Basic English for ...'. *Basic English for Polish Students* appeared in 1941 (Ogden 1941c) under the aegis of the British Council. It was adapted by Cecelia Halpern, one of Ogden's staff at the Orthological Institute. She was paid £40 for the translation (BW 2/255, 10 January 1940). *Basic English for Norwegian Students* appeared in 1941 (Ogden, 1941a), published 'in association with the Royal Norwegian government'. Ogden himself did the adaptation for the *Basic English for Dutch Students* in 1941 (Ogden, 1941b), and another version of this, entitled *Basic English for Dutch and Flemish Students*, appeared in 1942 (Ogden, 1942a), both with a foreword by the Netherlands cultural minister. *Basic English for Czecho-Slovak Students* appeared last, in 1942 (Ogden, 1942b).

These course books followed the '30 Steps' but were expanded from *Step by Step* in French (for example), to include an added section of sometimes quite long reading passages. These now included passages of dialogue, particularly in texts on 'The Bank', 'The Store', 'The Restaurant' and 'The Hotel', and to some extent foreshadowed the development of situational approaches in the 1960s. This general format of *Basic English for...* was the same for all the versions, with translations of explanations and the questions and answers and, of course, vocabulary lists. There were also woodcuts and line drawings – more than appeared in the French version. However, there were some differences among the different language versions, indicating that the authors had some flexibility and autonomy. The number and order of the reading passages varied. The core of eight passages was supplemented by up to five more, and these could vary. Passages on Livingstone and Stanley and on Captain Cook could give way to 'How and when the earth was formed' and 'The electric power industry'. There was an example of social sight vocabulary in 'DANGER: ROAD UP' in the Polish version, while the

Czech version had a whole new section on 'Basics for Business' with a number of model business letters.

As with all systems, it was acknowledged that there was a need for teacher training (BW 2/255, 20 April 1940). But the evidence from the French and Polish forces (above) suggests that in the right hands the programme could work effectively. Certainly the British Council and Evans Brothers, Ogden's publisher, devoted considerable time and resources to the production of the *Step by Step* books.

Reactions and responses of the wartime learners

The British Council's remit to support the wider educational needs of the newcomers meant that some Allied service personnel could take full advantage of the opportunities they were offered to become civil servants, doctors, architects and teachers of English, or to prepare for further and higher education. These were equipped at the end of the war either with useful qualifications, or with entrance qualifications to continue their studies.

The approach to learning English of the vast majority of service personnel, however, seems to have varied. The unwillingness of the Polish troops in St Andrews to attend classes has already been noted (above, p. 65), while English classes at the Norwegian House in London had to be abandoned (BW 108/1). But this does not mean that the servicemen were unwilling to learn English, especially if it helped in making social contacts. J. F Jaworzyn, a Polish airman, remembered:

> Formal lessons in English were started, and we were assigned to various station duties. The more adventurous of us, but not necessarily those knowing any English, began to go out on short passes. Most seemed to make it to Blackpool, the nearest resort, coming back with tales of their encounters with the English. (Jaworzyn, 1984, p. 15)

Jaworzyn continued with his studies long enough to pass his examination (unspecified) in English, but still felt his inadequacy in the language (Jaworzyn, 1984, p. 19). However, as he commented, most of the young Polish airmen preferred 'a journey to Blackpool than [*sic*] an hour with a book on English idioms' (p 19). The tribute he paid to the English for their welcome and friendliness, and their tolerance of any weaknesses in the English language, is echoed in many accounts by members of the Allied Forces. Certainly the warmth of their reception, plus their own youth and their wish to meet English speakers, provided a positive context in which to learn the language. This was certainly true in the case of Paul Lambermont, a member of the prestigious Lorraine Squadron in a mixed Franco-Britannique mess, who wrote of the mutual teaching of songs in the two languages (Lambermont, 1956, p. 76). On the other hand, many of the Allied Forces served in national, monolingual units or on board their own ships, so there were fewer opportunities for them to meet English speakers, and in any case the need to learn English was often not pressing.

However, for some there were very serious reasons for overcoming language difficulties. André Jubelin in the Fleet Air Arm offers a sobering reminder:

> I am still dreadfully handicapped by the language. Our wireless communi-
> cation is definitely poor and it is a torment to me to try to make myself
> understood while in flight. (Jubelin, 1953, p. 98)

Here knowing the language could make the difference between life and death.

For some members of the Allied Forces and refugees, not knowing English would assume a special importance. These were the Poles in particular. After the war had ended some of them wanted to continue to learn English at the Polish Hearth. A letter from the British Council dated 10 January 1946, replying to a request from Major Gulkowski for the continuation of free English lessons, stated that these could no longer be provided (BW 108/4).

Polish resettlement[12]

It can be presumed that these would-be learners were among the many Poles who did not want to, and in many cases could not, return to a Soviet-dominated Poland. They wished to stay in the UK or to emigrate to another English-speaking country, and chose to take the opportunity offered to them by Ernest Bevin in May 1946 to be demobilised into a Polish Corps here, then either staying in the UK or settling elsewhere (Anders, 1981, p. 294).

Following the passing of the Polish Resettlement Act in March 1947, a major resettlement programme was set up, with the National Assistance Board taking responsibility for the care of the families (including accommodation in hostels), the Ministry of Education for their education and the Ministry of Labour and National Service for helping them into employment. This programme included language tuition, the reason being:

> *Lack of knowledge of the English language was one of the most serious obstacles [sic] to the rapid absorption of the members of the Corps in industrial work, and accordingly provision was made for intensive courses of English within the resettlement camps.* (Zubrycki, 1956, p. 90)

The Committee for the Education of Poles in Great Britain was set up to oversee a broad programme of education.

The demobilised members of the armed services were soon joined by Polish refugees from across the world who knew no English at all, including many children who had had very little formal education of any kind since 1939. The children were not immediately sent to English schools. Education was first provided for them in the camps and hostels to which the families were sent, and this included tuition in English (Zubrycki, 1956, p. 94). The children were gradually enrolled in British schools, though by April 1950 there were still 4,000 Polish children in 39 Polish schools (Zubrycki, 1956, p. 94).

Provision for the adults included setting up the Polish University College in London to prepare Polish students for London University External Degrees in engineering and economics. The Polish Education Committee also took responsibility for courses in the English language and the British way of life (sounding very like the normal British Council courses); these were run in the National Assistance Board hostel where many Poles were living. The programmes encouraged the Poles to meet as many British people as possible. The take-up seems to have been considered satisfactory. In 1949 there were 17,000 Poles in 34 hostels, and in 1950 there were 13,000 Poles in 25 hostels. It was reported that 34 per cent of the residents of these hostels were taking advantage of these courses (Zubrycki, 1956, p. 94). The trades union movement too played a part, and a Polish section of the Transport and General Workers Union was established (Zubrycki, 1956, p. 99) which, for the first three years of its existence, ran classes in English (Zubrycki, 1956, p. 101).

Responses and experiences of the learners in settlement
There is a considerable amount of material on the Polish community and how they settled, and this provides a valuable insight into the

difficulties faced even by a group for whom settlement would seem to have been easy. Although valued allies in the war and from a Christian, European background, they still encountered hostility.[13]

Biographical accounts describe the continuing language difficulties that the Polish settlers faced. One young man had to give up a course at Hammersmith Technical College because he found the English too difficult (Barton, 2000, p. 64).

The experience of one woman in particular will chime with many ESOL teachers and learners today. When she arrived in England at the age of 18 from a Polish refugee camp in East Africa, she wanted to train as a nurse. Initially she had great difficulty with English. Even though she had had lessons in the camp school, 'English was just a noise.' She spoke warmly of her 'excellent English teacher' (Barton, 2000, p. 31) who helped her pass her examinations and qualify as a nurse. She married another Pole, and when they were unable to fulfil their dream and return to Poland they set up home in Lincoln and then in Nottingham to bring up their family. Despite the length of her stay in England, and the fact that she had qualified as a nurse in the English system, she could still write in 2000 (in English):

> I still felt self-conscious about my competency in the English language despite the years spent in Lincoln. It was difficult for me at parents' evenings or when I had to discuss problems, and it marginalized my involvement in school life. I felt that it was a barrier at times to understanding my children's educational needs, but they all succeeded in school. (Barton, 2000, p. 32)

The account given by this Polish nurse reminds us how easy it is to underestimate the tensions, conflicts and continuing lack of confidence experienced by adult ESOL learners, even in the most apparently successful cases. One wonders how far her perception of her inadequacy came from herself, her family or the responses she experienced in the wider community. This young woman drew enormous strength from her local Polish club.

The proliferation of Polish clubs across the country speaks of the profound need for many settlers to maintain their language and cultural identity in their unlooked-for exile. And at least one young woman, born here of Polish parents, spoke enthusiastically of being encouraged to maintain her cultural and linguistic heritage, even though this meant she could not speak any English when she started school here (Barton, 2000, p. 73). Jerzy Zubrycki (1956), in his study of Polish immigrants, underlines this powerful need to maintain a group and personal identity.

Such accounts also cast doubt on any crude black-and-white assumptions by governments about children's early language experiences and their need to start school being able to speak English. The UK in 2007 has many citizens from a Polish-speaking home background who are now making valuable contributions to our economic and cultural life – as there are from many other linguistic backgrounds.

Zubrycki identified 'The factors affecting the adjustment of the Polish community' in 1956, so his interviews took place within a decade of settlement. He described three possible states: assimilation, accommodation and conflict. In his view, knowing the language played only one part in resettlement, alongside personality, age, personal circumstances (including marriage and employment), war trauma, cultural isolation, social degradation and discrimination in employment. Assimilation was more likely in mixed marriages and might involve naturalization, but even this did not mean the loss of Polish identity. As one young male interviewee said:

> *In my opinion, naturalisation is by no means identical with assimilation. Personally I shall try to be naturalized as soon as possible if this will be in my interest. From what I know about England I am sure it would be no obstacle to my becoming a Polish citizen if a possibility of a return to Poland should occur.* (Zubrycki, 1956, p. 162)

This interviewee could envisage marrying either a Polish or an English girl, but he would want the Polish girl to learn English and the English girl to learn Polish. Another young man stated:

> *Sooner or later I am going to be naturalized, yet I do not intend to get completely assimilated with the British community.* (Zubrycki, 1956, p. 162)

He would maintain his cultural identity:

> *I think that a man may be naturalized, may speak perfect English and feel at home among the English, yet he may be fully conscious of his own nationality.* (Zubrycki, 1956, p. 162)

A third interviewee considered the act of naturalisation as 'a purely technical factor', but was troubled as he weighed the issues of cultural and national identity (Zubrycki, 1956, p. 163). A fourth saw naturalisation as a 'matter of legal character' and assimilation as a 'very long process' which would take two generations. He himself hoped to return to Poland (*ibid*).

Many British-born offspring of Anglo-Polish marriages report their own slightly different perceptions, particularly of their fathers settling and learning English. In these homes a recurring pattern seems to have been for the children to hear very little Polish; and indeed there was often a policy of speaking only English at home, since it was felt the children would otherwise be at a disadvantage at school. However, their fathers frequently had not mastered English fluently either, and they often drew support from the local Polish community clubs and organisations.

Conclusion

Once the Second World War had broken out, the refugees and Allied service personnel who came to the UK presented an unprecedented demand for English language tuition as well as other forms of training. Provision was made on the assumption that it would help the war effort in the short term, and in the longer term improve Britain's standing in the postwar world, when the temporary residents returned to their homes. So providing for ESOL learners became an arm of foreign policy. As in 1915, the government did not manage this extensive programme centrally, but this time used the British Council. Such delegation would continue with the programmes for future groups.

Zubrycki's analysis of the experience of the Poles who settled in the UK after the war highlighted the complexity of the language and the amount of information that was needed for successful settlement. The experience of the Poles also demonstrated the difficulty that many find in settling in a new country, and the lasting effects of dislocation and of the loss of national and linguistic identity.

The programmes to support the wider educational needs of the newcomers (including for the Poles who stayed on after the war) stand out in marked contrast to the attitude of governments to future groups of immigrants and refugees. The major groups of ESOL learners to come to the UK in the 1950s and 1960s would be immigrants from the New Commonwealth. The challenge they presented to governments, and the provision made for them, would be very different.

CHAPTER THREE

1950–1970: Immigrants from the New Commonwealth

Further groups of refugees arrived during the 1950s and 1960s. Following the Soviet invasion of Hungary in 1956, 17,000 Hungarians sought refuge in the UK. A further 5,000 fled from Czechoslovakia after the Soviet invasion of their country in 1968. But these arrivals in no way matched the numbers who came as immigrants from the New Commonwealth, often noted as beginning with the arrival of the *Windrush* from the West Indies in 1948. These new immigrants came to work, and indeed were often directly recruited for this in their homeland. Employers in the public and private sectors – London Transport, British Rail, managers of foundries in the West Midlands and mills in Yorkshire – welcomed the new recruits. They were providing the extra labour that was needed to rebuild Britain after the war, and so the numbers of such immigrants grew rapidly.

The general pattern was for the workers themselves – usually the men – to come first and for their families then to join them. So from the beginning of the 1960s there were recently arrived families with children to provide for, as well as the children who were then born to them in the UK. These newcomers presented a new challenge to governments in providing for their settlement.

Identifying and meeting the challenge

In 1969 an important and influential report by the Institute of Race Relations (IRR), E J B Rose's *Colour and Citizenship* (1969), traced the pattern of immigration since 1956 and its implications. It noted that, according to a PEP survey in 1966, there were about 900,000 immigrants from different parts of the New Commonwealth in the UK

(p. 99), though it also noted the difficulty of collecting accurate statistics (p. 94).

This lengthy and detailed IRR report identified the challenge that these new communities were presenting to the education, housing and other statutory services, as well as to the employment market, to voluntary organisations and to community relations. The report made detailed recommendations in all these areas.

While the educational analysis and recommendations concentrated on the school sector, the disadvantage faced by non-English speakers in the workplace were also highlighted (pp. 321, 323), and companies were urged to use the 1964 Industrial Training Act to provide employees 'with opportunities to learn English, whether by organizing instruction at the place of work or through day release' (p. 716).

The general focus of concern nationally tended to be on the immigrants from the Caribbean and India and Pakistan, but the 1969 report did identify other groups, notably the Greek Cypriots, who constituted the fourth largest group.[1]

The challenge for the government and voluntary organisations was to meet the new and different language learning needs of the new adult settlers. These could not be isolated from the responses in the school sector, which for a time led the way in developing appropriate forms of language teaching. For a time, also, the language needs of speakers of English as a second or other language and the needs of Afro-Caribbean learners who spoke a different dialect of English or Patois[2] were sometimes conflated. Also, the language needs of the new settlers could never be isolated from the impact of other factors, such as employment and housing, and of the increasing racism that many were encountering, which raised anxiety in successive governments.

The government's responses

The government responded in two ways: first by restricting immigration, and second by setting up programmes and passing legislation to ameliorate the situation of those already here.

Immigration legislation

The 1948 British Nationality Act allowed Commonwealth citizens to enter and settle freely in Britain. The government's concern at the number of immigrants settling in the UK led in 1962 to the passing of the Commonwealth Immigrants [*sic*] Act. This severely limited the number of immigrants entering the country by introducing a system of vouchers covering different categories. The majority of immigrants arrived under category A – those vouchers issued to employers in the UK to bring in workers; and category B – those issued to skilled applicants.

In 1968 the Commonwealth Immigrants Act restricted entry still further, giving unrestricted entry only to those who could prove 'close ancestral relationship with the UK' and establishing a quota of 1,500 Asian immigrants per annum. The rights of entry of children and elderly dependants were limited, and all such dependants were required to have entry clearance certificates. The voucher system introduced by the 1962 Act became non-statutory, to be run at the government's discretion.

In the meantime national, often virulent, hostility to immigration continued to grow, further fuelled by Enoch Powell's 'Rivers of Blood' speech at a local Conservative Party AGM in Birmingham on 20 April 1968. Although Edward Heath dismissed Powell from the Conservative Shadow Cabinet for his speech, there were rallies and demonstrations in support of what he had said.

Providing for the new immigrants

To counter the effects of such racism, and as part of the government's 'tough but fair' policy, the 1968 Race Relations Act was introduced. This Act made it illegal to refuse housing, employment or public services to people because of their ethnic backgrounds. There was some controversy over the exclusion of some government services from its provisions, but the Act was a significant step forward, particularly in its extension of the powers of the Race Relations Board to deal with complaints about discrimination.

The provision in the Act that most directly affected ESOL teaching was the setting-up of the Community Relations Commission (CRC) to promote 'harmonious community relations'. This replaced the non-statutory National Council for Commonwealth Immigrants (NCCI), set up in 1965, on the recommendations of the Second Report by the Commonwealth Immigrants Advisory Council in 1964.[3]

The NCCI had already played an important part in influencing the creation of teacher training programmes to meet the needs of immigrant children, and in establishing a network of local community relations councils.[4] The CRC as a statutory body would be in a stronger position to develop the NCCI's work in education; and, as will be seen, its continuing support for adult community language schemes would be crucial to the development of English language provision.

Integration v. assimilation

The various initiatives started in the 1960s have been labelled, then and since, as both assimilationist and integrationist, and this has led to some considerable confusion. In 1967 the Schools Council published a useful caveat as a footnote in *English for the Children of Immigrants*:

> *There is no general agreement regarding the use of the terms 'assimilation' and 'integration' in the context of an immigrant group's relation with the majority community. In this paper assimilation is used to describe processes of mutual adjustment by the immigrant group and the majority community. It does not imply that absorption, or near absorption, is necessarily the goal. The goal may well be 'integration', in the sense in which it describes a society in which the immigrant group continues to be an integer or unit on its own, but which as part of the greater whole is accepted by the majority.* (Schools Council Project, 1967, p. 3; see P Mason, 'What Do We Mean by Integration?', *New Society*, 16 June 1966)

This summary provides a useful characterisation of all the initiatives that are described below, none of which advocated the expunging of the cultural and linguistic identity of the newcomers.

English for immigrants

The Ministry of Education's Pamphlet 43, *English for Immigrants* (1963), was the first government publication dealing with how to respond to the new challenge facing teachers in schools; but it also clearly affirmed the need for adults to learn English, too. In fact, the pamphlet started from the position that these new learners were members of families and new communities.

The introduction to the pamphlet, though focusing on problems, was also sensitive to the needs of the immigrant community as a whole. Teachers should know and understand the position of newly-arrived families as well as how to teach their children. The pamphlet emphasised the need to respect differences in dress, religion, culture and language, and – anticipating the Bullock Report (below) – showed a respect for mother-tongue maintenance. The importance of good home–school relations was stressed. The pamphlet also expressed some concern at what it saw as an over-concentration of immigrant children in particular schools, and a wariness of British parents' hostile responses to this (Ministry of Education, 1963, p. 6).

The advice given in the first three chapters was bottom-up, in that the recommendations came from headteachers, drawing on good practice in the classroom. While the gradual introduction of graded vocabulary was recommended, there was a realistic acceptance that pupils picked up a great deal of language outside the classroom. All the advice and guidance offered in these chapters started from the assumption that English was learned not as a separate subject, but as a means to acquiring education.

In May 1950 HMI, dealing with Other Further Education (OFE), had been given a direct responsibility 'to consider the needs of the increasing number of immigrant workers who required help in learning English' (Elsdon, 2001, p. 26). This history bears testimony to the contribution that HMI would make to the development of ESOL for settlers living and working here.

However, the concluding chapter on adult learning in the Ministry of Education's 1963 report was from an HMI who drew almost exclusively on his experience of teaching English overseas. His chapter only briefly acknowledged the preceding three and, except for the section on Audio and Visual Aids, approached the teaching challenge completely differently. The assumptions about the learners, and the methodology that was recommended, were those appropriate for overseas students. There was no recognition of problems in literacy for adults who might be illiterate in their mother tongue, or who had mastered a different script; there was no dealing with the acquisition of the uncontrolled vocabulary that students had picked up outside the classroom. There was no focus on free and extended writing. In sum, it emphasised English as a subject, rather than English for education and life in the UK.

The Education of Immigrants

The next DES pamphlet, *The Education of Immigrants* (DES, 1965), was even more problem-centred, but it was significant in that it now emphasised the importance of disseminating information on the background of immigrants. This marked a significant watershed in the provision for ESOL learners in the UK. Up to this point the focus had always been on the learner acquiring a knowledge and understanding of the UK.[5] From the 1960s onwards, there would be an emphasis on the 'host' community's need acquire background knowledge of the new communities and an understanding of how to respond to their needs.

The 1965 DES pamphlet again expressed anxiety about possible hostility from (white) British parents; and a concern to keep the proportion of immigrant children to below one-third in any one school had led to LEAs' considering the possibility of 'spreading the children'.[6] British parents had to be reassured that their children's education was not being affected.

The importance of learning English was reiterated, and there were warnings to teachers not to be misled by superficial fluency in older pupils. A pilot training course for teachers at the University of London Institute of Education was commended.

The pamphlet's section on adult immigrants gave colleges the responsibility for teaching work-related English, accompanied by the hope that employers would release their employees:

> The Secretary of State considers that, even though adult immigrants may not intend to settle permanently in this country, they should have an induction course in English ways of living and learn to speak intelligibly. He believes that it is the function of the further education service rather than of employers to provide suitable courses. The government hope that employers will give all possible encouragement to their employees to attend these courses. (DES, 1965, p. 6)

Leaflets about courses were to be sent to offices of the National Assistance Board. Authorities were to contact personnel officers to encourage attendance at classes.

Mothers at home, too, should not be forgotten, the implicit suggestion being that they had a vital role in bringing the children up to standard:

> They should also make special efforts to reach the mothers in the immigrant communities and to provide for them education in the English language and in English social standards at times and in places that would encourage good attendance. (DES, 1965, p. 6)

Over the next half century, official attitudes would change less than might have been expected, and both exhortation to employers and injunctions to mothers would be repeated into the early years of the twenty-first century (see Chapter 7).

Finally, the pamphlet urged colleges of education to prepare trainee teachers for the fact that schools might have pupils from minority ethnic communities. There was reference to the University of London Institute of Education one-year diploma in Teaching English as a Foreign Language (TEFL); and the Schools Council Teaching English Project (Scope) was also noted (below).

Central government financial support for ESOL: Section 11

Central government funding for ESOL teaching in England and Wales was provided for the first time in 1967 under Section 11 of the Local Government Act of 1966. This empowered the Secretary of State at the Home Office:

> to pay grant in respect of the employment of staff to those local authorities who, in his opinion, have to make special provision in the exercise of any of their functions in consequence of the presence within their areas of substantial numbers of people from the Commonwealth whose language or customs differ from those of the rest of the community. (Bagley, 1992, p. 1)

Adults were included from the beginning. The legislation applied only to New Commonwealth immigrants and their children, who had been in the country for fewer than ten years (i.e. those who were seen to be culturally different from the norm, as opposed to those from the white Commonwealth). Local authorities could claim 50 per cent of their costs retrospectively. This was raised in 1969 to 75 per cent to be in line with Urban Programme funding (below). The policy also recognised the need to maintain separate cultural identities, especially in the maintenance of the learners' mother tongues.

Anomalies in the system immediately became apparent. There was a rule that local authorities could apply for funding only if more than 2 per cent of their population qualified. This was unfair, since local authorities could have pockets of New Commonwealth immigrants that far exceeded 2 per cent, but if the overall population was below that percentage they could not claim. The rule which said that New Commonwealth immigrants had to have been in the country for fewer than ten years to qualify was soon seen as totally arbitrary. The position of Pakistanis after Pakistan left the Commonwealth in 1971 was anomalous. The DES report, *The Education of Immigrants* (DES, 1971), noted another anomaly in that children born to parents in the UK did not qualify, while those born overseas did (DES, 1971, p. 25).

In July 1968, the first Urban Programme was initiated as a programme of aid for urban areas with special social needs. The 34 local authorities eligible to apply were chosen on the basis that more than 2 per cent of their households had more than 1.5 persons per room (using the 1966 sample census data) or that their school rolls contained more than 6 per cent immigrants. The funding covered revenue (including staffing) as well as capital costs for the duration of the particular programme.

After the UK joined the European Union in 1973, the government was able to apply to the European Social Fund for funding for Section 11 and other programmes, such as Urban Aid, which were aimed at relieving social or economic deprivation.

With the creation of the Manpower Services Commission in 1973, short-term employment-related courses such as Training Opportunities (TOPs) and Youth Opportunities (YOPS) courses could be set up. They were succeeded by other work-related programmes. These were useful but time-limited. All these other funds could be used to support ESOL work with immigrant communities in Scotland and Northern Ireland, too, if they fulfilled the relevant criteria.

However, the Section 11 programme, with all its deficiencies, was the only one in the UK that was aimed specifically at ethnic minority communities. This, plus the fact that it was not time-limited, meant that it made a major contribution to the development of ESOL in England and Wales, providing the only consistent source of funding for ESOL, year on year, until the incorporation of the colleges and funding under the Further Education Funding Council (Chapter 6). Until the early 1990s, Section 11 funding also allowed a number of local authorities to develop anti-racist, multicultural initiatives and to support the maintenance of the mother tongues of the learners who qualified for funding (below).

The history of Section 11 and its importance for ESOL provision is traced throughout the following chapters. At this stage it is enough to emphasise some general points. Local authorities used Section 11 money mainly for education and mainly for ESOL, and this included provision in the 16–19 years and adult education sectors as well as schools. However, the take-up was always uneven. From its inception, the fact that Section 11 funding made a contribution only to staffing costs was seen as a major disadvantage. Criticisms of the programme would also focus on its anomalies, inconsistencies, unhelpful restrictions and the difficulties in monitoring its effectiveness. Despite the changing nature of the ESOL population, its remit was not extended to other second-language speakers until 1993, but by then the funding had been cut substantially. It was finally abolished in 1998 and replaced by the Ethnic Minority Achievement Grant, processed by the DfES for schools, and for colleges by the Ethnic Minority Students Achievement Grant, processed by the Learning and Skills Council (LSC).

The abolition of the LCC and creation of the ILEA and GLC

The 1963 London Government Act saw the abolition of the London County Council and the creation of the Greater London Council, which incorporated the old LLC boroughs and the – many, newly created – outer boroughs.

This had a direct impact on ESOL provision in the Greater London area. The GLC did not cover the education functions of the old LCC area, and the Inner London Education Authority became the new education authority for that area, that is the London boroughs of Islington, Kensington and Chelsea, Westminster, Camden, Hammersmith and Fullham, Hackney, City of London, Tower Hamlets, Greenwich, Lewisham, Southwark, Lambeth and Wandsworth.[7] The ILEA was therefore able to continue, and to build on, the work of the LCC in providing ESOL tuition for adults, and it was able to develop work of national importance, too (below). However, many of the outer boroughs also had significant immigrant communities and made their own influential contributions to the development of ESOL. This was particularly true in Ealing with its Pathway Centre, in Waltham Forest, in Brent and in Croydon.

English language teaching in the 1960s

The dominant methodology in the 1960s was what became known as Situational Language Teaching, combining the structural with the situational approach, and continuing to emphasise the focus on the spoken language. This is usefully summed up by J Richards and T S Rodgers as follows:

92

1   *Language teaching begins with the spoken language. Material is taught orally before it is presented in written form.*

2   *The target language is the language of the classroom.*

3   *New language points are introduced and practised situationally.*

4   *Vocabulary selection procedures are followed to ensure that a general service vocabulary is covered.*

5   *Items of grammar are graded following the principle that simple forms should be taught before complex ones.*

6   *Reading and writing are introduced once a sufficient lexical and grammatical basis is established.* (Richards and Rodgers, 2001, p. 39)

The first major published course that followed the situational method was A S Hornby's *Oxford Progressive English for Adult Learners* (1954–6) which, in three volumes, progressed from absolute beginners to advanced learners. Illustrated with lively line drawings, it followed all the rules of the situational approach, with exercises to test comprehension and practise grammar points. The images and content reflected life in Britain from a white middle-class point of view, but the passages from newspapers and the use of maps located language learning in the real world. However, the author himself realised how rapidly the course moved and an alternative course, The *Oxford Progressive English Alternative Course*, was published in 1964. This moved much more slowly, and used accounts of the day-to-day life of a family, the Wests, and their friends, to develop the acquisition of vocabulary and grammatical structures. This also allowed for some mild humour. However, from the point of view of ESOL teachers at the time, it moved too quickly for those learners becoming literate for the first time or for those acquiring a second literacy, and it presented a view of life in the UK that few of the new learners would have had the opportunity to observe.

Also following the situational approach was *Situational English* (anon. 1967), adapted from materials especially developed for immigrants into Australia. Although illustrated with some small, humorous line drawings, the text was quite dense. It moved more slowly than even Hornby's alternative course, but there was still a heavy emphasis on grammar. The characters used in the dialogues were diverse, but the main emphasis reflected life in middle-class English families at home and work, with some stilted dialogues between two overseas students. There was no attempt at all to deal with literacy.

Finally, what many ESOL teachers in the 1960s still found in cupboards – as did their colleagues teaching overseas – were the course books produced by C E Eckersley.[8]

June Derrick provided a useful critique of current materials and their suitability for new learners in the UK in her annotated bibliography in *Teaching English to Immigrants* (1966, pp. 236–53). She divided the section into primary and secondary/adult. For the older students she recommended the Hornby courses, commending in particular the drills and exercises and pronunciation work (p. 243). While *Situational English* was generally commended for the way it prepared the learner for using English outside the classroom (p. 244), *Living English in the Arab World* was recommended for students who were having to acquire a new literacy (p. 242). Other courses were also noted briefly, including Hicks's *Foundation of English*, useful for European students, and *Present Day English for Foreign Students*, attractively presented but with very steeply graded grammar (pp. 243–4).

The Schools Council Project in English for Immigrant Children (Scope)[9]

Since it was very clear that none of these schemes adequately met the needs of the new ESOL teachers and learners in school, and later in the post-schools sector, the government funded the Schools Council Project in English for immigrant children (Scope), begun in 1967 and led by June Derrick. Published by Longman, the materials and the accompanying book (Schools Council Project, 1967–76) adapted the latest structural/situational theory in language teaching and learning to the development of the first ESOL syllabus, schemes of work, teachers' books and teaching materials. The project aimed to equip learners to enter mainstream education as soon as possible. Although the original focus was on children, the Scope project also influenced the development of materials for adults.

Scope 1, published in 1967, provided a structured grammatical framework, a systematic building-up of vocabulary and support for literacy, all within the context of everyday life at home, in the community and in school. The Project then went on to produce useful support material on the background (Butterworth and Kinnibrugh, 1970) and pronunciation (Rudd, 1971) of learners from India, Pakistan, Cyprus and Italy. The *Senior Course*, which was published in 1972, was planned for use with older students and school-leavers, and was used in adult classrooms and on training courses.

In 1976 *Scope 2* appeared as a series of packs about water, housing and travel for use with pupils between the ages of 8 and 13. These packs enabled pupils to undertake project work which would teach them the vocabulary and basic concepts of particular subjects – science, history, geography – and the language structures to deal with them, describing, comparing, using the passive voice. These paralleled similar develop-ments taking place for learners in further education colleges with the development of linked skills curricula (see Chapters 4 and 5). The Teachers' Book for *Scope 2* clearly identified the functions as well as the structures of the language being taught, thereby aligning the course with the new developments in linguistic theory (p. 1).[10] There were also associated project packs, which, although clearly aimed at pupils at school, could equally well be used in the post-schools sector. The *At Work* course book for *Scope 2* was written by Evelyn Davies and Shirley Hadi from the Pathway Centre, Ealing, who drew on their wider expertise in preparing students for the world of work

In 1967 the Schools Council published *English for the Children of Immigrants*, a statement of the principles and approach behind the project with some valuable background information. This revealed the spread of the immigrant communities across the country and the provision made for them. The survey included Hungarian, Italian and Polish speakers, as well as learners from the New Commonwealth, though it was these latter who were deemed to have the greatest need.

Of interest to today's reader was the citing of the Newbolt Report of 1921 on English teaching, with its statement on the existence of two nations divided by language and access to a cultural heritage. In 1921 the division was between the rich and the poor; in 1967 the Schools Council saw the division as between English and non-English speakers and the English language as the way to bring communities together across cultures:

> *What was true for Newbolt in respect of the education of the 'two nations' is equally true of the variety of nations in England today – the English language is the one indispensable means not only to enable them to communicate, but also to enable them to contribute to and participate in a national heritage and tradition. It is equally the means whereby most native English speakers can draw enrichment from the cultural heritage and tradition*

> *of the newcomers. The English language is the key to social and cultural*
> *assimilation* [sic] *and co-operation.* (Schools Council, 1967a, p. 4)

What was new and encouraging in this analysis was the possibility of a fruitful two-way exchange and enrichment.

At the same time as it was engaged on publishing the early Scope materials, Longman was also publishing Louis Alexander's *New Concept English* which first came out in 1967. This was publicised at the time as a ground-breaking new course. The back cover claimed it was a

> *… multi-purpose text which is used as a basis for aural comprehension, oral*
> *practice, reading oral comprehension, dictation, controlled comprehension,*
> *précis and composition practice, and written grammar exercises in recall.*
> (Alexander, 1967)

The course followed the situational method, with its emphasis on oral work, the use of connected texts with grammar rising out of the text, the ordered acquisition of vocabulary and an emphasis on pattern practice.

Scope materials vs. Alexander's *New Concept English*

If many of the linguistic assumptions and methods behind the *New Concept English* and Scope courses were similar, the outcomes were very different. A comparison between *First Things First*, the first book of Alexander's course, and *Senior Scope* Book 1, *We Live in England*, illustrates clearly the increasingly different and varied needs of adult learners resident in the UK from those of overseas students.

In Alexander's course, the learner was young, literate in the Latin alphabet, probably had at least secondary education, and was not living in the UK, though he/she could have been here as a student, visitor or tourist. The situations depicted were in the stereotypical contexts of a middle-class UK family or in public social environments. The language taught was that needed by a visitor or a pupil/student. The small cartoon illustrations often caricatured various nationalities and were in any case culture-specific, particularly in their humour. Equally culture-specific were the humorous dialogues, such as the one about getting rid of an unwanted admirer (p. 71) or of women gossiping in a restaurant about a famous actress (p. 129). Although the book covered the grammar much more slowly than the first Hornby course, by the end it had still moved from simple present to past perfect, past continuous and present perfect passive, and had tackled the forms of 'must' and the use of relative pronouns.

The *Senior Scope* Book 1, *We Live in England* by Greta Sealey and Gillian Skirrow, was more appropriate for the new learners living in the UK. It covered the simple present, past and future tenses, but overall focused much less on grammar than the Alexander course. It did not follow a narrow, restricting system for teaching grammar, recognising that even very early-stage learners living in the UK would need to understand the passive voice and to use and understand the imperative tense for giving and receiving instruction. The course accepted the central challenge of teaching literacy and was printed in a sans serif font, then favoured in children's reading books. Instead of cartoons and stylised characters, it used clear line drawings of two families, the Bassis and the Cottons, in familiar everyday situations – working as bus drivers, washing and cooking in the house, shopping in the neighbourhood. This also introduced the concepts of good neighbours and settlement, which were to be developed further in the 1970s with projects such as the BBC *Parosi* programmes, the CRE's *Home Tutor Kit* and the ILEA's *At Home in Britain* (Chapters 4 and 5 below).

The need to produce such materials and syllabuses for this new group of learners reinforced the growing polarisation between what came to be designated English as a Foreign Language (EFL) to overseas students and English as a Second Language (ESL) to settlers and residents. This is explored further in Chapters 4 and 5.

The professionalisation and training of ESOL teachers

Professionalising the workforce

During the 1960s the number of ESOL teachers was increasing nationally and internationally, and there were moves to set up professional associations to disseminate new thinking and share good practice. In the UK the Association of Teachers of English as a Foreign Language (ATEFL) was formed in 1967, becoming the International Association of Teachers of English as a Foreign Language (IATEFL) in 1971. ESOL teachers of learners resident in the UK would be influenced by the future debates in these forums (see later).

Teacher training: the university sector

During the 1960s some universities were beginning to develop courses to train teachers to cater for the new immigrants. The University of London Institute of Education had set up the first EFL course in 1935, and this was developed further in the 1960s. But new training was needed for the children in schools, and a new course was set up for this in September 1965. However, this was predated by the course established in Leeds in 1964, on which June Derrick taught. In 1967 the first course on education in a multicultural society was established at Edge Hill.

The work of June Derrick and her team at Leeds University was particularly important in these early years, and some of her thinking and sympathetic understanding echoes that in the 1963 Ministry of Education pamphlet. Her work influenced all ESOL teaching, and her involvement on the Scope project has already been noted.

In her *Teaching English to Immigrants* (1966), Derrick summed up the challenge faced by teachers ill-prepared for teaching the second-language learners in their classes. She was sympathetic to both the learner and the teacher. Starting from the perspective of a linguist and a language teacher, she was able to draw together the current theories on language teaching – Halliday, Palmer, Quirk (pp. 20–1) – to focus on the structural/situational method, and then adapt it to the needs of learners who had to acquire language in order to progress in school and adapt to life in Britain. She knew she had to emphasise to teachers that acquiring English as a second language was very different from learning it as one's mother tongue, and was more akin to learning a foreign language. However, as she wryly noted, British schools still taught foreign languages very badly, and certainly did not follow the belief that 'language is first and foremost sound' (Derrick, 1966, p. 4).

Building on a fairly standard structural/situational methodology, Derrick was both innovative and supportive (pp. 2–12). However, she was also realistic about the difficulties of developing an appropriate syllabus or scheme of work to meet the needs of a very diverse group of pupils. She believed that teachers should have 'an awareness of the problems that face the learner of English as a second language' (p. 22). Her work was timely and important, particularly in its focus on the spoken word and in putting the learner's needs first.

Derrick's work influenced adult teachers of ESOL through her publications, through the teachers who moved across from the school to post-school sector, and through the development of Senior Scope. The permeability of the barriers between the different education sectors at the time is illustrated by the fact that in the 1969–70 academic year students at Leeds University were trained as volunteer home tutors by Hilary Hester (a primary specialist) and given Scope materials to trial in schools.

RSA certificates

However, the developments in the university sector were not available to all teachers, and there was 'a gaping hole' in the provision of training at a basic level (Howat and Widdowson, 2004, p. 246). That gap was filled by the Royal Society of the Arts (RSA).

The RSA's training programme and qualification for English language teachers was inaugurated in 1967 at the suggestion of the ILEA. It aimed to cater for both groups of teachers: those teaching students coming to the UK to learn English as a subject, and those teaching adult immigrants. So initially the concept was of a unified certificate, catering for the different needs of EFL and ESL students. The adult certificate's first title, Certificate in the Teaching of English as a Second or Foreign Language, signalled this dual aim. From its inception, the certificate involved not only a written examination but, very importantly, an assessment of teaching or 'practical test'. In 1969 a similar scheme was set up for the training of teachers working with children in state schools. In the same year the adult certificate was renamed the Certificate in the Teaching of English as a Second or Foreign Language (Adults).

The quality of the preparation – based on the situational method – for this certificate, and the quality of the teachers it turned out, meant it gained credibility fairly quickly, and most teachers of ESL in the late 1960s and early 1970s were trained in this way, either on the new RSA courses or in programmes run along similar lines by International House and other language schools.

However, the difficulties in catering for teachers dealing with the two different groups of students grew. Adult residents needed the language for daily survival, for getting jobs and for 'dealing with the system'. They could not wait to progress through a neat language syllabus meant for overseas students, with its hierarchies of structures and controls, and general service vocabulary.[11] Teachers of adult residents were also faced with the challenges of dealing with the very different cultural and educational experiences of new settlers, and of coping with students who might be illiterate or literate but in a different script. A different set of skills and materials was needed.

None the less, it would not be until September 1975, again at the instigation of the ILEA, that a pilot course would be set up at Westminster College to train teachers in these new disciplines (see below, p. 121). Meanwhile it was left to local language schemes and community relations councils to try to provide appropriate training and materials for the teachers in the community, and for teachers of English in the workplace to develop syllabuses and materials for their learners.

At the same time, the realisation was beginning to grow that ESOL learners were actually part of a more heterogeneous and complex group than the crude division into EFL and ESL might suggest. ESOL teachers (both EFL and ESL) not only taught in schools, in the workplace or on free-standing language courses in colleges and community-based courses; they supported students into and on mainstream courses in FE and HE.

Responses on the ground

In the schools sector

It is important to consider the responses in the schools sector, since they had a direct influence on the teaching of adults. This was not only in the development of materials and methodologies, but also because in the early days many teachers moved across sectors, and some voluntary schemes supported not only children in school but also older teenagers and parents. This was particularly true in Coventry with its Community Education Project.

A pioneer LEA at this time was Birmingham. Bob Chapman, who had been on the National Committee of the NCCI, was the head of the Birmingham Education Authority's Language Department. Under him, while systematic language support was provided for pupils in schools, teachers were also running classes for adults, including those in the workplace, where LEA classes were also held. This provision was complemented by the Birmingham Association of Volunteer Teachers of English (BAVTE), which was among the first organisations of its kind in the country.

Aware of the need to improve the quality of the provision, Chapman oversaw the establishment in 1962 of the first Association for Teachers of English to Pupils from Overseas (ATEPO). The London ATEPO was formed in March 1965, and others followed across the country. They were then federated in May 1969 as the National Federation of Associations for the Education of Pupils from Overseas, and finally became the National Association for Multicultural Education (NAME). That organisation's journal and publications influenced teachers in the school and post-school sectors.[12]

Chapman was keenly aware of the situation facing adult ESOL learners. In 1967 he devised the first BBC Television programme for older ESOL learners, *Look, Listen and Speak* (see p. 104), and was later on the committee for the RSA Profile Certificate.

Chapman's work showed how, in local authority areas with far-sighted leadership, it was possible to see the language needs of the community as a whole.

In the workplace

While increasing provision was being made for children in schools, some attention was paid to workers who did not have English as their first language. As has already been noted, the Industrial Training Act 1964 allowed for training to be set up. However, by June 1969 the Report of the Select Committee on Race Relations and Immigration could note that its use had been minimal in teaching English to non-English speakers.

The value of such training was spelled out in two articles in *Race Today*: one by Len Squire (1969) and the other by Roy Williams (1969). Squire, in a piece devoted to helping industry to 'overcome some difficulties in the employment of immigrants', quoted from the 1966 PEP Report on the need for language tuition:

> *Employers argued that the two main sources of difficulty as far as immigrants were concerned was their lack of English and their lack of qualifications or the poverty of their indigenous qualifications by English standards.* (Squire, 1969, p. 39)

He then identified the opportunities that the Industrial Training Act offered, and explained that he believed such training was important for health and safety and company efficiency, as well for providing equality of opportunity for the workers and combating discrimination.

Williams (1969) reported on a survey he had conducted for the Foundry Industry Training Board. His main finding – that communication was the main problem – was unsurprising. Under the general heading 'Communication' he reported:

> *This is the most obvious problem area, and the training difficulties can be classified under three broad headings: firstly restricted linguistic and intercultural communication; secondly a relative low level of literacy; and thirdly a lack of feedback in the training situation.* (Williams, 1969, p. 41)

He then went on to identify the weaknesses in current training, particularly in relation to on-the-job communication, which often at its best was little more than 'Ali sitting by Nellie' (p. 43) and made a powerful case for an initiative on a national scale. This was indeed to happen in the 1970s with Industrial Language Training (see Chapter 4).

However, Williams noted that some good training was taking place, and quoted a project in Leicester in which a local firm was working with the LEA (p. 42).

At least two other LEAs took the initiative themselves. Birmingham LEA's classes on employers' premises have already been noted. The London Borough of Ealing set up the Pathway Centre in 1968, in conjunction with the Careers Service, providing courses for newly arrived bilingual teenagers to prepare them to move on to work. Both of these LEAs used Section 11 money for these initiatives.

In the community

The role of community-based classes and local language schemes was vital in providing English tuition for those adults – mainly women at home – who fell outside the provision already being made in schools, and the nascent courses for people in work. Drawing heavily on volunteers, the schemes began in the early to mid-1960s. Alan Little paid tribute to them in 1977 in his foreword to Mobbs's *Meeting their Needs* (Mobbs, 1977) and described the vital role of the local Community Relations Councils (CRCs) and the national Community Relations Commission:

> *Schemes using volunteers to teach English to ethnic minority women have been operating for about 14 years and have gradually increased in number and scope. The Community Relations Commission has been monitoring their progress and has provided advice, information and co-ordination for the schemes' organisers for eight years, during which time it has encouraged the*

102

schemes' development by grants and provision of teaching materials and has enabled many of them to expand their services. The expertise of the schemes has grown considerably and their methods have created a wide interest among those concerned with community relations and education. (Mobbs, 1977, p. 3)

The Birmingham Association for Volunteer Teachers of English (BAVTE) has already been noted. Other early schemes included the Wandsworth Council for Community Relations scheme;[13] and Ruth Hayman began her major contribution in 1969 when she established Neighbourhood English Classes across a number of north London boroughs, both inside and outside the ILEA.

The story of Neighbourhood English Classes, published as *Can You Speak English?* (Grant and Self, 1984), was a clear demonstration of the pioneering spirit noted by Celia Roberts.[14]

Provision proliferated, and the 1971 DES survey reported on good practice in 'classes for immigrant mothers', from Keighley and Sheffield to Warley, Hounslow and Croydon (DES, 1971, pp. 94–5). In Coventry the Priory Centre was singled out for combining information to help with daily life in the UK with language teaching, and 'with financial help from the Coventry Community Relations Committee'(DES, 1971, p. 95).

In the colleges

The same 1971 DES report went into some detail on college provision, reporting on both free-standing English language courses and work preparation and work-related courses.

HMI noted that English language classes were available in colleges across the country. Specially commended was the course at Park Lane College in Leeds set up in conjunction with the Immigration Reception Centre for 'young immigrants above school age' (DES, 1971, p. 92).

The Pathway Centre in Ealing (an LEA post-school centre not linked to a college) was praised for its emphasis on vocational guidance, contact with the local youth and community centre, and for developing work- and training-related language skills. Pre-training and assessment courses for learners with basic language needs had been set up by the Department of Employment and Productivity in conjunction with colleges in Leeds and Kennington (London).

HMI had observed some Industrial Language Training run by

colleges and supported by Industrial Training Boards, 'most of which are prepared to consider grant [*sic*] for such training' (DES, 1971, p. 93). Encouraging examples of good practice in part-time day and evening classes had been noted by HMI in colleges 'from Brixton to Bradford' and in some day release classes from industry. However, HMI entered an unwitting caveat in noting that

> ... *the immigrant provision may be combined with requirements of temporary overseas students from continental countries* (DES, 1971, p. 93),

citing evidence from the three London General and Commercial Colleges.

In the BBC

The BBC continued its tradition of providing EFL tuition with John Haycraft's *Getting on in English* (produced in 1964), a structurally based course with accompanying records. The Corporation then began to support the new learners resident in the UK, and developed radio broadcasts to accompany the Scope project.

A pioneering contribution to ESOL for adults came in 1967 at Pebble Mill in Birmingham with the *Look, Listen and Speak* programme, which has already been noted. This was devised by Bob Chapman in conjunction with the BBC Immigrants Programme Unit and in association with English by Radio and Television. The course followed a structural/situational approach, and learners worked through a series of situations – at the library, bank, post office, coach station and adult education centre; in a careers interview; letting the gas man into the house. The four workbooks progressed through grammatical structures from beginners' level onwards; they included translated word lists in four languages of the Indian subcontinent, and the course writers recognised that there might be problems of literacy. However, all the practice was paper-based, with comprehension questions on the written passages and practice tests in sentence completion and gap-filling – all of which depended on a good level of literacy in English.

The Immigrant Programmes Unit in Birmingham also made contributions to helping the new immigrants to settle with magazine programmes such as *Nai Zindagi, Naya Jeevan* (translated as 'New Life, New World') and with programmes on the backgrounds of various immigrant groups.

Evaluation of these early arrangements

The 1971 government publication *The Education of Immigrants*, (DES Education Survey 13), referred to earlier, was an important review of what had been achieved since the 1963 and 1965 reports. It was wide-ranging, detailed and very thorough. HMI had surveyed provision across England and Wales in the early (pre-primary) years and for the primary, secondary, post-16, further and adult education sectors and the youth service, as well as provision by voluntary and national organisations. But the report went wider than this, and evaluated the contribution to the education of immigrants of major statutory and non-statutory national organisations. Moreover, it did not shrink from describing the negative effects of some government policies. In its range, it remains unique in the history of ESOL in the UK.

The report started from the position that the aim of government policy was to create a non-divisive climate in schools, to support teachers, to safeguard against the lowering of standards and to encourage and promote relevant research (DES, 1971, p. 15). If the picture presented was sometimes negative and problem-centred, the report was also clear about to the challenges faced by teachers, and was sympathetic to their efforts. Some of the good practice it identified has already been cited.

The usefulness of Section 11 was acknowledged, but its anomalies and the unfairness inherent in it were spelt out (p. 25). The important role in teacher education of the National Council for Commonwealth Immigrants (NCCI), working closely with the DES, was noted, and the latest curriculum developments and the contribution of the Scope project were welcomed (p. 22). However, the report also recorded concerns over the dispersing of pupils, not least in terms of its being in breach of the 1968 Race Relations Act (pp. 18–21).

The chapter on the response of voluntary and other organisations (pp. 50–63) is particularly interesting. It described the extent of voluntary activity in education, from Sparkbrook in Birmingham to Huddersfield, and from Oxford to Manchester (pp. 51–2). Cambridge House Literary [sic] Scheme was identified as meeting the learning needs of West Indians (p. 51). The contributions of national organisations such as the Centre for Information on Language Teaching (CILT) (p. 58), and the BBC (pp. 61–2) were welcomed. The report noted in particular (pp. 54–5) the crucial contribution of the Institute for Race Relations, and especially its influential report *Colour and Citizenship* (Rose *et al.*, 1969), which was the source of much information on the makeup of multiracial Britain (see above, p. 84).

The chapter emphasised the crucial role of the Community Relations Commission (p. 53). Two of its duties were to '[p]rovide courses of training in connection with community relations' and to 'arrange and promote the holding of conferences on matters connected with community matters' (p. 53). The national organisation and the local community relations councils were able to interpret these duties to set up and/or support ESOL classes, run training courses and produce materials.

What is particularly interesting about this chapter, 'The Response of Voluntary and Other Organisations', was its focus on a whole-family approach to the needs of these new communities. So Oxford undergraduates volunteered to support children in school as well as newly-arrived teenagers and mothers at home (p. 52), and students in Manchester had helped in an immigration reception centre and in evening classes for parents (p. 52).

The good practice cited in the section on further education has already been noted. However, the tone here can at times also be negative, locating the difficulties in learners' own poor educational background and their 'inability to communicate' (p. 91) and the need for remedial courses. On closer investigation of one source for this view – the experience of a lecturer from Hammersmith College – it turns out that the problems are seen to lie with students from the Caribbean and not with second-language learners.[15] This illustrated the difficulties that lecturers at the time had in distinguishing between the language and literacy needs of those who spoke English as a second or other language and those who used non-standard varieties of English or spoke Patois. A greater understanding of the different needs would develop over the next two decades. However, as will also be seen, ESOL learners who were confident speakers of the language but lacked literacy skills could be successfully enrolled in adult literacy classes, while for other ESOL learners specialist ESOL literacy provision would be developed.

Immigrant ESOL learners in colleges in the 1960s also faced unfavourable comparison with overseas students, who might have had their own problems with language, but who 'in the main … are highly intelligent students, qualified to embark on their chosen courses' (DES, 1971, p. 98).

106

However, the 1971 DES report could also be perceptive about learners in the post-schools sector. Noting that orientation courses such as 'The English Way of Life' or 'Living in Britain' had been resented, it suggested that such content could be more acceptably and effectively put across in English language courses – thereby anticipating a model that would be followed in preparation for citizenship courses in the early years of the twenty-first century. The report further pointed out that school-leavers would need help if they were to progress on to technical, technological and GCE courses, although, unfortunately, it also warned that these young people should not be too ambitious academically. One experienced FE teacher was quoted on the importance of initial assessment.

On integration and harmonious race relations, the report was naively optimistic, believing there to be natural integration among students and very little, if any, racial intolerance. It believed that students learned and derived value from one another. However, the report did acknowledge that 'coloured immigrants' on courses of higher education met racism from employers when they were looking for industrial placements (p. 97).

This was a full and detailed report, which attempted to grapple honestly with the complex issues and challenges in making good provision for immigrants across the age groups. Although the tone was sometimes negative, there was also a celebration of good practice, and the difficulties facing teachers and learners were acknowledged. The report identified the wide range of needs among learners, the paucity of appropriate materials and the fact that teachers must be trained to meet the new challenges. These findings applied equally in the schools and post-schools sectors. In the post-school sector the report noted the reliance on volunteer and part-time teachers, although this was not interpreted as showing serious under-funding of ESOL provision.

All the weaknesses noted by HMI would be reconfirmed in the 1970s by the newly-created professional groups of ESOL teachers and organisers.

Conclusion

By the end of the 1960s a twin UK approach to immigration had been firmly established: curbing further arrivals and helping those already here with their settlement – including the introduction of anti-racist legislation. To a greater or lesser extent, these two approaches would characterise government intervention until well into the twenty-first century, but that intervention would also long continue to rely heavily on the contributions of voluntary and non-governmental organisations.

ESOL teachers of adults clearly had a leading role in helping the newcomers to settle, as did language teachers in all countries receiving immigrants. However, in the UK they faced a challenge not encountered by teachers in other Anglophone countries.

Over many years, the UK had provided teachers and teaching for overseas students, either in the UK or, more often, in their own countries. Harold Palmer drew on his experience in Japan and Michael West from his in Bengal. UK teachers had taught the students of the Empire, from Nigeria to Malaya and from Kenya to Hong Kong. In these countries English was often taught as the second but official language, essential for government and administration.

So there was a strong tradition of taking the English language and culture *out* to the learners. However, unlike in countries such as the United States and Australia, there was no tradition in the UK of pro-grammes for immigrants who had come *in* to settle. This history has shown that such government initiatives as there had been (for the Belgians in the First World War, the Allied service personnel in the Second World War, the Poles settling in the late 1940s) had been planned to meet the short-term needs of learners who would either soon leave the country or settle quickly and require no further provision.

By the late 1960s there were large numbers of learners who had settled in the UK. At the same time, the overseas EFL market was exploding, and the materials and syllabuses – but not the underlying linguistic approaches – being developed for this market were inappropriate to meet the needs of the much smaller ESL market at home. The tensions between these competing approaches and markets would emerge strongly as the ESOL provision developed in the 1970s to meet the needs of the existing settlers, as well as those of new arrivals – further groups of refugees and migrant workers. These tensions would be seen particularly in teacher training, in the developments of materials, and through the conferences, publications and representations of NATECLA.

CHAPTER FOUR

The 1970s: A time of expansion

The 1970s saw a rapid increase in ESOL provision for settlers already in the UK and the new groups that joined them. Teaching expanded in the workplace and in LEA college and community-based provision, as well as in the voluntary sector, and it continued to be influenced by new developments in thinking about language teaching. There were initiatives by the LEAs, the CRE, the BBC and the RSA. The new developments were supported by the newly-formed National Association of Teachers of English as a Second Language to Adults (NATESLA; later NATECLA and henceforward referred to as NATECLA except in titles of publications or where it is essential to identify the earlier acronym specifically). The shared concern of all these organisations was to develop provision appropriate to the ESOL learners living in the UK at a time of major expansion in teaching English as an international language.

ESOL provision was also strongly influenced by the recommendations of two major reports – the Russell Report in 1973 and the Bullock Report in 1975 – and by the development of policies in the ILEA. ESOL teachers and learners were also affected by the 1971 Immigration Act to restrict immigration still further (see p. 114) and by the 1976 Race Relations Act, which strengthened legislation to counter racism.

Combating racism

The 1976 Race Relations Act went further than the 1968 Act by making it unlawful to discriminate against a person either directly or *indirectly* on racial grounds in employment, education, housing and in the provision of goods, facilities and services. The 1976 Act also replaced the Community Relations Commission (CRC) with the more powerful Commission for Racial Equality (CRE), run by Commissioners appointed by the Home Secretary 'to tackle racial discrimination and promote racial equality'. The newly-formed CRE would use the new legislation to challenge racist behaviour through the courts. This would extend to language teaching (see below under 'Calderdale'). The CRE would also produce a number of reports which had implications for ESOL provision (Chapter 5).

In the media

National concern to combat racism was also expressed through the media. The BBC's role in relation to ESOL is explored at some length later, but also important was the series *Five Views of Multi-racial Britain*; broadcast on television in 1978; this series reflected the views of some major figures concerned to promote a harmonious, multi-racial society. The texts from this series were printed in conjunction with the CRE in the same year (CRE, 1978b). Similar concern prompted Thames Television's *Our People,* a series of six programmes looking at the history, background and contributions of immigrant groups, which was broadcast in 1979. The BBC and Thames took different approaches to the subject, but together they offered a broad coverage of the issues, and a frank tackling of the racism endemic in British society. They also challenged the refusal of many people to acknowledge the pernicious effects of racism and the fact that it had to be countered through positive institutional changes.[1]

Both sets of programmes were commended to NATECLA members in the 1979 NATESLA Catalogue of Resources (pp. 137–9).

Influence of the adult education movement

In 1973 the 'Russell Report', *Adult Education: A Plan for Development*, was published by HMSO to report on the Committee of Inquiry set up by the Secretary of State for Education and Science under the Chairmanship of Sir Lionel Russell (DES, 1973). Its vision was of 'a comprehensive and flexible service of adult education, broad enough to meet the whole range of educational needs of the adult in our society' (p. 1). Although its implementation has never been whole-scale or whole-hearted, it had a very important impact on the development of both literacy and ESOL provision for adults in the ILEA in particular, since it led directly to the adoption of 'An Education Service for the Whole Community' (ESWC) (see p. 111).

110

In 1975 the Alexander Report on adult education in Scotland was published (Scottish Education Department, 1975). This presented a vision of adult learning as inclusive, broadly-based and lifelong, and of a service that reached out to all members of the community, including the disadvantaged. This report, however, did not have the far-reaching effect and influence of the Russell Report in England and Wales (Cooke, 2006).

A Language for Life

In 1975 the Bullock Report, *A Language for Life* (DfES, 1975), strongly influenced thinking about adult and further education provision through its commitment to an 'education for all'. Its belief that language has the central place in all education led to the concept of 'language across the curriculum' and the belief that all teachers are language teachers – a view central to all subsequent initiatives to embed language skills in academic and vocational education and training. Its recognition that 'no child should be expected to cast off the language and culture of the home as he crosses the school threshold' stimulated initiatives to value and encourage the maintenance of the learner's mother tongue and to build on it. The maintenance of the learner's mother tongue was fundable under the Section 11 programme until the early 1990s.

The Inner London Education Authority (ILEA) and the Language and Literacy Unit (LLU)

Between the early 1970s and its abolition in 1989, the ILEA played a crucial role in the development of basic skills for adults, including ESOL. Underpinning this commitment were two important policy decisions.

The first in importance was the adoption of *An Education Service for the Whole Community* (ESWC, see p. 110) in the autumn of 1973. Written by the Education Officer Dr Briault himself, and drawing upon wide consultation, its purpose was 'to look at the education service in inner London as a whole and to propose development, designed to enable it to serve more fully the needs of the whole community' (Devereux, 1982, pp. 256–7). So, decades before *Widening Participation* (the 'Kennedy Report' of 1997 – see Chapter 6), the ILEA was concerned that its services should reach out to those previously excluded or alienated, and an analysis of the ethnic composition of those taking up opportunities in adult and further education was a powerful driving force in developing provision during the next few years.

This commitment to adult education was also reflected in the ILEA's own positive response to, and influence on, the 1973 Russell Report,[2] with its endorsement of the principle of lifelong education for the individual and its belief in the need to develop 'the enormous reservoir of human resources' for the benefit of society.

The second major policy decision was also taken in 1973 as a result of the ILEA's review of vocational further and higher education. This led to the mergers of technical colleges and colleges of further education. The resulting report (ILEA, 1973a) carried an appendix (Appendix II) which looked at General (non-vocational) Studies, i.e. general studies for mainly part-time courses and general education for mainly full-time courses. In 1973 the latter provided for only about 300 students. Appendix II stated that 'special concern for the needs of the younger, less able and less advanced students should be pre-served in any reorganisation,' focused on students' needs in 'the areas of literacy and numeracy,' and identified the needs of special groups, including immigrants (p. 15). The recommendations in Appendix II were used to support the case for special resources for these areas of work, especially in staffing, and became the catalyst for substantial developments in the curriculum, including in basic education and ESOL.

Once the decisions on Appendix II and ESWC had been taken, and using Section 11 and Urban Programme funding, the way was clear for the appointment of community education workers, literacy tutors and borough language co-ordinators and the establishment of the Language and Literacy Unit (LLU). In this, William Devereux's own commitment to adult literacy was fundamental.[3] However, two ILEA inspectors also made an important contribution.[4]

ILEA developments in ESOL

ESOL classes had long been run by the London education authority, whether this was the School Board for London, the London County Council or the Inner London Education Authority (above and Devereux, 1982, p. 268). By the end of the 1960s ESOL classes were taking place in adult and community education centres and some FE colleges, though in the latter they were perhaps more likely to be EFL classes for overseas students in which recently settled residents had enrolled themselves.

The ILEA's contribution to the development of what came to be seen as ESL (p. 119) accelerated in the 1970s. In 1975 it initiated and supported the pilot RSA teacher training course at Westminster College, aimed at meeting needs of ESL tutors teaching adults in the community (p. 121). It also developed a coherent staffing structure.[5] The appointment in 1977 of Sandra Nicholls as director for ESL, to work with Cathy Moorhouse, already in post as the director of adult literacy, led to the establishment in 1978 of the unified Language and Literacy Unit. The way was then clear for a co-ordinated approach to training, networking, curriculum and materials development, and to the planning and development of a range of different kinds of provision.

The strengths of the LLU in developing ESOL were soon apparent and were three-fold. The first was the commitment to push for full-time appointments, first in adult education (AE) and later in further education (FE) and higher education (HE), and then to create and lead a network of professionals. From this then came the second strength: the programmes of staff development to support the experienced and novice teacher alike. In 1979 a Training-the-Trainers working party was set up which published *Training the Trainers: Ideas for Training Volunteers in English as a Second Language* (ILEA 1979). Conversion courses were set up for teachers who wanted to move from EFL to ESL teaching. (See pp. 118–19 for a comparison of EFL and ESL.)

The third strength lay in the way the LLU would manage the production of a considerable range of materials to cope with the fact that EFL and adult literacy materials were rarely appropriate in themselves, though some aspects of good practice were held in common. In 1978 the LLU led a group of ESOL tutors in the production of a number of professionally-produced packs to support ESOL learners.[6]

The LLU responded to the changing industrial and economic climate in the late 1970s by diversifying staffing and provision. In 1979 the first Springboard programme, a job creation/job training scheme for unemployed 16–19-year-olds, was set up in north London. This was a model of cross-sector co-operation (below).[7]

Individual ILEA practitioners made their own contributions. Sandra Nicholls wrote, with Ranjit Arora, the *Parosi Teachers' Handbook* (Nicholls and Arora 1977), and Sandra Nicholls and Julia Naish wrote the BBC's *Teaching English as a Second Language* (Nicholls and Naish 1981) (see p. 128).

Finally, drawing on the findings of the Bullock Report in 1975, the LLU and the ILEA FHCE inspectorate would go on in the 1980s to encourage the development of language across the curriculum, and all colleges were urged to produce language policies, often developed in the context of a college anti-racist policy. These developments were part of the broader commitment to equality of opportunity and the positive encouragement of mother-tongue initiatives.

As this history will show, the Language and Literacy Unit (though under a different organisational structure after 1989) would continue to play a leading national role in the development of ESOL through teacher training, the delivery of the Skills for Life framework, the establishment of teaching qualifications for ESOL and the development of citizenship materials (below, Chapters 5, 6 and 7).

However, the ILEA was by no means alone in developing ESOL provision. LEAs across the UK continued to build on the pioneering work of the 1960s in centres like Birmingham, Coventry and Bradford, and their contributions are described below.

The new ESOL settlers

Patterns of immigration in the 1970s were strongly affected by the 1971 Immigration Act, nicknamed the 'Grandfather Act' because of the 'patriality rule', whereby applicants from the Commonwealth could be admitted if they had at least one grandparent who had been born in the UK. Such a ruling clearly militated against applicants from the 'new' Commonwealth countries in Africa, the Caribbean and the Indian subcontinent, who were very unlikely to have such a grandparent. This led to a rush to gain entry before the Act came into force in January 1972, and saw the arrival of further Asians from Kenya in 1970–71. The 1971 Act also affected those fleeing the civil war in Cyprus 1974, since they had no automatic right of entry into the UK.

One large group of New Commonwealth citizens who were given specific permission to enter were some 28,000 Asian refugees expelled from Uganda by Idi Amin in 1972. There were attempts by the government to control the settlement of the Ugandan Asians through the Ugandan Asians Resettlement Board, which set up camps to house the refugees and tried to encourage dispersal. However, speedy secondary migration soon ensured that the new arrivals resettled with friends and family – albeit in crowded conditions – in existing immigrant areas.

Perhaps because of this, the Ugandan Asians were considered more as 'immigrants' than refugees' (Kusher and Knox, 2001, p. 287). They certainly met some of the hostility experienced by these established communities (Kuepper et al. 1975, p. 111).

Refugees from Latin America were generally received more cordially than those from Uganda, though admittedly they were smaller in number. The first group came from Chile after the coup by General Augusto Pinochet on 11 September 1973, when nearly 3,000 were admitted to Britain as political exiles. The newcomers were often sponsored by local and national organisations such as trade unions and academic bodies, and were welcomed by particular local councils (Kusher and Knox, 2001, p. 289). A Joint Working Group for Refugees from Chile was set up.[8] The Chileans formed part of a general exodus from the military dictatorships in Latin America at the time, including from Uruguay, also in 1973, and from Argentina in 1976 (Kusher and Knox, 2001, p. 290). Some of these arrived in the UK.

Some 3,000 refugees fleeing from the conflicts between Ethiopia and Eritrea, or from Ethiopia itself (by those opposing the Mengistu dictatorship) also arrived in the UK, to be followed by groups from Iran. Then the Vietnamese began to arrive in the late 1970s (but since their impact was felt more in the following decade, they will be covered in the next chapter).

Finally, with Britain's entry into the EEC in 1973, the way was open for the arrival of citizens from other member states.

Views of Britain and attitudes to settling and learning English

It is always difficult to assess the attitudes to learning English when the groups of potential learners differ so greatly, and in any case individuals within the groups respond differently. However, the 1970s provided two examples of broadly contrasting responses. The refugees from Latin America hoped to return home once the regime had changed, and often saw their stay as enforced and temporary. While many learned English, others, as the writer's own experience testifies, resisted. This had been true of many Belgians in 1915, who also anticipated an early return home. The arrivals from East Africa, on the other hand, saw their stay as long-term, and those from Uganda were initially very favourably disposed to settling here and to learning English. However, as they encountered difficulties in settlement and became exposed to racist hostility, they became more uneasy (Kuepper *et al.*, 1975, pp. 107–14). None the less, it is their group – along with the Asians from Kenya – that now is held up as having settled successfully.

Effect of the new arrivals on ESOL provision

Refugees from Latin America faced the same problems in settling and learning the language as other arrivals, but they had the advantage of speaking a European language and writing the Latin script. So they had no difficulty with literacy, and at times their language needs were judged to be the same as those of migrant workers from Europe, or even overseas students. This could lead to some inappropriate allocations into classes but, more significantly, to ignoring the effect of the stress and trauma they had faced as refugees. They encountered less hostility than those from Uganda because their numbers were fewer, they were treated more sympathetically (Kusher and Knox, 2001, pp. 290–1), they were sponsored from within the UK and they were not so exposed to racist attacks. Even so, it was always easier to make arrangements for their settlement, and for their learning English, if they were in areas of existing immigrant settlement such as London with its Latin American Centre.

Asians from East Africa too arrived with nothing, and after a period of dramatic upheaval; but as has already been noted, they were less likely to be seen as refugees (Kusher and Knox, 2001, p. 287). It was also often initially assumed by organisers that, because by and large they came from business and professional backgrounds, Ugandan Asians had a greater knowledge of English and the systems in the UK than other groups of settlers from the Indian subcontinent. Although this could often be true (Kuepper *et al.*, 1975, p. 102), it was by no means always so (Kuepper *et al.*, 1975, p. 95; Romijn, 1976, pp. 25–6), and organisers had to use their initial assessments carefully if they were to ensure that learners were found the right classes.

In Scotland, too, organisers were dealing with new arrivals, both immigrants and refugees. A handbook was produced for teachers in the Glasgow area giving guidance on teaching plus information on the background of the different groups, from the longer established Italians, Cypriots and Pakistanis to the new refugees from South America (Jordanhill College, 1979). (The difficulties in funding ESOL in Scotland are detailed in Chapter 5.)

In England and Wales, the main source of funding continued to be under the Section 11 programme. However, until 1993 this money was unavailable to support newcomers from countries outside the New Commonwealth, so organisers often had to struggle to fund tuition for many of the newcomers.

Language teaching in the 1970s

The main development in the 1970s was the move from the situational approach of the 1960s to the identification of 'common core' language, based on the concept of functions and notions that all languages have: the language of request, agreement, disagreement, evaluation, and so on (Howatt and Widdowson, 2004, pp. 328–9). The view was that *all* learners of foreign languages needed to master this common core of functions/notions[9] before moving on to acquire the language of their particular specialisms. For the first time, the emphasis was on what languages had in common, rather than on where they were different. (A more detailed account is given in Chapter 5.)

The main leaders in this were D W Wilkins in the UK, supported by D Trim at the Centre for Information on Language Teaching (CILT) (below) and J A van Ek in Holland.

European Threshold System

These new developments were encouraged by the increasing inter-national need, in the new economic world order, to communicate across language barriers, particularly in the new Europe. Van Ek and others worked together to develop the European Threshold System of credit accumulation and transfer, an international system for learners seeking to acquire the languages of the member states of the Council of Europe.[10] (This has been succeeded by the Common European Framework.)

The Threshold Level built on both situational and functional approaches. The scheme's language learning objectives were summarised as identifying:

- *the situations in which the foreign language will be used, including the topics which will be dealt with;*
- *the language activities in which the learner will engage;*
- *the language functions which the learner will fulfil;*
- *what the learner will be able to do with respect to each topic;*

117

- *the general notions which the learner will be able to handle;*
- *the specific (topic-related) notions which the learner will be able to handle;*
- *the language forms which the learner will be able to use;*
- *the degree of skill with which the learner will be able to perform.*
(van Ek, 1975, p. 5)

In 1979, Professor Trim from CILT led a small delegation of teachers, which included three members of NATECLA as well as EFL teachers, in a week's conference in Sweden to discuss the teaching and learning of second languages, whether Swedish to Finns or English to South Americans.

The importance of the Threshold System lay not only in the structure it gave to language teaching and learning. It also reflected the fact that the international movement of labour had placed language learning at the centre of the lives of many workers and employers. Language learning was no longer either an optional extra subject at school or the preserve of those who might use it vocationally in the diplomatic service or international trade. However, the equal weight that the Threshold Level System gave to all languages was counterbalanced by the growing influence of English as a world language, a growth anticipated and hoped for by C K Ogden and Winston Churchill in the 1930s and 1940s with Basic English (see Chapter 2).

To the functional approach would soon be added the communicative approach, which derived from 'the conviction that language teaching should take greater account of the way that language worked in the real world and try to be more responsive to the needs of learners in their efforts to acquire it'.[11]

All these developments had a considerable influence on provision for ESOL learners.

EFL for overseas learners and ESL for learners resident in the UK

In the 1970s there was an international explosion in the teaching of English as a world language. In 1971 the UK-based Association of Teachers of English as a Foreign Language (ATEFL), founded in 1967, became the International Association for Teachers of English as a Foreign Language (IATEFL). A lucrative market for materials to teach English as a foreign language grew up to meet the needs of these overseas learners. Inside the UK this market expanded in the hands of the traditional

English language publishers like Longman, but many other major publishing houses, including Cambridge University Press, published course books and studies.

These publications were aimed at overseas learners of English, whose needs were different from those of the immigrants and refugees settling in the UK. They were also different from the needs of migrant workers, who, although they might intend to make only a temporary stay in the UK, required the same language skills and information as the refugees and immigrants settled here.

In order to describe the different approaches to these two different groups, the terms English as a Foreign Language (EFL) for the needs of overseas learners and English as a Second Language (ESL) for the needs of residents came into use. This polarisation between EFL and ESL characterised the debate about English language teaching in the UK for the next decade, and led to the development of two different approaches to teaching, to the development of materials and to teacher training. No longer could it be assumed there was one homogeneous group of learners – if there ever had been such an assumption, and if it had been useful.

The term 'English for Speakers of Other Languages' (ESOL) is normally used throughout this history; however, it is useful at this point to employ the specific terms ESL and EFL in order to discriminate between the two approaches.[12] They had much in common. The best materials and teaching methods followed the same theories of good language teaching and learning (functional, communicative) that were developing at the time. Teachers from both approaches shared their experiences at national and international conferences and gave papers.[13] These international contacts showed that, at its best, ESOL (EFL and ESL) in the UK was forward-looking and effective.

However, the new settlers were making entirely new demands in terms of materials, syllabuses and teacher training. There was a constant struggle to provide materials for the small ESL market, and these would generally be produced by non-profit-making organisations like the National Extension College (NEC) or by the CRE, LEAs, NATECLA or local community groups. Also, the 'host' community – including ESOL practitioners themselves – continued to need information about new groups of settlers as they arrived. Such material was not needed for the EFL market.

119

Catering for the 'ESL' learners

As experience of teaching adults resident in the UK developed during the 1970s, so an understanding of these different, and differing, needs deepened. Teachers, whether they worked in community centres, adult centres, FE colleges or the workplace, were dealing with very large number of adults, who were all working, living in Britain and (for many) bringing their children up here. But they came from very different social, economic and educational backgrounds, and from countries across four continents. Their backgrounds ranged from the illiteracy of rural and urban poverty to educated affluence. Most were eager to find work of any kind. Some were concerned to build on their existing professional and academic skills and knowledge. Migrant workers needed language for their employment and day-to-day life, but often also wanted to gain qualifications in English to take back home with them. Whatever their background, language aptitude and knowledge, these settlers were all under pressure to acquire or improve their English; but they also needed information about life and work in the UK.

Teachers were faced with two tasks: language teaching, and helping the newcomers settle into a new society – what HMI Inder Geera characterised as the language model and the social intervention model. The social intervention model had to take account of competing ideologies of integration, assimilation and cultural pluralism, as well dealing with the day-to-day practical problems of settlement, and in the context of racial prejudice and cross-cultural misunderstanding. The wider UK community and its institutions also needed practical initiatives to improve communication and increase cross-cultural understanding to help them deal with these new communities. To the background material provided by the Scope initiative on immigrants from India, Pakistan and Cyprus were added publications such as Alix Henley's *Asian Patients in Hospital and at Home* for workers in the Health Service (Henley, 1979),[14] and the background materials published by the National Centre for Industrial Language Training (p. 130).

An examination of the new EFL materials and syllabuses being published at this time[15] shows how, once again, they were inappropriate for most learners living in the UK. By and large, EFL course books assumed a common literacy, and often access to a shared culture, and were predicated on a certain basic level of education. Above all, they represented the learners as transient residents in the UK – businessmen, tourists, students – drawing on services, rather than as regular members of the workforce, contributing to the economy. Or else they were seen as students living in other countries who were seeking an additional qualification to add to their repertoire.

A typical EFL dialogue set in a restaurant, for example, would present the learner in the role of the patron. In ESL classes for immigrants and migrant workers, the learners would be more likely to identify with the waiter. Above all, with the exception of specific texts for English for academic or specific purposes[16], EFL courses represented the learner as someone mastering a subject rather than acquiring a tool for immediate use in the urgent business of day-to-day living. Finally, EFL courses rarely assumed responsibility for the students' acquisition of the information and access skills that were essential to ESL learners if they were to make use of their new linguistic competence to settle in the UK. So new materials and methods were needed.

The EFL/ESL distinction was particularly useful in teacher training. The RSA's Certificate in the Teaching of English as a Second or Foreign Language, set up in 1967, had provided useful training, but it became increasingly clear that a further set of skills was required, including the skill to develop new syllabuses and new learning materials. Adult residents needed the language for immediate daily survival, for getting jobs, and for dealing with 'the system'. ESL teachers also had to learn how to deal with the widely different levels of educational experience among the new settlers, and with differing levels and kinds of literacy.

In 1975 a specially developed RSA Certificate was piloted in the ILEA at Westminster College under Sandra Nicholls and Elizabeth Hoadley-Maidment. The pilot was successful, and it became known as the Certificate in Teaching English as a Second Language in Further, Adult and Community Education (TESLFACE). The certificate found wide acceptance and was soon run across the country,[17] gaining the status of a diploma almost immediately. This qualification was built on the same training in linguistics and pedagogy as the original RSA certificate, but it also focused on teaching literacy and developing the materials and curriculum appropriate to learners who were settled in the UK. In 1981 the Certificate in Initial Training in the Teaching of English as a Second Language to Adults was introduced to provide a basic training, initially for volunteers and home tutors as well as part-time teachers.

121

A recurring issue for these RSA language certificates was the position of teachers of English who were not themselves native speakers of the language. Here the ESL and EFL fields had very different approaches. ESL organisers actively recruited teachers with backgrounds similar to those of the students, and these teachers then undertook the same training and gained the same qualification as native speakers of English. For EFL teaching there were different qualifications for teachers who spoke English as a second or other language.

Crossing the boundaries between EFL and ESL

The boundaries between EFL and ESL were frequently crossed by teachers, often very productively. And the very complexity and heterogeneity of ESOL learners, many of whom needed English for academic purposes (EAP), English for Specific Purposes (ESP), linked skills and/or embedded courses, encouraged and increased this permeability. This was particularly true for courses in further and higher education, where ESOL teachers from both EFL and ESL traditions found themselves supporting students. Some of these courses were tailor-made, developing language for specific academic and vocational courses.[18] ESOL teachers in the 1970s were also preparing students for free-standing tests to gain entry to further and higher education – the JMB Test in English (Overseas) – and this extended in the 1980s to preparing students for International English Language Testing System (IELTS) examination. ESOL teachers also taught and continue to teach on courses to prepare doctors for the Professional and Linguistic Assessments Board (PLAB) test.

However, despite the movements of teachers across boundaries, difficulties did arise from the bipolar EFL/ESL approach, particularly since it led increasingly to two different kinds of provision. The existence of EFL and ESL courses within the same college or institute and often, in the 1970s, at the same cost, raised the difficult problems of the proper assessment and placement of students. Women in saris could be directed straight to ESL classes in the community if they did not manage to state quickly enough that they were doctors seeking to practise in NHS hospitals and wanted a course in the local college to prepare them for the PLAB test. Furthermore, the existence of separate provision often made it difficult for students to move from one kind of course to another. This would lay the organisers of community ESL open to the criticism that their courses failed to prepare students to move on into other areas of vocational or academic study, and colleges that their courses were not available to students from community-based provision. Differences in fee structures would also complicate the decision of where to allocate the students.

Providing English language tuition

A useful insight into what leading providers and practitioners believed ESOL provision was for, and for whom, came with the BBC radio series *Teaching English as a Second Language*, broadcast in 1979. The accompanying book stated that:

> *English as a Second Language provision is designed for people living, working and bringing up their families in this country. Like all adults, they need to*
>
> *(a) make informed choices about their own lives and the lives of their children*
>
> *(b) be able to take advantage of any opportunities for further education and training*
>
> *(c) understand the institutions and structures of the society in which they live so that they can play a full part in it if they so wish.* (Nicholls and Naish, 1981, p. 12)

The book identified a network of ESOL which covered community-based provision, classes in college and work-based training. These combined to provide a menu of free-standing language classes, 'linked skills' (now 'embedded') courses, and training in the workplace for both workers and management, run by Industrial Language Units. These are useful categories under which to describe the provision at the time in more detail.

Language schemes and community-based provision

Since the early 1960s, the Community Relations Commission nationally, along with local community relations councils, had played a vital role in developing and supporting language schemes across the UK. Alan Little's tribute to these schemes in his foreword to *Meeting their Needs* (Mobbs, 1977, p. 3) has already been noted (see p. 102).

An important part of the CRC's support, remembered with

gratitude by many early ESOL practitioners, was the newsletter *Language Teaching and Community Relations,* published quarterly. This went some way towards breaking down the isolation that many practitioners felt by including reports from individual schemes and printing examples of their materials or 'hints for tutors'. A *Home Tutor Kit* was also produced.

The early 1970s saw a rapid expansion in these schemes. In 1974 the Community Relations Commission published a list of 86 Home Tuition Schemes across England and Scotland (CRC, 1974), and by 1976 these had increased to more than 90 and included schemes in Wales (CRC, 1976a). The 1974 report noted that many schemes had started ten years before and explained the focus on Asian women at home:

> *Asian women face a variety of difficulties in this country; some are obvious – namely social isolation, adjusting to a cold climate, trying to accept a new pattern of life and coping with unfamiliar surroundings. The social and cultural background they come from, as well as shyness and apprehension, makes* [sic] *it difficult for them to attend statutory classes for learning English, which are organised by Adult Institutes. For this reason Home Teaching Schemes were started.* (CRC, 1974, p. 1)

The teaching notes recommended 'the Direct Method', and 'structures and vocabulary are taught using common situations in the home and family ...' (CRC, 1974, p. 2). The CRC's local and regional conferences for tutors and 'informal meetings for organisers' were also noted (p. 4).

This identification of the one particular group of ESOL learners who could be correctly characterised as 'hard-to-reach' would recur over the next forty years, appearing in the Kennedy Report in 1997 (p. 215) and again in the early years of the twenty-first century (Chapter 7). Its longevity is probably due to the fact that it most easily enabled funders and policy-makers to equate ESOL learners with the stereotype of the adult literacy student.

The 1974 CRC account described how volunteer tutors working with Asian women in their homes needed training and support. In 1977 the BBC therefore produced a Worktalk film, *Teaching English at Home* as part of the *Parosi* initiative (BBC, 1977) (p. 127). The programme was developed with help from a number of home tutor organisers, including Ruth Hayman, who would go on be founder members of NATECLA (see p. 134). The *Teachers' Notes,* written by Denise Gubbay of the Pathway Centre (Gubbay, 1977), gave background information and included notes for trainers and teaching notes on using role play, following the latest functional approaches to language teaching.

However, local schemes did more than provide home tuition, and their students were not only Asian women. In Wandsworth, for example, there were classes for elderly Ugandan Asian refugee businessmen. Then the new refugees from Latin America were beginning to arrive. Across the country organisers were also faced with how to deal with teenagers who had come to join their families late in their school career and could not be found places in schools.

The responsibility of the language co-ordinators, therefore, was not just to train volunteers and paid teachers, undertake outreach work, set up classes across the statutory and voluntary sectors and establish links with the social and health sectors. There was also the need to work with schools and schools language centres, and to establish links with FE provision. The absence of good, relevant teaching and learning material led to the schemes' creating their own (below). By the time the CRC commissioned Michael Mobbs to produce a national survey in 1976, there were 110 such schemes nationwide.

For his *Meeting their Needs; an Account of Language Tuition Schemes for Ethnic Minority Women*, Mobbs (1977) examined and evaluated the work of language schemes across the country (p. 20), focusing on the Asian women who made up the majority of learners in many schemes, but accepting they were not the only students. For the survey Mobbs visited 14 schemes – Bethnal Green, Blackburn, Bolton, Chesham, Glasgow, High Wycombe, Lancaster (Adult Literacy), Neighbourhood English Classes, Nelson, Newport, Preston, Reading and Wandsworth – and received information from a great many others. He found that the schemes were managed under widely different organisational structures, from FE colleges and AE institutes to local community relations councils, adult literacy schemes, independent charitable trusts and various voluntary organisations.

Mobbs recognised the contribution made by the volunteer teacher and was sympathetic to the value of close personal relations between teacher and learner. He paid tribute to the hard work and dedication of many of the schemes and described in some detail the materials and teacher training programmes developed by both large schemes such as the Birmingham Association of Volunteer Teachers of English (BAVTE) and small ones such as the one in Leamington Spa. He also covered schemes in Wales and Scotland.

However, he noted that there were considerable problems in developing an appropriate methodology, and he identified the need for good volunteer/teacher training. Building on his work in the linguistics department of the University of Lancaster, he offered guidance on how to develop 'non-formal provision of language teaching for adults', which was an example of 'an increasingly adopted "alternative" approach to the formal institution-based class provision characteristic of Adult and Further Education' (Mobbs, 1977, p. 5). He drew on the new theories of language teaching to suggest syllabuses and methods relevant to these particular students – especially for those with different or no formal education. In this, he demonstrated an understanding and approach similar to that which underpinned the new RSA teacher training course. He emphasised that good teacher/volunteer training should include knowledge and awareness of language. He saw the greater value of small-group over one-to-one tuition in language learning. He identified the contexts in which the learners needed English – at the doctors, school, clinics, and so on – and offered a model, based on the work of Christopher Candlin, of how to carry out a language analysis in such situations. He noted the paucity of relevant material, apart from *Senior Scope* and *Situational English* (the latter aimed at European immigrants into Australia), and that the gap was being filled by a wealth of locally produced materials which often duplicated each other.

By the time Mobbs's book was published, most of those working in the field – including those in language schemes – had already moved their thinking beyond the world of 'Asian ladies' and the sometimes unfortunately patronising attitudes that could be adopted towards them. (That particular imbalance would shortly be redressed by Amrit Wilson's feisty and feminist *Finding a Voice: Asian Women in Britain* (Wilson, 1978), adaptations from which were published a year later by the NEC, supported by the CRE, as *Asian Women Speak Out* (Wilson and Naish 1979) and used to the end of the century as a reader in ESOL classes.)

Most of Mobbs's concluding recommendations were already, or shortly would be, addressed. For example, group tuition was already accepted as good practice in the vast majority of language schemes.[19] However, his recommendations on funding were unfulfilled. He called for organisers of large schemes, and those in areas with a high proportion of ethnic minorities, to be paid on a full-time basis. He acknowledged that a major barrier to this lay in the uneven take-up of Section 11

126

funding in England and Wales, and that, even when funding was available, only a small proportion was allocated to further and adult education. He therefore called for the amount of finance available to ESOL tuition schemes to be increased:

> *along the lines of the annual grants to the Adult Literacy Campaign; this would be a gesture of public recognition for the work of the schemes in opening up communication channels between minority and host communities, and in breaking down the isolation of many of our fellow citizens.* (Mobbs, 1977, p. 53)

This was an early public recognition of the disparity in the funding systems for ESOL and adult literacy provision. In the event, parity in funding would have to wait until 1993.

To remedy the lack of guidance and materials for home tutors, the CRE produced a new *Home Tutor Kit* (CRE, 1977), published by the National Extension College (NEC). The kit is by today's standards homespun and perhaps over-simplified. However, created by teachers working in the field, it provided up-to-date guidance, following a functional approach, but in clear non-technical language. It supported tutors in deciding what to teach and covered the language structures, vocabulary, literacy and numeracy required for particular situations and how to teach them – syllabus design, lesson plans, and so on. It also provided sets of pictures and cards to reinforce learning.

The PEP report and Parosi

The national focus on Asian women intensified with the publication of David Smith's *Racial Disadvantage in Britain: The PEP Report* (D Smith, 1977), with its findings that 82 per cent of Asian women interviewed who were over the age of 44 were judged to have little or no English (p. 56). These findings influenced the production of the BBC *Parosi* initiative.

In 1977 the BBC, with money from the EEC, produced a series of 26 weekly English-language television programmes, *Parosi*, aimed directly at the learners themselves, Asian women at home. The series had good coverage.[20] The programmes presented familiar daily situations in language that was carefully graded in terms of structure and vocabulary. It reinforced the ideal of neighbourliness (*Parosi* means neighbours), with its logo of two facing profiles, one white and one black.

127

Accompanying the series were two publications issued jointly by the CRE and the BBC. The first, the *Parosi Students' Book*, contained information about the UK in Panjabi, Urdu, Hindi and Gujerati, and covered topics such as education, housing, health, employment and transport, with illustrated dialogues in English. *The Parosi Tutor's Handbook*, by Sandra Nicholls and Ranjit Arora (1977), gave tutors information on the background of their students and some of the challenges they faced in settling into a new life in the UK, quoting from the PEP Report (above). There was up-to-date guidance on what to teach and how, and information on the structure of post-school education to help the students move on. The reading list included *Scope* materials and *Industrial English* (Jupp and Hodlin, 1975), but also the *Ladybird* books.

However, the *Parosi* programme was less successful than the adult literacy campaign had been in attracting the target group of learners into tuition (Devereux, 1982, p. 276). The next BBC initiative aimed at ESOL learners, *Speak for Yourself*, would therefore be carefully planned to attract minority language groups (below, Chapter 5).

The *Speak for Yourself* television programmes were preceded by a Radio 4 series for teachers, *Teaching English as a Second Language*, written and presented by Sandra Nicholls of the LLU and broadcast in the autumn of 1979. This was accompanied by the BBC book *Teaching English as a Second Language* (Nicholls and Naish, 1981), cited above (p. 113). The radio series brought together structural, situational and functional approaches. They were both part of an ongoing BBC Further Education project, which would later include *Speak for Yourself*.

The nationwide consultative meetings for *Parosi* had one very important effect in that they led to the setting-up of NATECLA (from p. 134).

College-based provision

The 1971 HMI report had already shown that ESL provision was being offered in FE colleges across the country for both adults and young people. During the 1970s this provision expanded considerably. There were free-standing language courses, but there was also support for students on vocational and academic programmes. The specific courses to train doctors or prepare students to enter higher education have already been noted.

The importance of the provision in FE colleges and the role that colleges could play in combating racial disadvantage were recognised by the Community Relations Commission in *A Second Chance: Further Education in Multi-Racial Areas*, published in March 1976 (CRC, 1976b). Intended as a discussion document, this was a thoughtful and thought-provoking survey of the problems that the CRC believed were now facing FE lecturers, and which their colleagues in schools had been encountering for more than ten years. The focus was on racial disadvantage, but there was also considerable concern about the linguistic experience of both Afro-Caribbean and ESOL students.

The introduction to *A Second Chance* identified general problems: how to deal with different languages and cultures in the classroom, and whether to discuss race; how best to cater for students who spoke a different language or dialect at home. Should there be separate courses? Should FE take responsibility for the unemployed? The introduction emphasised that the report was not dealing with overseas students.

Chapter 1, 'Ethnic minorities in further education', drew on the latest statistics and surveys[21] to show how school-leavers from ethnic minorities were at a disadvantage in the workplace and turned therefore to further education courses. Chapter 2 identified the variety of appropriate courses that were needed, and offered as case studies work in Bradford College, Bethnal Green Institute and Brixton College

Chapter 3, by Tom Jupp, whose *Industrial English* had appeared the year before (Jupp and Hodlin, 1975), and Evelyn Davies from the Pathway Centre, identified the generic language skills needed by students from Afro-Caribbean and ESOL backgrounds if they were to succeed on an FE course, and described the cross-cultural understanding required by teachers. It again emphasised the belief that, despite the reluctance of many vocational and academic lecturers to acknowledge it, all teachers are language teachers. The chapter reflected the latest understanding of cross-cultural communication on which the work of Industrial Language training was built, and Appendix 3 detailed the work of the National Centre for Industrial Language Training (NCILT).

Many recommendations in this report would become familiar by repetition over the course of the next 20 years. In addition to asking the government to set up a national initiative to develop appropriate courses for 'disadvantaged 16–17-year-olds' and pressing for an HMI responsible for the oversight of multi-racial further education, the report urged

LEAs and colleges to take full advantage of the funding available to them under Section 11 and the Urban Programme and from the Training Service Agency (TSA) of the Manpower Services Commission (MSC). Colleges should adopt a language policy and set up language training courses for non-specialists. Examining bodies should ensure that their examinations and syllabuses took account of the fact that 'we are now a multi-racial society'.

Good practice for post-16 learners

There were some excellent developments in FE work in the 1970s. Teachers in Shipley College, Yorkshire, were beginning to adapt their experience of teaching in industrial language units and FE and community-based courses to develop a coherent framework to support young students across the FE curriculum, to be published as *Building a Framework* (McAllister and Robson, 1984). FE colleges were also involved in co-operative work-related schemes. One scheme in north London – Springboard, already noted – was particularly interesting in the way it brought together different agencies and employers to address the specific needs of young learners who had had some schooling in the UK, but were not ready to enter the employment market.[22]

Springboard was particularly useful in highlighting the disadvantage faced even by learners who had arrived in the UK in time to enrol in primary or secondary schools. Of the 23 students who finally enrolled on the first course in September 1978, four had been in the country for six years, five for five years, nine for three years, two for 18 months and three for only six months. The course therefore addressed the core language and social and life skills of learners – and particularly the need to build up their confidence – as well as work-related skills and language.

ESOL in the workplace

Industrial language training

The early initiatives in Industrial Language Training have already been noted (Chapter 3). During the 1970s the Pathway Centre in Ealing, London, became the focus of some very important developments in teaching English in the post-school sector. Driven by an emphasis on careers through the appointment of Evelyn Davies from a careers background, classes were set up in 1970 at the Greenford site of J Lyons, and two full-time lecturers – Tom Jupp and Susan Hodlin – were appointed. The Department of Employment Race Relations Employment Advisory Service became interested, and the work began to develop.

The next stage was the establishment of a national framework for ILT. This came in 1974 a result of the Report of the Home Affairs Select Committee on Race Relations and Immigration, Session 1973–4, which reported that '100,000 immigrant workers, the majority of whom were Asians, were unable to develop their skills and abilities because of language difficulties' (Roberts et al., 1992, p. 383). Section 11 and Urban Programme funding was made available to local authorities for local Industrial Language Units (ILTUs).

In 1974 the National Centre for Industrial Language Training (NCILT) was set up at the Pathway Centre with Tom Jupp as director. The funding for this came centrally through the Department of Employment Training Services Division (TSD) of the Manpower Services Commission (MSC).

In 1978 the MSC took responsibility for the funding of all industrial language training. This made it vulnerable to alterations in the labour market and employment, and to changes in government policies. So, set up as it was in 1974 by a sympathetic government, another government's withdrawal of funds would see the demise of the National Centre in 1987, followed by the local units in 1989 (below, Chapter 5). In the meantime, some innovative and influential work had been accomplished.

A clear initial articulation of the Industrial Language philosophy came with the publication of Jupp and Hodlin's *Industrial English: An Example of Theory and Practice in Functional Language Teaching* (Jupp and Hodlin, 1975). The strength of this approach lay in its bringing together a well grounded understanding of the latest theories of language teaching and learning – and practical experience of how to incorporate this into good practice – with the belief that communication between the second-language learner and his or her employer is two-way, and so both sides need support.

To achieve this, Industrial Language Training drew on the theories of cross-cultural communication being developed by John Gumperz, who analysed the cultural and behavioural aspects of communication and, more important, miscommunication.[23] To this was added a clear understanding of the powerful influence of racist attitudes in the workplace. The constant aim, therefore, was to accompany English lessons for

131

the workers with information, cross-cultural training and language awareness for the employers and employees who did not share the language and culture of the immigrants. This approach resulted in a number of very practical initiatives.

In 1974 the Runnymede Trust, with ILT practitioners, published *The Background and Employment of Asian Immigrants* to support 'short courses talks and discussions for non-Asian supervisors, managers and trade union officials' (Jupp and Davies, 1974). Further background material appeared on immigrants from Hong Kong, East Africa, Bangladesh and Cyprus.[24] At the same time, there was support for teaching ESOL to catering staff (Laird, 1977), for laundry staff (Hodlin *et al.*, 1974) and for the assessment of workers in the Health Service (Opienski, 1973), all with the Kings Fund Centre. In 1979 the West Yorkshire Language Link published *Signing Off: English for Adult Immigrants Seeking Work* (Sayers *et al.*, 1979) as part of their work with the unemployed. A valuable reminder that not all Asian women were basic level learners came with S Cogill and D Gubbay's *Materials and Lesson Plans for an Advanced Intensive English Language Course for Women in the Community* (1978).

Between 1972 and 1976 the BBC produced *Work Talk*, a series of four training films, all contributing to an analysis of the basic communication difficulties that arise 'when workers have little command of the English language', and accompanied by a training manual. The films – often aiming for a light-hearted touch – tried to help managers empathise with the experience of second-language learners, showed the positive results of language training schemes, offered a case study of a Sikh worker seeking promotion and used a series of sketches to illustrate different kinds and levels of language problems.[25]

The work of ILT was timely. In 1977 the Community Relations Commission published *Industrial Training Boards and Race Relations* in co-operation with the Runnymede Trust (CRC, 1977). Discussing language training and communication problems, the report praised the good practice of three industrial training boards, contrasting this with the inability of many other employers to understand the importance of communication and pointing out that failure to overcome communication problems could lead to stereotyping, low expectations and a 'them and us' culture.

In 1979 the BBC broadcast *Crosstalk* as part of its important national series, *Multi-racial Britain*, already noted. This demonstrated how misunderstandings could arise in various situations: in an advice centre interview, at the bank, in a job interview. It was accompanied by *Cross-talk: A Study in Cross-cultural Communication* (Gumperz *et al.*, 1979), which gave background materials and notes to help trainers use the film.

By engaging in research and producing learning and training materials – and it has been possible to note only a few here – the National Centre (NCILT) itself and individual Industrial Language Training units and their staff across the country made a considerable contribution to the development of work-related ESOL.

It is important to emphasise that this work, and these practical materials, were useful to *all* ESOL teachers, and that the National Extension College's commitment to publishing and publicising so many of them testifies to this. The ILT recognition of the effects of racism and inequality of opportunity, and its ability to produce materials that took account of these, gave an impetus to the shared commitment to anti-racism that was a feature of much ESOL work in the 1970s and 1980s.

Funding

Section II

Dissatisfaction with Section 11 funding continued into the 1970s. In 1976 the NUT produced a trenchant critique of the provision with its pamphlet *Section 11: A NUT Report* (NUT 1976). Accepting that some useful provision in schools had been set up (and authorities could now reclaim 80 per cent of the cost with the government's use of ESF funding), the report criticised the 2 per cent and the ten-year rules (above), commented on the unevenness of take-up nationally, identified the problems in interpreting guidelines and deplored the absence of statistical information. (The government had stopped collecting statistics on ethnic minorities in 1973.) At this time there was no monitoring of whether the staff appointed were in any way helping immigrant children or just being used to swell staff numbers. The only monitoring was by financial audit. Above all, the NUT report pointed to what it saw as an outdated integrationist attitude. It also called for school employees to be brought under the 1976 Race Relations Act and bound by its terms. This would not happen until December 2000. Although focusing on schools, many of the criticisms in the report applied equally to the way the programme operated in further and adult education.

MSC TSD courses

The other major source of funding for ESOL was the training provided by the Manpower Services Commission (MSC). Reference is made in this account to Youth Opportunities (YOPs) and Training Opportunities (TOPs) and their successors. It is not possible to embark on a lengthy account, but it is certainly true that some good provision was made, for example, the North London Springboard. However, the difficulty with such funding was that, unlike Industrial Language Training while it lasted, it was too often short-term and piecemeal, and depended for its success on the skills, training and understanding of a very wide variety of training and educational organisations.[26]

The founding and contribution of NATECLA

(*Note:* The term NATECLA is employed throughout this history unless it is specifically important to identify the earlier acronym of NATESLA.)

In the autumn of 1977, the BBC ran two regional conferences to pilot the *Parosi* series and invited the national network of organisers of ESL tuition to take part. These two conferences provided the first major opportunity for large numbers of teachers and organisers to meet and share views and problems. Both groups decided unanimously that the opportunity to do this was invaluable, and that a national organisation should be set up for this to continue.

To understand why there was such an immediate and enthusiastic response to this proposal, it is only necessary to remember the isolation in which so many practitioners had been operating and the challenges they all faced, whether they worked on employers' premises, in the classroom or in the learners' homes. For all of them there was the need to develop a suitable curriculum and materials. By 1977, too, practitioners knew well that the student body was growing and diversifying to include not only the older women focused on in the *Parosi* initiative, but also men in and out of work, young people of both sexes leaving school and newly-arrived refugees.

In February 1978 the BBC hosted a conference that drew delegates from across the UK, and from adult and further education and Industrial Language Training units. The main speakers were Robbie Robinson, vice-chair of the CRE, HMI Eric Bolton and Sandra Nicholls from the London LLU. Eric Bolton spoke eloquently from a national perspective of the challenges facing ESOL, and was remarkably prescient on the difficulties which would be encountered in the fight for resources. These were located in:

> the debate about the redistribution of resources within the limits of the financial cake. Within education, the priority of English schemes for adults must be judged alongside demand and need for more provision for adult illiterates, the under-fives, special schemes for the school leaver, the need for curricular change to better reflect the needs of technological multi-racial Britain and very specifically, the growing pressure for mother-tongue development and maintenance. The National Association for English Schemes ... will have to address itself to those questions of relative priority as well as drawing together the knowledge and experience of the schemes that are scattered across the country. In effect, your new association will have to present a well reasoned case as well as be a reservoir of experience and expertise if you hope to bring about the developments and changes you believe necessary and desirable.[27]

The Association was to discover over the next 25 years that even the most well-reasoned case would often fall on very deaf ears.

Since they represented teachers from across the spectrum of ESOL providers, the conference reluctantly abandoned the suggested name of the National Association of English Language Schemes, with its doughty acronym, NAELS, and chose instead the National Association for Teaching English as a Second Language to Adults (NATESLA). This was based on individual membership, and would be organised on a branch basis and run by a management council drawn from locally elected representatives. The first chair was Marion Moselle from the Birmingham Association of Volunteer Teachers of English (BAVTE), and the first secretary was Ruth Hayman from Neighbourhood English Classes in north London.

Despite its poverty – and maybe because it was not dependent on grants from central government – NATECLA survived and was successful.[28] The original plan to have an organisation only of individual members was changed to allow for institutional membership, and in that way more teachers had access to the publications and the opportunity to attend local and regional training. On the other hand, this may perhaps have led to less personal commitment for some members. In the beginning the vast majority of members were volunteer or part-time teachers who paid their own conference fees; at the time of writing the majority were full-time, or fractionally-paid teachers, and their organisations were often able to pay towards their attendance at training events.

The triple role of NATECLA

From the outset NATECLA had to perform a triple role. The first was to disseminate good practice, to set up in-service training locally and nationally, and to promote the publication of materials. The second was to ensure that the focus of language teaching was placed constantly within the broader perspective of the changing economic and social reality of the UK, relating the work to other areas of concern and activity – health, employment, access to education and training, community relations and immigration. The third was to represent second-language speakers and their needs to, and on, national bodies. To do this, the organisation was in a unique position to report on the quality and extent of ESOL provision across the UK.

The first issue of *NATESLA News* was published in Spring 1979. From the beginning, the aim was to share information about teaching and learning, to provide up-to-date information on current topics and events affecting ESOL, and to publicise the association's activities. The first issue included a long, welcoming review of ITV's *Our People*, alongside reviews of *Asian Women Speak Out* and of readers from Coventry and Milton Keynes. There was also a double-page spread on ESL/Literacy, offering practical support and suggestions. The lead article in that first issue, 'Second Language, Second Class Subject?' identified the challenges facing ESOL teachers, cited the opposition and even animosity of some local authorities, and noted with concern that ALRA's submission to the Training Services Division (TSD) stated that the TSD had no responsibility to fund ESOL courses. The article concluded:

> as long as there are students on waiting lists, as long as it is assumed
> that minimal provision is enough, and until ESL is no longer seen as low-
> level work with low-status teachers – a second-class subject for second-class
> subjects – there will be a fighting role for NATESLA. (NN no 1, Spring
> 1979)

The newsletter maintained this balance of information, reviews, teaching notes and editorial comment, and it provides an invaluable resource for the history of ESOL in general, as well as the history of the organisation itself. The presentation remained home-spun and even amateurish for many years, until the new format and design was introduced in the autumn of 2001.

The NATECLA journal, *Language Issues*, was introduced in 1986 to complement the *Newsletter* by offering the opportunity for longer and more considered articles on topics of interest to ESOL practitioners (Chapter 5 below).

Materials and resources

As soon as it was set up, NATESLA organised a travelling exhibition of books and materials for use at local and national training events. This was not finally disbanded until the mid-1990s, when more nationally-produced ESOL materials were available (Chapter 5). A list of resources was compiled as the *NATESLA Catalogue* and published and updated regularly until 1986. From the start, NATECLA members were involved in developing materials, from locally produced readers through the *Home Tutor* packs and BBC programmes to the Skills for Life and citizenship materials.

Teacher training

Annual national weekend conferences, managed by branches in rotation and held in an appropriate regional venue, provided a balance between teacher training workshops and opportunities to consider the wider issues affecting ESOL providers and their students. The conference themes included bilingualism with Professor Harold Rosen as main speaker (1983), anti-racism with Peter Newsam and Faroukh Dhondy as speakers (1985), multilingualism (1996) and inclusive learning (1999); other keynote speakers included Buchi Emecheta (1988) and Tuku Mukerjee (1980). The main theme of the 2000 conference was the Moser Report. In 2006 the main speaker was Professor David Crystal and the conference theme was Language and Identity.

Conference workshops had a very practical focus: using classroom observation in teachers' professional development; dealing with refugees who arrived as unaccompanied minors; teaching basic literacy; improving learners' listening skills and providing ESOL in the workplace. There were also regular workshops on the requirements of the various examinations available to learners. A one-day conference, initially usually held in Birmingham, was introduced to deal with pressing issues in teacher training as they arose through the year.

The branch organisations also provided training and forums for discussion, though this was patchy. The NATECLA Teacher Training Working Party was crucial in establishing and maintaining good, relevant ESOL training and its accreditation (p. 206).

ESOL research and publications

NATECLA commissioned its own research and also published jointly with other bodies. A number of the most important reports and the submissions, and the recommendations it presented to government bodies and national committees of inquiry from Swann to Kennedy to Moser, will be examined in some detail in the following chapters.

In sum, as the rest of this history will show, NATECLA (the name was changed in 1988 to include other community languages with English) played a unique role in the development of ESOL. Its members and former members included almost everyone who was leading the new thinking about ESOL, whether from the point of view of work-based training and embedded learning, or the education of teachers, or the development of curricula and materials. Their quality and commitment ensured not only the development of good teaching and learning programmes, but also that a professional voice would be heard in national debates on ESOL. How far that voice would be listened to would vary.

Supporting ESOL: evaluation of resources

In October 1979 NATESLA produced the second edition of its annotated *Catalogue of Resources*. A spiral-bound A4-size book with critical comments on the works listed, this provides us with an invaluable insight into the thinking about ESOL teaching at the end of the 1970s and the range of resources available to teachers.

The introduction to the catalogue is interesting for its identification of the learners who were seen as the main focus of ESOL work:

- people employed attending part-time classes;
- new arrivals – brides, bridegrooms, young dependants (mainly teenagers)
- the unemployed (work-seekers, pre-TOPS)

- housewives (in class or home tuition)
- people needing special provision (industrial, ante-natal, etc)
- older people (retired; unemployed but unlikely to find employment)

In this edition of the catalogue there was no specific reference to refugees.

The introduction also provided a summary of the various approaches to language teaching: the grammatical, the situational and the functional. The compilers of the catalogue then listed books that they judged to be useful for ESOL teachers themselves: works on the pedagogy of language teaching and on teaching adults; studies on the particular languages and cultural backgrounds of their students; and wider materials on multi-racial, multi-cultural Britain. There was an enthusiastic two-page review of Amrit Wilson's *Finding a Voice: Asian Women in Britain* (1978), and the publication of *Asian Women Speak Out* (Wilson and Naish 1979) was announced. NATECLA members were also recommended to read the background materials produced by the Scope project, Ann Dummett's *A Portrait of English Racism* (Dummett, 1973), *Between Two Cultures: A Study of Relationships between Generations in the Asian Communities in Britain* (CRE, 1978a), the PEP report (Smith, 1977), the BBC's *Multi-Racial Britain* (CRE, 1978b) and Thames Television's *Our People* (1979). Works on language teaching included standard EFL and adult literacy materials and titles, alongside the Threshold Level publications, June Derrick's *Teaching English to Immigrants* (1966), the *Parosi* materials and Jupp and Hodlin's *Industrial English* (1975).

For use in class, teachers could draw on some EFL and adult literacy materials, including the 'functionally based' EFL *Strategies* series (Longman) and the literacy materials, *Seven Days a Week*. However, these were only partially useful, and the *Scope Senior Course* (Schools Council Project, 1972) 'is the only scheme of work written specifically for the ESL market … based on a structural [approach] … presented in everyday situations'. It had its limitations, but the Teachers' Book 3 was 'very useful'.

The catalogue listed the growing amount of local material being developed specifically for ESOL, a testimony to the activity taking place across the country. It included the *Asmat* Readers from Bradford; the ILEA's *At Work, Telephone* and *Newspaper* packs; the Nelson and Colne ILTU's *New Start*, later published by Heinemann (Furnborough *et al.*,

139

1980); north London's Neighbourhood English Classes *Can You Speak English?* materials; the *Neighbourhood Book of Asian Cookery* from Blackburn; readers from the Bolton Language Scheme; the CRE Home *Tutor Kit*; the *Talkback* materials and readers from the Coventry Community Education Project; *The New Baby* from the Milton Keynes Language Scheme and *Living in England* from Bedford. All were evaluated critically from the point of view of the busy ESOL teacher.

The catalogue thus reflected the diversity of subjects with which ESOL teachers had to be familiar, and the paucity of suitable commercially-published materials.

Influence of the adult basic education movement

When the adult literacy movement started in the early 1970s, local links were sometimes established with ESOL schemes. This was particularly true in London, where the Language and Literacy Unit, under Cathy Moorhouse and Sandra Nicholls, was able to encourage a series of fruitful joint projects, especially in the development of ESL literacy. However, such links were local. At a national level the literacy movement developed separately, and received national funding.

The national adult literacy campaign gathered momentum with the success of the BBC's *On the Move* programmes in 1973–4, and in 1975 the Adult Literacy Resource Agency (ALRA) was established under the directorship of William Devereux from the ILEA, initially for one year. The organisation was allocated £1 million a year for three years to support the development of LEA literacy provision. This was the beginning of central government funding for adult literacy. ALRA was replaced by the Adult Literacy Unit (ALU) in 1978, with a remit to finance special development projects and develop and publish materials for adult literacy work. However, the annual budget was reduced to £300,000.[29] In the same year, NATESLA was founded with the blessing of the CRE, HMI and BBC, but with no central government funding.

ACACE Report

In 1977 the Labour government set up the Advisory Council for Adult and Continuing Education (ACACE) and Shirley Williams, the then Secretary of State for Education, commissioned a strategy report on adult basic education (ACACE, 1979).

This was in many ways a far-seeing exercise which, despite the use of terminology that now tends to grate – 'mentally handicapped' – aimed to empower diverse groups of adult learners: those with literacy and numeracy needs; those who spoke English as a second language or used another dialect of English; those such as the recently-retired or school-leavers who had not achieved at school and needed a number of life and coping skills.

Although the report did not emphasise them as a separate category, it also identified those who, in the 'social, technological, occupational and economic changes' (p. 6) that lay ahead, would be at a disadvantage in trying to enter vocational or other training.

The strength of the report lay in its call for clear structures and continuous and stable funding, and in its recommendation on the changes necessary in central and local government organisation to deliver this vision. To this end, it was recommended that a government Development Board for the Education and Training of Adults[30] be set up which would involve all the relevant government departments. A centrally-funded Adult Basic Education Unit would encourage and fund innovatory schemes, provide advice and guidance to local authorities and set up a central referral system. Local authorities would co-operate with local voluntary organisations and ensure that any fees charged to students would be at a low enough level not to deter basic education learners. In terms of funding, LEAs should ensure that the net expenses for adult basic education were 'incorporated into the factor of "students in further education", to which the 'needs' element of the Rate Support Grant is related' (p. 8).

A final recommendation went to the heart of the difficulties faced by all ABE tutors: their salary. ABE tutors were generally paid at the lowest rates on the scale, with few prospects of promotion, perhaps on the unspoken assumption that low-level students require low-level teachers. The ACACE report recommended a review of the pay structure for this work.

The report then described the current provision for adult basic education. A detailed account of ESOL provision was given in an appendix. This described work-based ESOL under Industrial Language Training Units. It identified other providers, including colleges of further education, voluntary organisations, community relations councils, ethnic minority organisations and training courses funded by the Training Services Division of the MSC (p. 58). The detailed account of community provision 'owes much to information provided by the National Association for Teachers of English as a Second Language to Adults (NATESLA) in their evidence to the Advisory Council's Adult Basic Education Committee' (p. 59). This NATESLA submission noted that tuition was normally in small groups, that many learners needed help in adapting to life in this country, and that the student's mother tongue could be a very useful aid to learning. Students needed flexibility in the timing and siting of classes, and crèche provision was important. A functional curriculum was generally followed, adapted to the needs of many different groups of learners, and this could include classes on welfare rights and linked skills courses in subjects like car maintenance.

There was no reference to the needs of the more advanced learners and those already literate in the Latin script in the NATESLA submission. That being said, the complexities of the different communities of ESOL learners and the differences between ESOL and adult literacy provision were clearly articulated.

The submission demonstrated that demand was outstripping provision:

> There are large numbers of students who could be recruited if there were staff to make the necessary contacts. Indeed, in some authorities, waiting lists are often closed because the existing provision cannot absorb more students.
> (ACACE, 1979, p. 62)

This would continue to be the case for the rest of the period covered by this history.

The fate of the ACACE report was decided at the general election in 1979, with the return of a Conservative government and a new Secretary of State for Education. ALRA was replaced in 1980 by the Adult Literacy and Basic Skills Unit (ALBSU), which was given a remit to serve the literacy and numeracy needs of ESOL learners orally proficient in English, but not others. ALBSU's role in the provision of ESOL, and the difficulties that ensued, will be traced in the next chapter.

Scotland

Following the BBC *On the Move* programmes, and in the same year, the Scottish Education Department also received money to support adult literacy, and the Scottish Adult Literacy Agency was set up. This was succeeded by the Scottish Adult Literacy Unit, which in turn was followed by the Scottish Adult Basic Education Unit. However, unlike in England, these organisations did not have responsibility for, or even much connection with, ESOL (see Chapter 7 for the position in 2007).

Save Adult Education

The new government also aimed to cut back in all areas of public expenditure, and in this to remove funding from all adult education not directly related to employment and skills. A vigorous national campaign was mounted to oppose this (Clyne, 2006, pp. 173–4).

Conclusion

The 1970s was a period of intense activity for ESOL, with the arrival of new learners from across four continents and the diversification of programmes and materials to meet their needs. However, demand always exceeded provision. The development of materials and provision was accompanied by a growing divide between ESL and EFL. ESOL learners continued to be affected by legislation to limit immigration but were also influenced by laws and positive programmes to combat racism. All these trends would continue in the 1980s.

The new challenge in the 1980s would come with the establishment of ALBSU, the more permanent national organisation to encourage adult basic education. The government's decision to give this organisation responsibility for limited support for some aspects of ESOL – but with no additional funding – would ensure the continuing under-funding of ESOL as a whole. It would also encourage the often unhelpful conflation of the needs of ESOL learners with those of adult literacy students. The newly-established NATECLA would have to argue for more funding for all ESOL, and to make the case that ESOL learners had a *range* of learning needs.

CHAPTER FIVE

The 1980s: Consolidation, retrenchment, adult literacy and incandescent youth

This chapter deals with a complex period in the recent history of ESOL, and focuses on the different factors influencing ESOL provision and the experience of both teachers and learners.

The 1980s saw further new arrivals – refugees, asylum-seekers and economic migrants. National concern over the increasing numbers of legal arrivals, and a growing alarm over the number of illegal entries, led to more legislation to limit and control immigration. This affected many learners in ESOL classes. There was a consolidation and extension of provision for ESOL, and a growing consensus on what constituted good practice. At the same time, there were attempts at government level to bring ESOL under the ALBSU umbrella, reflecting some national perceptions of ESOL and affecting its funding.

The 1980s was also a period of retrenchment and increasing concern over the quality and extent of ESOL provision nationally. The retrenchment coincided with a period of national recession and the cutback in all public-sector funding, but especially in the reduction in the funding of adult education, which had begun in the late 1970s (Clyne, 2006).

Finally, the decade was a time of national self-examination regarding the plight of young people in minority ethnic groups, fuelled by the riots in Brixton, Bristol and Liverpool; and there was concern about racism and the failure of the education system to meet their needs. ESOL speakers were at the heart of this concern.

To deal with this complex period the chapter has been divided into three main sections: the learners and legislation affecting them; ESOL provision; and ESOL as a national concern.

The learners

Further groups of refugees arrived in the 1980s, this time fleeing conflict or persecution in Ghana, Sri Lanka, Iran Pakistan, Somalia, Turkey, Congo and Sudan.

Also, the refugees from Vietnam, who had begun to arrive in the late 1970s, increased in numbers in the early 1980s. They presented a particular challenge, and special arrangements were made for them. The original 1,500 arrived from October 1978 onwards and were managed by the British Council for Aid to Refugees (BCAR, now the Refugee Council). They were housed in Kensington Barracks, where English language classes were set up for them by the ILEA. Once Mrs Thatcher had agreed, at an international meeting in Geneva in July 1979, to take a further 10,000 refugees and their dependants, an extended programme was set up. The newly-arrived refugees were initially housed in camps (often ex-army and RAF camps) across the UK, including Scotland, and were managed by the Joint Committee for Refugees from Vietnam (JCRV), which had representatives from the Home Office, and three voluntary organisations – the BCAR, the Ockenden Venture and the Save the Children Fund. English and reorientation classes were run in the camps, but the refugees were often far from the nearest centre of English-speakers. They were then rehoused across the UK in accommodation released by local authorities. So ten separate families could be rehoused in ten separate villages in a mining area in the North-East.

It was clear that these rehoused refugees would continue to need support, and that many of the areas in which they found themselves had no experience of teaching ESOL. So in 1981 the Home Office funded a year's tutor-training project, managed by the JCRV. Although some useful training was done, it was, as the final report suggests, too little too late (Rosenberg et al., 1982). Once again, the folly of dispersal was demonstrated. This policy had been fuelled by old fears of 'swamping' and meant in reality that the refugees found themselves isolated, without community or educational support or access to realistic opportunities for employment. Not surprisingly, they took matters into their own hands, and there was a great deal of secondary migration to the major urban centres for immigrants and, for the ethnic Chinese refugees, to centres of Chinese settlement.

However, some useful work did come out of the programmes to deal with the Vietnamese. Drawing on the experience of the successful

145

publication in 1979 of Alex Henley's *Asian Patients in Hospitals and at Home*, the NEC, in conjunction with the Health Education Council, produced a well designed and informative handbook, *The Vietnamese in Britain: A Handbook for Health Workers* (Mares, 1982), which aimed to bridge the gap between the new settlers and the Health Service.

More important still, the teachers who had originally taught the newly-arrived refugees in Kensington Barracks produced an excellent handbook for ESOL teachers, *Lessons from the Vietnamese* (de la Motte *et al.*, 1981), again published by the NEC, and funded by the Home Office. This combined useful background information on the new arrivals with good teaching guidelines and material. The latest theories of functional language teaching were incorporated into a relevant, student-centred syllabus, uniting language structures, situations and functions. Although more homespun in appearance, *Lessons from the Vietnamese* bears favourable comparison with the best glossy EFL materials published at the time. It can still provide useful guidance for teachers facing newly-arrived groups of students, and the consequent need to develop an appropriate basic syllabus and materials.

All refugee groups faced difficulties, but some groups seemed to encounter particular problems. For example Turkish-speaking Kurds often found particular difficulty in asserting their special identity.[1] Kushner and Knox also cite compelling evidence that the 23,000 refugees from Congo (the former Zaire) who were admitted in 1989 faced special hostility as public animosity towards bogus asylum-seekers was fuelled by scare-mongering press reports (Kushner and Knox, 2001, pp. 384–7).

ESOL providers had always to be alert to the difficulties facing their students, and to be especially aware of the positions of particular groups of refugees; but they accepted that their main responsibility was to provide their learners with the language skills and information needed by all new settlers.

Attitudes to learning English

An important survey of the adult use of language, the Adult Language Use Survey (ALUS), was carried out by the Linguistic Minorities Project, based at the University of London Institute of Education,[2] and the results were published in *The Other Languages of England* (Linguistic Minorities Project 1985, pp. 134–222). ALUS was conducted in Coventry, Bradford and London in 1981, and asked adult speakers of

Bengali, Chinese, Greek, Gujerati, Italian, Panjabi (two forms), Polish, Portuguese, Turkish and Ukrainian about their use of English and their mother tongue. Although the results were perhaps unsurprising, the report was valuable in its recounting of the views and experience of the speakers themselves.

By their own evaluation, all groups felt that their skills in spoken English were lower than in their mother tongue – except for the Italian-speakers in Coventry. This was equally true for groups that had been in the UK for some 30 years – the Poles and Ukrainians; all felt they had poor literacy in English. When asked where, when and how they used English, the newer groups of Bengali- Sylheti- and Cantonese-speakers reported little use in the home, while longer-established Italians and Greeks reported more.

The survey showed that, as one might have expected, there was a direct correlation between little use of English at work and the presence in the workplace of fellow workers and/or a boss who spoke the community language. At work the Cantonese and Bengali/Sylheti speakers used and needed English the least, raising the question of whether perhaps some people might be tied to a particular workplace because they lacked the language skills necessary to move on and out. These were all issues familiar to practitioners working in the Industrial Language Training field

The section of *The Other Languages of England* dealing with children's use of English looked at the intergenerational use of the mother tongue and English (Linguistic Minorities Project 1985, p. 364). ESOL practitioners working with families were familiar with children switching languages when they moved from communicating with each other to communicating with adults. But the report's findings that the mother tongue might be used more frequently among female family members was interesting, and perhaps echoes some of the reports of language use in the East End in the earlier part of the twentieth century (above).

Another value of the full report was the reminder it gave of the many and diverse languages spoken in the UK; in 1987 more than 170 languages were spoken in ILEA schools alone. It also reinforced the rich multilingual context in which these communities often operated. Students in ESOL classes with little, or even no, formal education frequently had a sophisticated understanding of how languages worked and differed from each other. The full report also gave very useful backgrounds on the various language groups.

Commission for Racial Equality (CRE)

The Commission for Racial Equality continued to make an important contribution to the thinking about ESOL and its development. It produced discussion documents and good practice guidelines which are discussed in the following pages. In 1985 it published a new edition of the *Home Tutor Kit*, which was welcomed as an improvement on earlier versions.

A particularly important contribution came with the Commission's widely-publicised inquiry into Calderdale LEA's provision of ESL in the schools sector. The Calderdale Report (CRE, 1986) found that the Calderdale LEA was in breach of the 1976 Race Relations Act, because pupils who had English as a second language, and were for that reason withdrawn from the mainstream curriculum, suffered indirect discrimination. The report also criticised assessment and enrolment practices and other arrangements the authority had put in place.

Although the Calderdale report related to the statutory provision in the schools sector, there were powerful implications for further education. These lay in emphasising the right of learners who speak English as a second language to have access to the full curriculum. These cross-sector implications were explored by Evelyn Davis of the Pathway Centre in Ealing at a meeting of RSA tutors at the ILEA Centre for Urban Education (*Language Issues (LI)*, vol. 2.1, p. 36).

The Calderdale ruling, therefore, reinforced the already growing consensus that good practice in FE must ensure that ESOL learners have access to the full curriculum, and, equally important, have the appropriate support to enable them to do this.

Legislation to cope with new arrivals

The first piece of legislation related to nationality and citizenship, the 1981 British Nationality Act, redefined who was and who was not a British citizen. It was no longer sufficient to be born in the UK: one parent had to be a British citizen already. Similarly, the right of a child born in the UK to stay in the UK depended, with a few exceptions, on its having a parent who had the right to stay.

Concern over the number of immigrants who were entering the country illegally led to the 1987 Carriers' Liability Act, whereby carriers were subject to a fine of £1,000 for each passenger who travelled without papers, or with incorrect papers. Although the regulation itself probably did not touch ESOL learners already in classes, the growing climate of fear and hostility towards immigrants did.

The 1988 Immigration Act affected many adults already settled in the UK, since it dealt with family reunions. The Act required male Commonwealth immigrants to prove they could accommodate and maintain their families independently and forbade entry to second wives. Overstaying the time permitted to be in the UK became a criminal offence, and the right of appeal for overstay was limited.

ESOL provision: influences and reflections, policies and practice

The 1980s saw a number of reflections on the wider issues affecting and influencing ESOL, and an explosion in the production of materials, in curriculum development and in teacher training. The main players were NATECLA, the BBC, the RSA, ILT, NEC, the LEAs – particularly the ILEA – and the CRE, often working together. These developments drew on current thinking in linguistics and ESOL pedagogy, and a commitment to anti-racism, multiculturalism and bilingualism. The adult literacy movement also had a role to play.

NATESLA/NATECLA

During the 1980s the association broadened its basis and developed some administrative structures.[3] In 1982 NATECLA set up its own charity, the Ruth Hayman Trust (in memory of its first secretary and founder member), and has ever since actively supported the Trust's work to help bilingual adults in their education and training. The organisation consolidated the triple role it had set itself (p. 136):

- to disseminate good practice, set up in-service training locally and nationally, and promote the publication of materials;
- to ensure that the focus of language teaching was placed constantly within the broader perspective of the changing economic and social reality of the UK;
- to represent second-language speakers and their needs to, and on, national bodies.

These aims continued to be pursued through the annotated catalogue, the travelling exhibition of resources and *NATECLA News* (*NN*). To these were added *Language Issues* (*LI*) (p. 154) and the Association's surveys, reports, representations and formal responses to committees of inquiry. These will be covered at appropriate points in the remainder of this history.

Particularly significant in the 1980s were the Association's active moves to value and validate other community languages in the UK. In 1988 a conference resolution was passed to change the organisation's name to the National Association for Teachers of English and other *Community* Languages to Adults (NATECLA). This was more than a token recognition of the importance of the other languages spoken by residents in the UK. The organisation had always drawn on the experience of those of its members, like Rakesh Bhanot, who themselves had come from minority ethnic and linguistic communities. Many of them had learned English as their second or other language, although this may have happened at a very early age; others had grown up in families where several languages were spoken. Whatever their personal language history, they were all able to reflect on and share their own, their family's and their community's experience with their monolingual and monocultural colleagues. This important dimension of the organisation's thinking came out very clearly in the pages of *NATECLA News* (*NN*) and *Language Issues* (*LI*) and enriched the debates at national conferences.

To deal with the separate special issues of mother-tongue maintenance, the organisation set up a Community Languages Working Party. However, in an editorial dealing with Section 11 in the Spring 1992 issue of *NATECLA News* (vol 39, p 1), Rakesh Bhanot and Jane Taylor, the co-chairs, wondered whether including 'Community Languages' in the organisation's name had in fact been wise. Little had been achieved for community languages, and the main aims of the organisation seemed to have become obscured. Some debate on the issue followed, but in the end it was decided to keep the links with the other languages spoken in Britain and try to strengthen the Association's work in community languages.[4] The Association therefore retained the 'C' in its name but acknowledged that it was not easy to promote community languages, particularly after Section 11 funding was no longer available to support them (p. 208).

In 1984, NATECLA Scotland was established to deal with the fact that, while the challenges and problems facing ESOL learners and teachers were the same, the funding and organisation of education were different north and south of the border. Two UK-wide national conferences were held in Scotland, and professional contacts north and south of the border continued to be strong.

Developments in teaching and learning: establishing the consensus

The themes and workshops at NATECLA conferences and a good many articles in *Languages Issues* (see p. 154–5) reflected both the overall philosophy and the day-to-day concerns of ESOL practitioners.

Current Issues in Teaching English as a Second Language

However, one publication in 1988 was particularly useful in drawing together and reflecting on the major issues, themes and influences in the 1980s, and it is worth some attention here. This was Sandra Nicholls and Elizabeth Hoadley-Maidment's *Current Issues in Teaching English as a Second Language* (Nicholls and Hoadley-Maidment, 1988).

The body of the collection concentrated on how good policy was put into practice in further and adult education, with chapters offering a range of practical support for teaching and learning in the adult and further education sectors, including how to deal with newly-arrived teenagers and adults who had recently been made redundant.[5]

The introductory section grouped four articles under 'influences and developments'. In 'ESL Provision in the Post-schools Sector: Historical Perspective' (pp. 3–10), Sandra Nicholls looked back over the period since the mid-1970s and noted how ESOL practitioners had begun to recognise the need to throw off the 'monocultural yoke' (p. 5) and to challenge the 'deficit model of minority communities' (p. 5). They were also beginning to question an earlier naive belief that language alone 'would inevitably lead to better education and employment prospects' (p. 6). Nicholls believed that practitioners should challenge earlier assumptions about adult language learning, including a preoccupation with a linear progression: 'Did such a step-by-step model help or hinder adult bilinguals ...?'(p. 6). She also asked: 'was the implied goal of "native-speaker competence" either realistic or even desirable?' On a practical level, she supported the MSC's development of courses to increase adult skills (TOPs) and to prepare young people for work

(YOPs) in a period of economic downturn. But in addition she argued for more language support and training in study skills for ESOL learners. She looked forward to further work building on linguistic and cultural diversity, and to the development of bilingual methodologies. Euan Reid, in *Minority Languages in England: A Neglected Resource?* (pp. 10–20), gave an account of the Linguistic Minorities Project Adult Language Use Survey (1985) already noted (see earlier, p. 146).

Celia Roberts's article, 'Maps of Interaction for the Language Traveller' (pp. 20–8), was a detailed and academic account of the influences on language teachers of the latest linguistic theories.

Roberts looked back to earlier developments in ESOL in the 1970s as 'small scale and *ad hoc*' but also with 'shining with pioneer spirit' (p. 20). She then traced the influence on ESOL teaching of developments in applied linguistics, sociology, anthropology and psychology. She noted the role played by linguistic philosophers such as John Austin and John Searle with their Speech Act theory, showing how language performs a social function, and pointed out that there might be a difference between surface meaning and intended meaning. 'Can you open the window?' is in fact a polite request, not an inquiry into a physical ability. Anthropologists like Dell Hymes had looked at how 'speech events' differ across cultural and ethnic groups, concluding that there were rules of use 'without which rules of grammar would be useless' (p. 22).

Language teachers had also learned, from the work of Michael Halliday, to understand in greater depth the powerful social role of language. But they had drawn above all on the work of D W Wilkins, who built on these theories to develop his 'notional' syllabus. This brought together the grammatical, the functional and the modal (concerned with the speaker's perspective), and Wilkins put great emphasis on 'needs analysis and specifications based on observable behaviours' (p. 23). His major contribution to the development of the Council of Europe's Threshold Framework has already been noted (see p. 117).

It is probably true that many ESOL teachers were relatively unfamiliar with the works of these scholars. However, the new thinking influenced the production of materials such as *Lessons for the Vietnamese* (de la Motte *et al.*, 1981), and Roberts noted too the influence on NCILT's *Role Play* (Gubbay, 1980). Books by Wilkins in particular were also to be found on reading lists for training courses.

As has already been noted, NCILT was also influenced by John Gumperz's work on the embeddedness of language in culture, and his examination of the power based in the relationship between the native and non-native speaker. Roberts outlined his main arguments:

1   *There is a communicative dimension to discrimination which is rarely perceived as such.*

2   *Different ethnic and cultural groups may differ systematically in the way they convey information and attitudes in talk, and this can lead to communication breakdowns and negative stereotyping.*

3   *By analysing communication breakdowns, it is possible to isolate what these differences are; to help both native and non-native English speakers to look out for and try to repair these breakdowns; and to help those in positions of power and responsibility to appreciate the consequence of not taking action.*
(Nicholls and Hoadley-Maidment, 1988, p. 24)

Effective communication depended on linguistic features such as intonation, pausing, pitch or ways of organising speech. Mistakes in these could cause an ESOL speaker's meaning to be misunderstood or mis-interpreted by a native speaker, seriously affecting the outcome of the communication. This was particularly important in the case of 'gate-keepers', who held the keys to college courses, training or employment. Misunderstandings in these situations could seriously undermine any attempts to ensure equality of opportunity and equal treatment. The solution was for *both* sides in the communication – the ESOL speaker and the native speaker of English – to understand what was happening. This was the approach Roberts followed in *FE in Black and White* (FEU, 1987; see also p. 186).

The fourth article in the opening section of *Current Issues in Teaching English as Second Language to Adults* was a timely reminder that the best and most up-to-date practice was not always followed. Rakesh Bhanot and Yasmin Alibai wrote their 'Issues of Anti-racism and Equal Opportunities in ESL' (pp. 29–35) to challenge the patronising assump-tions behind some traditional ESL material in which learners were presented as hapless, passive and 'appallingly accident prone':

> *There are some things they never do: argue, express opinions, go to meetings, study, laugh, tell stories, protest, run their own business. After unblocking all those loos, they don't have the energy.* (Nicholls and Maidment, 1988, p. 30)

The authors offered guidelines for teachers on how to scrutinise materials for often unintended racism, and urged them not only to deal with solvable practical problems, but to look at the full picture, which included confronting racism.

Language issues

Another valuable source of information on the thinking and new developments in ESOL was the NATECLA journal *Language Issues*. The first issue appeared in spring 1986. From the outset, the policy was to include longer and more substantial articles than could be covered in *NATECLA News,* and on a wide range of subjects that were felt to be of interest to ESOL teachers and providers. The first editorial stated the intention to cover inter-ethnic communication, bilingualism and discourse studies; the dissemination of good ESOL practice; up-to-date information on relevant social and political issues; reviews of books and other materials.

This was an avowedly eclectic approach. The first issue was a good, though not totally representative, example. It included an interview with the eminent linguist, Michael Halliday.[6] Other articles covered in the first issue included the use of the students' mother tongue in teaching English (especially in developing writing), making English language provision for refugees, the position of ESOL learners in relation to the many available tests in English, a report on the Chinese community in Britain, and the history of NATESLA.

The editorial statement – 'We intend to explore the middle ground between academic research and ESL classroom practice' – was generally sustained throughout the issues that followed, and that is perhaps why – at least to date – there were only a few further articles on specific linguistic theories. However, the journal always closely reflected and met the concerns of ESOL practitioners, with well-informed articles on the background and languages of each new group of arrivals, considerations of adult learning, evaluations of good classroom practice, articles on adult literacy, regular reviews of books and materials and very useful summaries of all relevant new government initiatives and legislation. These last were often accompanied by accounts of NATECLA's own response and representations.

Language Issues also regularly reported on what was happening for ESOL learners in schools through the provision of English as an Additional Language (EAL), the term used in the school sector for second-language learning. In this way, the journal sent a powerful message that, since ESOL learners came from identifiable communities and usually lived in families, it was important that ESOL practitioners should share ideas and concerns, and pool experiences and approaches across the education sectors. There had been some valuable cross-sector work in ESOL: the Scope programme in the 1960s, and some excellent initiatives in community education in LEAs like Coventry and Leicester. Older teenagers had been helped through local arrangements between schools and post-schools providers, and these had led to developments such as North London Springboard and the Pathway Centre in Ealing. Across the country, English classes for mothers had been set up in primary schools, though this had been a practical strategy to encourage learners to enrol, rather than a sharing of ideas on teaching and learning.

Nevertheless, the rigid divisions within the education system generally made cross-sector co-operation difficult.

The adult literacy movement

In 1980 the new Conservative administration replaced ALRA with the Adult Literacy and Basic Skills Unit (ALBSU), with the aim of developing adult literacy and numeracy. ALBSU was given a very limited remit for ESOL: 'to serve the literacy and numeracy needs of ESOL learners orally proficient in English'. This totally excluded the majority of the learners described in the ACACE strategy report (see earlier, p. 140). However, the *NATESLA News* (no 5, pp. 1–2) report on the change urged ESOL practitioners to take advantage of the new opportunities to develop ESL literacy materials. Some useful projects and publications followed, as a result of the cross-fertilisation of ideas and approaches from the two movements.

In 1985 ALBSU published two works, seen as complementary. Monica Turner's *Literacy Work with Bilingual Students* (Turner, 1985) was based on work carried out between 1981 and 1983 in an ILEA/ALBSU Special Development Project (ALBSU, 1983) with 'fairly fluent speakers of English', in line with ALBSU's remit for ESOL at the time and when Turner was the ILEA literacy development officer.

ALBSU's second publication (in which Monica Turner was also involved) was *ESL/Literacy: An Introductory Handbook for Tutors* (Booker *et al.*, 1985). It included work for students 'at more basic stages', in line with ALBSU's changed remit for ESOL in 1984 (below).

In his review of both works for *Language Issues* (vol. 1, no 1, p. 47), Mike Baynham suggested that, while the *Handbook* was useful, it exemplified the fact that the 'functional approach can become rather mechanical and dull without the edge of personal involvement and self expression that some of the methods described in Monica Turner's *Literacy Work with Bilingual Students* can give to the literary process'. The question this raised for practitioners was whether personal involvement and self-expression could be developed with students at an early stage of learning English.

There were certainly useful developments in ESL/Literacy under ALBSU. An Open Learning Centre for ESOL at Gloucester College for Arts and Technology was reported on in two consecutive issues of *Language Issues* (vols 5.1, pp. 25–34 and 5.2, pp. 15–22). This very detailed account was positive about the value of open, supported and flexible learning, but emphasised the dangers of short-term funded projects which could arouse expectations that could not be fulfilled.

Despite such useful developments, however, ALBSU's new national role for ESOL, initiated in 1980 and expanded in 1984, did very little to support the funding and development of ESOL (below).

ESOL and adult literacy

Relationships between the two movements were also complicated by the gulf that often existed between them at both local and national level, a gulf that it should perhaps have been easier to bridge. This is often explained in terms of the differences between the two fields in terms of ideology, political acceptability and pedagogy (Hamilton and Hillier, 2006).

For most practitioners, adult literacy provision was driven by a commitment to empower the individual. Governments on the other hand believed that adult literacy must be funded in order to improve the UK skills base. The individuals who needed support often lived in social groups identified by governments as under-achieving, and, despite the emphasis on core skills in the National Curriculum in schools, this under-achievement persisted. Also such learners were often difficult to reach. The pedagogy for adult literacy still relied quite heavily on one-to-one teaching.

ESOL practitioners saw their learners as members of minority communities, at a disadvantage within the larger, dominant society because of language, but not necessarily as under-achievers, and, except for one or two groups, by no means hard to reach. Practitioners frequently challenged governments in their thinking and practice on racism, immigration and asylum. Successive governments veered between funding ESOL to promote integration and community cohesion (Section 11, 'Citizenship'), and justifying funding in terms of the need to up-skill the workforce, along with native speakers needing basic skills training. The ESOL 'problem' was often seen as short-term, and there were tensions between government departments concerning who should fund provision – the Home Office or the successive departments of education. The provision was over-subscribed and there were waiting lists. The pedagogy for ESOL, too, was different in that the preferred practice for developing oral skills was to teach groups.

Policy into practice

Local authorities and local schemes

Individual local authorities, institutions and language schemes continued to make significant contributions to the development of methodology and materials in ESOL. In Leicester a series of radio programmes, *Chalo Kaam Kare*, sponsored by ALBSU and Radio Leicester, focused on helping the local Asian community with functional literacy and giving essential information on services. In Coventry the Community Education Project produced a series of readers in addition to *Keep my Name a Secret*. In Leeds the Harefields English Language Project produced the *HELP Maternity Language Course*. In Sheffield the City's library compiled a collection of bilingual accounts of arrival and life in Britain. Many schemes, like Bradford's, produced their own graded ESOL readers aimed at their own language communities, and these included the *Forest Readers* in Nottingham and *Speak/Teach* readers in Bolton. In 1987 the first of a series of successful readers, *Our Lives,* based on students' own experience, was launched in Croydon, funded by the teachers themselves. The list is long, and it is probably true that all the centres of immigration developed materials. Individual colleges such as Shipley College in Yorkshire, Clarendon College in Nottingham and Stevenson and Jordanhill College in Scotland also made contributions to local and national developments.

• *ILEA Language and Literacy Unit (LLU)*

The LLU continued to be very important in the development of ESOL, nationally as well as locally. This was to some extent inevitable, considering its size and centralised structure and the fact that such a high proportion of the national ESOL population was found within its boundaries. According to the ALBSU estimates (p. 172), it accounted for between 21 and 25 per cent of the provision in England and Wales. But its leading role was also the result of significant pioneering policies and practices, which developed apace in the 1980s.[7]

A series of four packs entitled *At Home in Britain* was published by the NEC in 1980, with financial support from the CRE (ILEA 1980a). This dealt with access to services such as housing, and contained teachers' notes, work sheets and up-to-date photographs. An ESL Publishing Group was established, and five books of students' own writing were published, including a whole collection devoted to refugee writings. The Group also published discussion papers in a series called *ESL Issues*. These included *Mother Tongue and ESL* (ILEA, 1982) and *ESL and Unemployment* (ILEA, 1986). Recognising the need for language support for particular vocations and academic studies – today identified as 'embedded learning' – a Linked Skills Working Party was set up. This produced *A Linked Skills Handbook for Skills and ESL Tutors*, published jointly by ILEA and NEC in 1983 (ILEA, 1983). The Unit then established an FE/ESL Curriculum Development Project, which supported, among other projects, the development of English for science by teachers in Hackney College. A Teacher Training Working Party was also set up (p. 206).

The LLU recognised that, as the needs of learners were changing, staffing and provision must change too. Concern over growing unemployment led to the Unemployment Project and the appointment of four area-based ESL specialists to promote courses in colleges that would prepare learners for employment.

Finally, ILEA and LLU ESOL practitioners continued to make their individual contributions, particularly in ESOL literacy and to the BBC *Speak for Yourself* project (p. 162) and with *Current Issues in Teaching as a Second Language* (Nicholls and Hoadley-Maidment, 1982) (p. 151).

One aspect of the LLU's work of importance to ESOL teachers and learners was the development of work with Afro-Caribbean learners under Roxy Harris. In 1985 Irene Schwab and Jud Stone from the Hackney Reading Centre and City and East London College produced

Language Writing and Publishing: Work with Afro-Caribbean Students (Schwab and Stone, 1986). Gone were the days of the 1960s, when ESOL and Afro-Caribbean students were conflated just because they were all black immigrants. But the work of Roxy Harris and colleagues went still further. It sharpened practitioners' understanding of varieties of English, engaged them in the debate about Creole, and deepened their language awareness, not the least through the publication of *Language and Power* (ILEA, 1990), with its suggestion that we all have language histories to examine and recount.

In these developments, the LLU was working along lines similar to those followed at the ILEA's English Teachers' Centre and the Institute of Education Linguistic Minority Project, all of which reflected the reaffirming philosophy of Professor Harold Rosen: that each of us has a rich language repertoire.

The Language and Literacy Unit survived the abolition of the ILEA in 1989 and continued to provide national leadership in literacy, numeracy and ESOL. Its further contributions are traced in the following chapters.

Publishers and publications

On the whole, commercial EFL publishers did not consider publishing teaching aids and materials for the small ESOL market. There were some exceptions, however.

In 1980 Heinemann Educational produced *A New Start*, a functional course in basic spoken English aimed at South Asian immigrants, written by Peter Furnborough and other colleagues from the Industrial Language Training Unit at Nelson and Colne College (Furnborough *et al.*, 1980). In 1981 Hodder & Stoughton published what could arguably be said to be the first ESOL general course book: *Use Your English: A Course in English as a Second Language for Adults* (Beech *et al.*, 1981). This was a useful, functionally-based course written by Bridget Beech, Clarice Brierley and Marianne Moselle, three very experienced ESL practitioners from backgrounds in community education and Industrial Language Training in Birmingham. The publisher's claim that the course could also be equally used by home tutors and those with low-level EFL students in class was perhaps indicative of a wish to increase sales.

In 1983 Hodder & Stoughton published Vivien Barr and Clare Fletcher's *Topics and Skills in English* (Barr and Fletcher, 1983b), a book and cassette that could be used for self-study or in the classroom. As the title suggests, it was arranged under useful topics such as filling in forms and getting and attending an interview, with the opportunities to practise the relevant language functions and grammar. It was clear and practical and was widely used.

However, there was still relatively little interest from the commercial market, so the National Extension College's contribution to the development of ESOL books and materials was invaluable, and some titles have already been noted. Working closely with teachers and organisers in the field, and as a non-profit-making organisation, it contributed to developing the theory of ESOL teaching and to the production of good materials. It published teaching packs like *At Home in Britain* (ILEA 1980a), working with the ILEA and teachers in London, and the groundbreaking *Building a Framework* (McAllister and Robson 1984), working with teachers in Shipley College, Yorkshire, who had developed a framework for language across the academic and vocational curriculum. The list of titles grew with *Lessons from the Vietnamese* (de la Motte *et al.*, 1981); Robert Leach's *Coping with the System* (1980), *Communicating with the System* (1983) and *Making, Using and Adapting Materials* (1985); and Suzanne Hayes's *Drama as a Second Language* (1984). Then there were Vivien Barr and Clare Fletcher's *English for Driving* (1983a), accompanying the BBC TV series, *L-Driver: English for Driving,* and Suzanne Looms's *English for Business* (1986a) and *You and your Business* (Looms 1986b), accompanying the BBC TV series *Talking Business.* The NEC also produced accompanying booklets in Bengali, Chinese, English, Gujerati, Punjabi and Urdu to accompany *Talking Business.*

The evaluation of Barr and Fletcher's *English for Driving* by Morpeth and Lo (1985) provides an insight into the careful thought, planning and co-operation necessary to ensure good ESOL linked skills work, especially when it combines print and broadcast media. All those involved drew on considerable experience – the BBC of its ESOL programmes, especially of *Speak for Yourself* (below); the NEC of its previous work with ESOL and also of distance learning; and the writers of the students' book who were experienced ESOL practitioners. The success of the venture depended on co-operation between all these. It also involved consulting learners, ensuring that the students' book and television series were as closely linked as possible, consulting the Department of Transport and publicising the series and learning materials widely, especially through NATECLA. The evaluation reported that the series had been well received by learners and by teachers who had used the materials in class. However, it also noted how expensive good translated materials were, and noted that other languages would have been welcomed.

In 1989 the NEC produced its own open learning course in reading and writing, *Help Yourself to English* (Johnson, 1989), covering communication skills in a social context, a vocational context and an academic context.

ILT in the 1980s

The influence of the National Centre for Industrial Language Training (NCILT) continued into the 1980s, with the publication of material for ESOL literacy such as Sheila Cogill's *Writing Business Letters and Memos* (1980) and *Personal Business Letters* (1982) and support for classroom practice such as *First Language Support in an ESL Classroom* (Lewis *et al.*, 1981), *Role-play: The Theory and Practice of a Method for Increasing Language Awareness* (Gubbay, 1980). There was more background material on the groups from which the learners came, and training manuals to help staff such as those working in the Health Service. The catalogue for 1984–85 lists some 70 works produced by the national centre or local units or by individual ILT practitioners. In 1985 the BBC produced *The Interview Game*, influenced by *Crosstalk*.

Funding for NCILT ceased in 1987 and for the local Industrial Language Training Units in 1989. The reasons advanced for this have varied. Certainly the national economic situation was making it increasingly difficult to persuade employers to release workers for training. However, one authoritative view suggests that the government was reluctant to support the core philosophy and practice of Industrial Language Training.

> The decision to cease funding was in line with government policy to move from nationally organised, long-term-funded training to employer-led, financially competitive short-term courses. This decision, no doubt, also reflected a lack of commitment to fund a service with a substantial research and development element, and one which aimed to tackle issues of racism and equal opportunities as well as language. (C Roberts *et al.*, 1992, pp. 380–1)

Some units did continue work within wider further and adult education provision, and the former Lancashire ILT became a free-standing unit called Equality at Work. Following the demise of Industrial Language Training, the money was reallocated to the Training Services Division for the development of regional training through the Training Standards Advisory Service (see below, Chapter 6).

The BBC

The next BBC initiative after *Parosi* (above, Chapter 4) was an ambitious multi-part project. This built on and learned from the experience of *Parosi*, which had been disappointing in the numbers of new learners it had attracted. The project illustrates how setting up programmes for ESOL learners was more complex than devising them for adult literacy students.

The project involved producing a television series, *Speak for Yourself*, broadcast from October 1980; publishing students' books in 12 languages; and setting up a telephone referral service. These were preceded by the radio series on ESOL teaching by Sandra Nicholls, broadcast in 1979, which was followed by a handbook *Teaching English as a Second Language* (Nicholls and Naish, 1981), both of which have already been noted.

A detailed account of the television project was given in *Speak for Yourself: The BBC Project on English as a Second Language* (BBC, 1981). The first challenge was to identify the client group and estimate its needs. The BBC engaged in a wide range of consultations of both teachers and students, using mainly NATECLA networks. The pilot programme was shown widely to similar groups. The outcome was the decision to use a soap opera format of 20 x 25-minute programmes which would both teach the language – especially survival English – and give information about institutions such as the DHSS. A major concern expressed by those consulted was that the BBC should present positive images of black people and combat stereotyping (p. 34).

The attention of potential viewers was to be caught through the broadcasting of a series of foreign language films under the title *International Success*, which would be used to trail the *Speak for Yourself* programmes. There was evidence that viewers enjoyed these films, and they were pleased that the BBC had put them on.

A wide range of institutions was involved in this complex project, wider than would have been required for an adult literacy series. They included NATECLA, the CRE, local CRCs, LEAs, NIACE, the adult literacy support services, the DES for money for research (BBC, 1981,

p. 34), the Birmingham Interpreting and Translation Agency (p. 35), the Library Association and library authorities (p. 35), Leicester University for the research and a chain of grocery stores for the distribution of leaflets (p. 38). The Rowntree Trust provided money for the multilingual support service and print back-ups (p. 39), and the Cadbury Trust for printing the students' booklet (p. 37). Money also came from the European Social Fund.

The BBC's evaluation of the project, drawn from 150 responses to a questionnaire, showed that viewers clearly enjoyed the series and that native speakers of English, too, were interested in the information on coping with the system. Probably the major conclusion was the value of using the mother tongue to contact and motivate viewers and learners. But outside funding would always be needed for this.

Speak for Yourself was followed in 1985 by *Switch on to English*, a more limited venture to support the development of the literacy skills of ESOL learners and involving collaborations between ALBSU, the BBC and ESOL practitioners. The ESOL consultants were two experienced ESOL specialists, Brigit Bird and Clarice Brierley from the Birmingham Industrial Language Centre, who produced an accompanying handbook providing further practice in functional literacy, such as following instructions, understanding flow charts and filling in forms (Bird and Brierley, 1985). This was also available in bilingual versions of an increasing number of languages, reflecting the new groups of arrivals: Bengali, Chinese, Gujerati, Panjabi, Spanish and Urdu. Once again, a BBC venture in ESOL had to draw on some charitable support, this time from the Baring Foundation, for assistance in development and distribution costs.

Evaluations and use of the materials and programmes

The *NATESLA Catalogue* again offers a useful insight into how the materials and publications available to the ESOL teacher were evaluated and used. The third edition in 1981 was in a smaller format and better organised than the second, though the print was very small. The practitioners' critiques were especially useful.

Again a number of EFL readers, course books and books for teachers were noted, including W Littlewood's *Communicative Language Teaching*. New ESOL materials included the ILEA's *At Home in Britain* – 'a well-produced and practical resource pack'– and the BBC's *Speak for Yourself* handbook (Gubbay and Cogill, 1980) to accompany the TV series was also recommended.

The number of NCILT publications listed and recommended showed its increasing influence. These included *Signing off* (Sayers *et al.*, 1979), 'a valuable resource for ESL teachers in general', and *The Teaching of Communication Skills through the Use of Role Play to Speakers of ESL* (Gubbay, 1978/9), 'an important teaching technique in ESL'.

In addition to Jupp and Hodlin's *Industrial English* (1975), the 1981 Catalogue listed *Crosstalk: A Study of Cross-cultural Communication* (Gumperz *et al.*, 1979), which provided background material and notes for the TV programme of the same name and was judged to be 'stimulating, contentious, recommended reading'. There were a number of books on the background of the various immigrant groups, and even more dealing with the disadvantage and racism they faced, including *Language Disadvantage and Ethnic Minorities* (Jupp, 1981).

Readers for students now included autobiographies published by the ILEA English Centre, including *Small Accidents* (Bandali, 1979), *Asian Women Speak Out* (Wilson and Naish, 1979), and a pioneering reader from Coventry, *Keep My Name a Secret* (Youett, n.d.), all drawn from the students' own writing about their own experiences. In this way, philosophy of the adult literacy movement and the language experience practice in schools was being incorporated into ESOL work.

Adult literacy materials themselves were again included in the Catalogue. However, as the commentary on *On Sight* shows, ESOL learners often found difficulty with adult literacy schemes when they encountered words that were simple and phonically regular but had a number of, often idiomatic, meanings. In this case it was the three meanings of 'lift' – to raise up, to give someone a ride in a car and to steal. These presented no difficulty to the native speaker, or to the ESOL learner with advanced listening and speaking skills, but required pre-teaching for most ESOL learners.

Books on teaching ESOL that were recommended were *Training the Trainers* (ILEA, *c* 1979), a 'useful source of practical ideas', and *Teaching English as a Second Language* (Nicholls and Naish, 1981) 'an excellent overview of the whole field'.

The 1981 Catalogue also acknowledged the special difficulties faced by refugees and was enthusiastic about *Lessons from the Vietnamese* (de la Motte *et al.*, 1981): 'a very useful teachers' reference book and resource for all ESL teachers and not just those working with the Vietnamese'.

164

The ten years that followed saw more developments in ESOL methodology and understanding and some new materials, particularly in ESOL/Literacy. The situation was summed up in the 1992 Language and Literacy Unit's publication of the *ESOL Materials Database* (Sunderland, 1992a), based on a survey ESOL practitioners. This noted that, although a number of resources had been published, there were still too few that were appropriate. By then, however, publications that practitioners had felt were relevant and useful, such as *Lessons from the Vietnamese* (de la Motte *et al.*, 1981) and *Teaching English as a Second Language* (Nicholls and Naish, 1981), were out of print. The ephemeral nature of good material – including the publications of ILT – would continue to characterise the development of ESOL up to the beginnings of the Skills for Life initiative. At that point, many practitioners found that comparatively little had survived that they could draw on to develop new curricula and materials, especially for embedded and work-based learning. It was left to those who had been in the vanguard in the 1980s and early 1990s to draw on their personal experience and collections.

The 1992 survey also showed that some teachers continued to rely on materials that had clearly outlived their usefulness. This unevenness of practice was unsurprising to NATECLA, since its own surveys demonstrated how piecemeal and patchy ESOL provision was nationally. This would be confirmed by other reports and surveys.

The 1992 *Database* then formed the basis for Helen Sunderland's *Tutor's Guide to ESOL Materials for Adult Learners* (Sunderland, 1992b), an annotated critical bibliography that not only covered course and textbooks, ESOL pedagogy and teacher training, but also included a very clear and useful section on how to evaluate materials.

Growing concerns

Despite the emerging consensus on what constituted good practice in ESOL, and the commitment and energy of practitioners, publishers and national organisations like the BBC to put this into practice, the 1980s saw the emergence of a number of very serious concerns. There was insufficient funding for ESOL nationally, and provision was extremely patchy. Teacher training was inadequate to ensure that there was consistent good practice, and ESOL learners had few relevant, and even fewer marketable, qualifications to work towards. At the same time, governments were becoming increasingly alarmed at the unrest and under-achievement of many younger members of minority ethnic communities.

Inadequacy of ESOL provision

NATESLA Survey

The NATESLA Survey, carried out between January 1980 and January 1981, demonstrated the wide variations in the quantity and quality of ESOL provision in England and Wales (NATESLA, 1981b). The resulting report drew upon 188 questionnaires returned from across 86 LEAs, covering 23,250 students in adult, further and community education.

Some good initiatives and developments were identified. However, the survey demonstrated just how uneven the provision was across the country, and that it was insufficient to meet the needs of the estimated 500,000 potential learners who had been identified. (This number would persist in successive ALBSU reports throughout the 1980s.) These potential learners included the newly-arrived refugees from Vietnam, who were presenting organisers and teachers with new challenges. Across the country there was an over-reliance on volunteers, and too many staff were untrained. The survey found that funding was mainly through Section 11, but noted that this was not available for tuition for the Vietnamese. Courses were also run using money from the Inner City Partnerships, the Urban Aid programme and the MSC's Preparatory and Youth Opportunity (YOPs and TOPs) programmes. However, there was still a considerable shortfall in funding, and the report was pessimistic about the future. This was largely because of cuts in adult education funding; and the report cited the *Report Prepared for the Expenditure Steering Group on Education by HMI* on a survey carried out in autumn 1980 to monitor the effects of cuts in education (NATESLA 1981b, p. 43).

The concluding recommendations were addressed to LEAs, urging them to increase the quality and quantity of staff and provide in-service training; and to the DES, encouraging it to appoint inspectors with ESOL experience and asking it to support the work of NATESLA. The Home Office was urged to revise the terms of Section 11, and the MSC to recognise the special disadvantages faced by second-language speakers as they sought work and training, with particular emphasis on the disadvantage faced by second-language speakers in a time of high unemployment. This last tied in well with Tom Jupp's submission to the Race Relations and Immigration Subcommittee of the House of Commons Home Affairs Committee in January 1981 (Jupp, 1981).

The Home Affairs Committee's final report acknowledged that not having a sufficient command of necessary English was a primary disadvantage, and the one 'which could most readily be affected by government action' (NATESLA, 1981, p iii). This report, conducted by a fledgling, under-funded, voluntary organisation, presented as useful a picture of ESOL in England and Wales as any that would follow later in the 1980s.

The position in Scotland

In 1989 NATECLA Scotland published *Language Matters?* (Matheson and Weir 1989), a survey of both ESOL and community languages provision, the latter mainly for Cantonese, Bengali, Panjabi and Urdu speakers. The list of the 36 responses gave an interesting insight into how widely the provision was made, and countered some stereotypical assumptions about the dispersal and ESOL needs of second-language speakers in Scotland. Although the majority of responses came from the Strathclyde and Lothian regions, as was to be expected, they also came from six other regions, including the Highlands. The main respondents were FE colleges, many in Glasgow and Edinburgh, but also in Falkirk, Dumfries and Galloway and Dundee. There was information from home tuition schemes and responses from community and voluntary groups.[8] The universities of Edinburgh, Glasgow and Stirling also submitted responses.

There was no funding for community language and ESOL provision in Scotland comparable to the Section 11 funding in England and Wales, so the 36 responses reflected the commitment of local authorities and voluntary organisations. The majority reported that funding came from their local authority, 11 through further education and nine through community education. Two respondents said that funding came from a mixture of local authority money and from income generated from fees for EFL courses. Seven said that money came from a mixture of voluntary organisations and local authority funding, and three said funding was from voluntary organisations alone. One respondent was hoping for funding under the local authority from the Urban Aid programme. Two responses from universities reported that courses were self-financing, but the authors of the report believed that these responses showed a failure to understand the difference between EFL and ESL.

The main findings of the report identified shortfalls in funding and a failure to understand the kind and extent of the need for ESOL provision, and there was a recommendation for more research. There was also a great need for staff development and training. There were too few ESOL classes compared with EFL classes, and too many providers did not understand the difference between the two. The picture was not entirely bleak, however:

> *some excellent and interesting work was found and the overall picture is perhaps fragmented rather that irreparable. But until coherent and positive action is taken, minority ethnic adult learners will continue to find themselves marginalized, with inadequate and inappropriate English language provision and with unnecessary barriers to taking part in 'mainstream' adult and further education of whatever sort they wish.* (NATESLA, 1981b, p. 2)

NATECLA members in England already knew of the pioneering work of Flick Thorpe at the YWCA Roundabout Centre and the contributions of Stevenson and Jordanhill Colleges.

ALBSU, ESOL and central government funding

ALBSU

The very limited remit for ESOL ('to serve the literacy and numeracy needs of ESOL learners orally proficient in English', see p. 142) that ALBSU was given in 1980 totally excluded those basic learners whom the ACACE strategy report had identified as needing the most support (p. 141). However, Sir Rhodes Boyson, the new Secretary of State for Education, made it clear in May 1980, at a conference on the new organisation, that there was no extra funding for ESOL, and that ALBSU was *not* to be concerned with basic ESOL (*NN* no 5, p. 1). This resulted in a damaging division of ESOL learners into arbitrary categories. Particularly important, it excluded from any support the many new arrivals who were already highly literate, but who needed tuition in the English language itself.

In March 1984 the Secretary of State agreed to extend ALBSU's funding for another four years, but the remit in relation to ESOL had not been decided. On 9 May 1984 a delegation from NATECLA, comprising the then current chair and two previous chairs, attended a meeting at the DES. The Director and Chair of ALBSU were also present. The NATECLA delegation put the case that, while ESOL and adult basic literacy provision had some things in common and there had been some useful developments in ESL/literacy, there were important differences between the two fields. These related especially to different levels of oral competence among ESOL learners, and also to the fact that many ESOL learners were already highly literate, successful and qualified in their own language. Furthermore, ESOL support was provided for students on vocational and academic courses in colleges of further education, and for some students aiming for, and even in, higher education. The NATECLA delegation argued for separate government support for ESOL. This failed.

In spring 1985, in the *ALBSU Newsletter* no 12, ALBSU was pleased to announce that the restrictions on its previous remit for ESOL had been lifted. In describing ALBSU's existing involvement with ESOL, the article cited not only the ESOL/literacy projects, but also the new BBC programme, *Switch on to English*.

However, the article was keen to establish that 'this amendment to the Unit's remit does not make ALBSU the central focus for ESL in England and Wales' (p. 2), since there would again be no additional funding. The piece continued with a clear admission of the differences between ESL and literacy provision, but stated that ALBSU would now be involved with basic ESOL:

> *ALBSU recognises that not all English as a Second Language work could be said to be a part of basic education and that many significant strands would not fit comfortably within the Unit's primary concern with basic communication skills. Moreover the development of ESL provision (and to some extent its funding) has been somewhat different from the development of literacy and numeracy funding for adults, and thus any attempt to make basic education an entirely homogeneous service is likely to lead to hierarchies of skills and the attachment of greater value to some parts of the service than to others. (ALBSU Newsletter no 12, Spring 1985).*

One can only guess what this coded warning referred to. It was followed by the decision to contact ESOL organisers directly about the Unit's service, including teacher training, accompanied by a wary caveat that the Unit was really not empire-building. The minimal involvement of

169

ALBSU with RAC training is described in the NATESLA/DES 1985 report (below).

- *English as a Second Language Provision for Adults in England and Wales*

In 1987 ALBSU published a quite lengthy report, *English as a Second Language: Provision for Adults in England and Wales* (ALBSU, 1987). In this it agreed that ALBSU had made only a limited contribution to ESOL teacher training, but maintained that the two regional workshops to evaluate the ILEA project had been well attended.

The report is most interesting for the light it throws on the debate behind the scenes in 1984 over the extension of ALBSU's remit for ESOL. ALBSU disagreed with the ACACE (1979) Strategy Paper, which 'saw English as a Second Language work as a core component of basic education … for its part ALBSU acknowledged that some ESL work was above the very basic level' (ALBSU, 1987, p. 2). But that still left ALBSU's role in relation to ESOL unclear. The then Secretary of State for Education, Sir Keith Joseph, saw 'a need for further clarification on the interface between language and literacy where English is the second language' (p. 2). This led to more discussion, the outcome of which was a masterpiece of civil service avoidance and fudging:

> At the end of 1984 the Education Department agreed that the interpretation of the Unit's remit would be to allow ALBSU to involve itself with ESL work where the involvement arises sensibly, naturally and logically from the Unit's primary concern with literacy and other basic skills. (ALBSU, 1987, p. 2)

The report went on to record that, in the view of the DES, ALBSU was not the central focus for ESOL and there would be no additional funding for it:

> The amendment was not intended, according to the DES, to make ALBSU the central focus for ESL [sic] in England and Wales, but rather to remove the practical difficulties that the restricted remit had led to. The Department also made it clear that additional funds could not be made available, and that any new initiatives that ALBSU wished to take in respect of second language provision needed to be financed from within the Unit's existing grant. (ALBSU, 1987, p. 2)

In fact, ALBSU did allocate resources from within its existing budget, and the report noted that in 1986–87 some £140,000 had been spent on ESOL work. This included an ESOL database (p. 172) and a referral system and teacher training. However, much more money was needed – according to ALBSU's estimate, £2 million over the next three years.

The main body of the 1987 ESOL report was devoted to describing the position of ESOL in England and Wales as drawn from ALBSU's annual survey of LEAs. This presented no surprises for NATECLA in particular and ESOL practitioners in general. It showed that in some areas with few ESOL students, they were enrolled in inappropriate EFL and basic education courses. There was some continuing confusion between EFL and ESL. Organisational structure varied, with some colleges including ESL with general studies and others including it with communication studies or basic education. Similar differences existed within adult and community education. In November 1985, 37,203 adults were reported as receiving help with ESOL. (ALBSU had some reservations about these figures, a concern shared by ESOL practitioners.) Most students were taught in groups, but 16 per cent were in one-to-one provision. Fees varied widely, with some LEAs remitting fees entirely and others charging up to £16 an hour. Only 1.8 per cent of the students were in MSC-funded provision. The ILEA accounted for 21 per cent of all the students being taught across England and Wales.

Again, the figure of half a million adults needing tuition was quoted, but the only source given was that this was the belief of the ALBSU Advisory Group in 1983. It is a matter of conjecture that this figure derived from the 1981 NATESLA survey.

The statistics on teachers seemed rather more convincing: of the 2,551 paid teachers across England and Wales, only 220 (fewer than 1 per cent) were full-time, and provision relied heavily on 4,934 volunteers. Opportunities for teacher training varied widely. Access to RSA courses depended on where you lived. Adult literacy training was inappropriate. NATECLA provided a very valuable source of training, but most practitioners had to pay for this themselves, and with such a preponderance of part-time tutors and volunteers 'this is a considerable burden'. There was a shortage of suitable materials. In sum:

> *What is lacking is not the dedication and commitment of staff and volunteers, but rather the necessary resources to turn all of this effort into high quality provision.* (ALBSU, 1987, p. 10)

171

The database on ESOL materials that ALBSU compiled was limited. It cited the Publishing Resource Unit in Leeds, NCILT, the NEC and the BBC as main sources of ESOL materials, but there were some very surprising omissions. This was despite the fact it included the *NATESLA Catalogue*. ALBSU identified a lack of simple and culturally suitable readers, but a great many were listed in the *Catalogue*. The ALBSU statement that 'there is a lack of materials for teachers about English as a Second Language work with adults both for the specialist and for those involved in adult education in general' suggested that the compiler of the *Database* was unaware of the *Parosi Handbook*, the BBC radio series *Teaching English as a Second Language to Adults* and its accompanying handbook, the CRE's *Home Tutor Kits*, the NCILT *Crosstalk* materials, NEC publications such as *Drama as a Second Language* and the works on linguistics and language teaching listed for RSA courses. While these may not have provided an ample or even a sufficient resource for teachers, they were not negligible. Such omissions and blind spots in ALBSU's work in, and for, ESOL undermined the confidence ESOL practitioners had in it.

- *A Nation's Neglect*
ALBSU continued to express concern over ESOL provision. In 1989 it conducted a survey of a sample of speakers of English as a second or other language (ALBSU had begun to use the now-accepted term ESOL), the results of which were published as *A Nation's Neglect. Research into the Need for English amongst Speakers of Other Languages: A Summary Report* (ALBSU, 1989a). ALBSU believed that this showed that there were between 1,600,000 and 1,875,000 speakers of English as a second or other language in England and Wales. Respondents were asked to assess their own competence in reading and writing in their mother tongue and their ability to understand and speak, and read and write, English. Using the respondents' own assessments, ALBSU found that 21 per cent were illiterate in their own language. Extrapolating from the sample, the report estimated once again – despite the increase in the number of new arrivals in the UK – that 500,000 needed basic ESOL provision (and more women needed help than men), but only 44,000 were receiving it and 25 per cent were in the ILEA.

The main motivations that the respondents gave for learning English were to gain access to employment and promotion and to help their children. However, younger people were more motivated by their own leisure and enjoyment requirements. A summary report was produced in eight languages, including Welsh.

• *A Programme for Action*

Following this survey, ALBSU proposed *A Programme for Action*, which covered employment training and youth training schemes as well as provision in adult and further education (ALBSU, 1989b). This programme opened with a rather thin historical account of ESOL provision, and, in describing the work with immigrant groups in the 1960s and early 1970s, omitted college and work-based ESOL provision altogether. However, the account accurately reflected the piecemeal and underfunded development of ESOL over the previous 25 or so years.

Two reasons were offered for the lack of any planned national programmes for ESOL. The first, and most illuminating, was the assumption [by central government?] that the problem would disappear once Commonwealth immigrants had integrated. The second was the continuing lack of data on ESOL learners. However, even with the statistics it had now collected, and its recognition of the complexity and diversity of the ESOL population, it is remarkable that ALBSU's estimate of the numbers of learners it believed needed support at a basic level remained at 500,000.

The *Programme for Action* noted the withdrawal of funding from Industrial Language Training, although the reason given was inevitably more benign and less critical of government policy than that offered in *Language and Discrimination* (Roberts *et al.*, 1992):

> *In recent months the Training Agency has decided to withdraw the £2.2 million funding available to Industrial Language Training Units, particularly as the location of the ILTUs does not, in the Training Agency's view, fully represent the distribution of the ethnic minority workforce.* (ALBSU, 1989b, para 38)

ALBSU believed that a new and important role had been identified for the Training Agency, now it had been allocated, and augmented, the ILT money:

> *The Training Agency has, however, agreed to make £2.5 million available to improve, in a variety of ways, ESOL provision made as part of Employment Training as well as part of a new programme aimed to improve business*

performance called Business Growth Training (BGT). In his speech at ALBSU's National Conference in June 1989, Norman Fowler, the Secretary of State for Employment, drew particular attention to English for Speakers of Other Languages. (ALBSU, 1989b, para 39)

The Training Agency's dissatisfaction with the quality of the ESOL training that it funded would culminate in a highly critical report in 1991 (see p. 218).

An article in *ALBSU News* (autumn 1989, pp. 2–3) summarised the finding of the survey, reported that there had been three national conferences to discuss its findings, and proposed ways forward. This article openly admitted that ALBSU's own remit in relation to *ESOL* 'has been confused for some time', and that 'clarification over the years has helped a little but has not produced the resources necessary to stimulate and develop provision on a scale that recognises the level of need and demand' (p. 2). To deal with the problem, it advocated a 'partnership approach', which would include the Further Education Unit, NIACE, UDACE, the Home Office and the Department of Employment. It should also include NATECLA, which had 'played a creditable role in raising awareness and encouraging development with scarce resources over a number of years and will play a significant role in future development' (*ibid.*).

In accepting that ALBSU had a continuing responsibility for ESOL, the article admitted that this was not a unanimous view within the Unit itself. ESOL practitioners had long been aware of differing attitudes towards ESOL in the Unit, and this admission left them to conjecture which positions were being put forward, by whom and why.

In support of ALBSU's continued involvement with ESOL the article quoted the words of Peter Davies, the ALBSU chairman, in commending the report to John McGregor, Secretary of State for Education, and Peter Walker, Secretary of State for Wales. Davies's support for making ESOL provision available had less to do with the empowerment of the individual learner and more to do with the national economy – the acceptable face of adult basic education:

If we fail to deny access to the crucial skill of English, we will continue to deny opportunities to a substantial minority of our population and waste a resource – the skills and attributes of people – crucial to the well-being of our society (ibid.).

The article continued in a vein that would become increasingly familiar in the next decades:

> With changes in the employment market following from reduced numbers of school leavers, employers will be looking increasingly to retraining workers. It is vital that non-English-speaking adult members of ethnic minorities should be provided with any necessary basic language tuition to allow them to make full use of the opportunities this will provide (ibid., p. 3).

However, the focus on only low-level basic education for ESOL learners would remain.

The article ended with a 'Programme for Action' in five key areas which ALBSU had identified for itself:

- supporting, evaluating and monitoring ESOL;
- sponsoring development projects;
- improving staff development and training;
- producing learning materials; and
- undertaking research.

ALBSU estimated that at least £3,450,000 would be needed for this over the next three years. This funding was not forthcoming.

Funding: Section 11

Concerns over funding in the 1980s were exacerbated by changes in the rules for Section 11 support. The management of Section 11, and the criteria for claiming it, continued to attract considerable criticism. There was some improvement for the large number of learners originating from the Indian subcontinent when, in 1982–83, the government redefined the terms 'Commonwealth immigrant' to include (i) all those immigrants in this country who were born in another country of the Commonwealth (including those born in Pakistan before it left the Commonwealth in 1972), no matter how long their residence in this country; and (ii) all children of the above, whether born in this country or elsewhere, aged 20 or under. The term 'substantial numbers' replaced the 2 per cent, enabling more authorities to claim funding. However, many groups of new learners, especially the refugees, were still excluded from Section 11 funded provision. Criticisms continued to grow.

Some of the most significant came through an ESRC-funded study at the University of London Institute of Education, *Education Funding for*

Ethnic Minorities (Crispin and Hibberd, 1987). This listed a catalogue of continuing and disturbing failures: the Home Office's unwillingness to offer advice and monitor recent changes; LEAs' unwillingness, or inability, to understand the annual circulars and their consequent over-reliance on headteachers; the difficulties of identifying the teaching posts that were funded and the lack of co-operation from the teachers' associations; the failure of LEAs to consult local communities and CRCs; and the problems with ethnic monitoring. It also reported with concern the fall in take-up over the previous five years. It deplored the fact that Section 11 staffing did not come under the provisions of the 1976 Race Relations Act.

The report suggested that the reason for the reluctance of successive governments to monitor and evaluate the use of Section 11 was 'an inexplicit style of administration in terms of race' (Crispin and Hibberd, 1987, p. 3). It cited and quoted from a number of academic studies to aver that, far from being a policy of neglect, there was a commitment to 'doing good by stealth', which was 'a deliberate policy choice, motivated by benign liberalism and political pragmatism' and 'an enduring commitment to an assimilationist perspective of Blacks in Britain' (p. 3).

Carl Bagley's useful history of Section 11 (Bagley, 1992) illustrates a further positive use of Section 11 money, in that local authorities used the grant to employ multicultural, anti-racist advisers and mother-tongue teachers, who made a major contribution to the development of anti-racism and multiculturalism.

However, this was not a planned policy on the part of the Home Office, whose approach differed in two major aspects from that of the CRE, the Further Education Unit of the DES and Industrial Language Training (funded by the MSC). First, all their work was predicated on an overt acceptance and understanding of racism and cross-cultural mis-understanding. Second, these organisations drew on data provided through ethnic monitoring.

What remained true, however, was that, with all its failings, Section 11 was the funding stream that most consistently survived changes in administration and the economic downturn, and continued to be the main source of funding for ESOL in the post-schools sector throughout the 1980s and into the 1990s. The *NATESLA Survey* (NATESLA, 1985) found that, although some provision was funded under the YOPs and TOPs programmes and a small minority from other sources, the majority of ESOL provision for adults was financed under Section 11.[9]

The appendices included in the *NATESLA Survey* report (NATESLA, 1985) give a valuable insight into how much Section 11 money was allocated to pay teachers in FE and AE and what kinds of provision could be supported. They show that for 1982–83 only 9 per cent of the money for salaries went to pay teachers in FE and AE. A copy of claim form (97/1982) listed the range of courses eligible for funding – home tuition, access and return to learning, literacy, vocational preparation and so on. Most important, the guidelines accompanying the claim form accept that 'it is unlikely that a post-holder will spend 100 per cent of his or her time teaching a group made up entirely of Commonwealth immigrants'. Here at last was an official recognition that classes contained learners who had nothing to do with the Commonwealth, old or new, and who spoke many languages.

In 1988 the government finally undertook a belated *Scrutiny* of Section 11 provision (Home Office, 1988). This argued for much tighter monitoring and reporting, much clearer targeting and an extension of the funding to the voluntary sector. *Language Issues* for autumn/winter 1989–90 (vol 3.2, pp. 39–41) carried a report of the *Scrutiny*, noting that the study had found that a yearly allocation of £100 million was spread over a number of public services, including race relations and leisure services, but that there were 'no clear objectives for the grant nor any effective system for assessing the results' (p. 39). Furthermore, although the bulk of the grant went to education, housing and social services, there was no system for consulting the relevant government departments. Local authorities were still reluctant to undertake ethnic monitoring, and this issue would have to be confronted. There were also continuing complaints from local authorities about the shifting of goalposts.

ESOL practitioners were interested, but not surprised, to learn that although 82 per cent of S11 money went to education, the proportion of this allocated for 'ESL to adults' was just over 1 per cent. The *Scrutiny's* recommendation that the restriction to Commonwealth immigrants should be removed was to be welcomed. However, in the event, the funding was not extended to other groups until 1993.

The changed arrangements for Section 11 funding in the 1990s, partly influenced by the *Scrutiny*, would raise difficulties for all ESOL managers and organisers.

Teacher training

The quality and extent of ESOL initial and post-experience teacher training (outside the university sector) was a constant concern for ESOL providers in the 1980s and into the 1990s. NATESLA's second, and major, research project, *Research Project into Training Teachers of English as a Second Language in the Post-16 Sector* (NATESLA, 1985), was carried out by Elizabeth Evans from Waltham Forest College, with a Steering Group that included representatives from the DES, the MSC, a support group of practitioners in colleges and adult institutes and the ILEA Language and Literacy Unit. The research was funded by the DES, which did not necessarily accept the conclusions.

The report was detailed and authoritative. It identified the major nationwide training providers of teaching English as a second language to adults (TESLA), as the ILEA, NCILT, NIACE and ALBSU, with an acknowledgement of NATECLA's contributions to training through its national and branch conferences.

In her evaluation of all the TESLA training on offer, Evans found none that satisfactorily fulfilled an adequate national function. Although in 1984 ALBSU had been allocated a national training role for TESLA under a grant for

> ... *developing within the general education service in England and Wales provision designed to improve the standards of proficiency for adults, whose first or second language is English, in the areas of literacy and numeracy, and those related basic communication and coping skills without which progress in and towards education, training or employment is impeded* (NATESLA, 1985, p. 38),

its contribution had necessarily been minimal. Some useful ALBSU-funded training had been run by ESOL practitioners using the Regional Advisory Councils, but there was money for only one ESOL training weekend per region per year (p. 115). So ALBSU funding could provide only a modest supplement to that offered by LEAs, voluntary bodies and NATECLA.

The main finding of the NATECLA report was that TESLA training was insufficient, piecemeal and uncoordinated, and its recommendations were that co-ordination should be achieved either through existing organisations or by establishing a new national teacher training body.

178

ESOL practitioners in general, and NATECLA members in particular, were struggling to affirm the pedagogy appropriate to their field. It was agreed that this should be built on a respected international understanding and agreement about good language teaching, and demanded four interlinked skills, knowledge and ability:

- the acquisition of a body of knowledge about language in general and the ability to put this into practice (linguistics and pedagogy);
- competence in the target language;
- a sound understanding of how adults in particular learn, and the ability to put this into practice; and
- a recognition of the impact of the wider social, economic, legal and administrative context on their learners.

These issues would emerge in the debates in the 1990s over the suitability of the City and Guilds teacher training qualifications for ESOL teachers, and in drawing up the subject specifications for ESOL teachers in 2002–6, where attempts were made to bring the four strands together (p. 180).

Meanwhile, practitioners in the 1980s were concerned about the currency and development of the RSA teaching certificates and diplomas in the increasingly competitive and intransigent world of the accreditation of teacher training controlled by ACSTT.[10]

Accreditation for learners

At the same time as ESOL teachers were looking for appropriate training and accreditation for themselves, they were casting around for appropriate accreditation for their students. In this they were faced by the complex array of examinations and assessment schemes (Rosenberg, 1988). These ranged from the Certificate in Pre-Vocational Education (CPVE) to the Certificate in Secondary Education (CSE), O-levels and general EFL examinations, such as the Cambridge First Certificate, to English for Academic Purposes (EAP). All these had their disadvantages. Those that had currency with employers and further and higher education were generally designed for native speakers of English. EFL qualifications were often inappropriate in themselves and, except for the very difficult Cambridge Proficiency examination, had little currency in the UK.

There were a few qualifications that could be said to have some relevance for ESOL learners. There was a special O-level English language examination, which was not designed to be culturally specific but set from the position of English as a *lingua franca*. This was the University of London Syllabus B examination. However, it could be taken only by students living overseas.

Two qualifications were aimed at ESOL learners on academic courses in further education and were based on the work of Pat McEldowney, who had analysed the listening and reading skills needed for the advanced study of the sciences. The first of these, the North Western Regional Advisory Council's English as a Second Language Test, was taken by students in the UK, and was seen as an equivalent to a CSE. The higher-level Joint Matriculation Board Test in English (Overseas) was taken in the UK and abroad as an assessment of suitability for study in higher education. These were useful courses for students, and the framework for language teaching was very clear. But they offered a simplistic, black-and-white view of language, with no attention to nuances and subtlety, or consideration of register or connotation.

There were also some local arrangements. The Open College of the Northwest (OCNW), established in 1975, had developed its Foundation Accreditation in Maths and English (FAME) for adult literacy students, and this was judged to be appropriate for some ESOL students. (OCNW went on to accredit ESOL qualifications under the Skills for Life framework, see p. 226).

The lack of an appropriate accreditation for adult ESOL learners led in 1981 to the establishment of the RSA ESOL Profile Certificate, criterion-referenced and assessing the four skills of listening, speaking, reading and writing. The profile sentences themselves indicated levels of difficulty, and students could achieve at different levels in different skills. This allowed for the measurement of a 'spiky profile', in which learners' levels of achievement in listening, speaking, reading and writing differed. This was just as useful for students who had lived in the UK for some years and were orally fluent but had difficulties with reading and writing, as it was for newer arrivals who could read well, but found difficulties in understanding and using the spoken language.

The pilot was a success, and the certificate was soon being run across the country including in Scotland. Moderation was undertaken locally, often using Open College networks. This encouraged the cross-fertilisation of ideas and the sharing of good practice. The RSA ensured consistency and quality through a team of assessors who visited centres regularly. This too encouraged the dissemination of good practice. However, the cost and the teaching time needed for assessment and for the completion of the Profile statements deterred some adult education centres and colleges from using the Certificate, and in any case it was not available in all areas.

Catering for 16–19-year-olds

While ESOL practitioners were struggling to make adequate provision for the growing numbers of newly-arrived ESOL learners who were presenting themselves for tuition, the government was becoming increasingly alarmed at the under-achievement and disaffection of many young people from ethnic minority backgrounds already here, and a number of important studies and reports ensued.

Youth in Multi-racial Society

A CRE report that appeared in March 1980, a year before the Brixton riots of April 1981, anticipated something of what was to come. Entitled *Youth in Multi-racial Society: The Urgent Need for New Policies* (CRE, 1980), the report identified the urban deprivation, racial prejudice and un-employment experienced by many black teenagers, which were leading to dangerous levels of disaffection and alienation. Its main recom-mendations were to the youth service, but the valuable role of further education in providing 'second chance education' was acknowledged. However, it believed that FE had failed to set up an appropriate range of courses that might attract some of the most alienated young people (CRE, 1980, p 12).

When the riots in Brixton erupted in April 1981, they sharply focused the attention of the government and national bodies on young people from ethnic minority backgrounds, and a flurry of reports and good practice guidelines followed. Although those actively involved in the unrest were from Afro-Caribbean backgrounds, speakers of English as a second or other language were included in all the reports and good practice guidelines. These were commissioned by different bodies, with differing aims and objectives, but they combined to build up a consistent and powerful picture of the position of ESOL, especially in the FE sector, and to draw the same conclusions on the inadequacy of the

181

education provision being made and, in most reports, on the racism and disadvantage faced by learners.

Underpinning all the reports and surveys was an acceptance of the recommendations in the Bullock Report (DfES, 1975): to ensure that the education system provides an 'education for all'; recognises that learners do not leave the language and culture of the home behind them as they cross the school threshold; values and ensures the maintenance of pupils' mother tongue and builds on it; and – most important, since language has the central place in all education – ensures the widest acceptance of the concept of language across the curriculum and acknowledges that all teachers are language teachers.

The Scarman Report

The government's response to the 1981 riots was to set up a Committee of Inquiry, initially chaired by Tony Rampton, who was then succeeded by Lord Scarman. Although in the final report (Scarman, 1981) the major focus was on young people from Afro-Caribbean backgrounds, the general findings applied equally to those from homes where English was spoken as a second or other language. Starting from the Home Affairs Committee's findings that 'we have not got ethnic minority education right' (Scarman, 1981, p 26), the Scarman Report focused a great deal on the language skills necessary for education and employment. Notably, Scarman concluded: 'I endorse the Home Affairs Committee's view that reform of Section 11 of the Local Government Act 1966 must not be long delayed' (p. 205).

Further Education in a Multi-Racial Society

At nearly the same time, the CRE published its report *Further Education in a Multi-Racial Society: The Urgent Need for New Policies* (CRE, 1982). This examined in some detail the difficulties facing ethnic minority students in FE colleges and the failure of the colleges to meet their needs. It addressed both of these issues in the context of developing multicultural policies and combating racism. The implications for colleges of the 1976 Race Relations Act were spelt out, including the support the Act gave for the employment of teachers from the same backgrounds as the students (CRE, 1982, p. 30). Appendix 2 was devoted to fighting racism in colleges and Appendix 3 to the ILEA's multi-ethnic policy The foreword referred directly to the recent unrest across the UK:

> *The need for our institutions to adapt to, and cater for, the needs of a multi-racial, multicultural society is being posed with increasing urgency. The events in Bristol, Brixton and Liverpool and elsewhere emphasise the cost of failing to meet those needs.*
>
> *The booklet aims to show how colleges can become more responsive to community need, how curriculum can be developed and how staff can be trained in ways that take into account centrally the multicultural nature of our society. It backs up its recommendations with practical examples of various policies and schemes in operation in different parts of the country.* (CRE, 1982, p. 5)

Considerable attention was paid to ESL teaching and the failure of colleges to provide adequate support:

> *Despite the fact that language is the core of all education, by and large further education does not give sufficient priority or consideration to ESL and the language teaching needs of ethnic minorities. The ESL provision in further education is patchy both in the physical availability of courses in some areas and in the suitability of existing courses to meet the specific needs of ethnic minority students. Too often, existing syllabi have been imposed on students without sufficient effort being made to question the relevance to the needs of the particular group. A clear distinction exists in both aims and content and in aspects of methodology between ESL courses for ethnic minority and general EFL teaching. However, in some areas language teaching provision has been regarded as sufficient if immigrant Asian workers are included in classes designed for European au pairs.* (CRE, 1982, p. 48)

Today's ESOL specialists might reject such simplistic equating of language needs with race, colour, nationality and gender. However, the report was intelligent and sensitive in its analyses of the differing needs of different learners – language for education, work and day-to-day life. It stressed the importance of good assessment procedures, the accreditation of previous learning and experience, and the provision of language support for specific courses. The report again took the position that all teachers carried the responsibility for the language used and needed in their classroom.

The CRE's estimate of need was far higher than ALBSU's, believing that some 200,000 people from an ethnic minority background were hindered in finding work because of a 'lack of adequate English' in a 'period of industrial contraction', and it urged the necessity for some for Trade Union activity too (p. 49).

183

Further Education in a Multi-Racial Society gave to the ESL [*sic*] teacher an idealistic and pivotal role which reflected the latest thinking on best practice and was clearly influenced by the ILT/Gumperz analysis (p. 153):

> *Responsibility does not end with the provision of a functionally based language course aimed at a specific topic area. Constant liaison between the subject teacher and the ESL teacher is necessary to ensure that the student and the subject teacher are in full communication with each other. The involvement of teachers from ethnic minority backgrounds in such programmes gives an added dimension, profitable to both sides. The socio-linguistic implications of second-language use and cross-cultural communication still are not fully understood. For ethnic minority students to make the best use of opportunities in further education, it is imperative that all teachers be aware of the factors involved and in a position to call on the necessary support.* (CRE, 1982, p. 50)

Examples of good practice were noted in the Bradford College Multi-cultural Education Unit, and in access courses in LEAs across the country.

Many of the CRE report's recommendations echoed those of the NATECLA submission to the Swann Committee (below). The CRE urged the government '[t]o develop a co-ordinated comprehensive system of education for the 16–19 year age group as a whole'(p. 10), and urged colleges to develop a language policy and train their staff.

The Swann Report

The Swann Report (Swann, 1985) focused specifically on the education of young people from ethnic minority groups in schools. NATECLA presented a submission (NATESLA, 1982) that focused on the special needs of the 16–19 age group and provision for them in further, adult and community education, especially provision for those arriving in the UK as older teenagers – 'late arrivals' – who had had little or no schooling in the UK. These often found it difficult to enrol in schools, which were only too aware that they had inadequate facilities to help them. Once more, NATECLA used its own networks to conduct a national survey, and it also cited and drew on the one conducted in 1981 (NATESLA, 1981b). The new survey again found that staff needed training. It also showed how, because there were few links across the different sectors of post-16 education, it was difficult to plan for coherent provision, and for learners to progress from one sector – perhaps community-based classes – to another – say, a further education college. It found practical obstacles to study in the form of the three-year rule whereby learners recently arrived in the UK could find themselves liable to pay fees, an obstacle not faced by school pupils.

The report's recommendations to the government included another plea for the revision of the terms of Section 11, a recommendation that the three-year rule be reviewed and a request for a national policy to monitor and evaluate the quality and take-up of provision for ESOL students in this age group. The recommendations to the MSC were for an overall policy that would recognise the situations faced by these particular learners and their need for 'catch-up time', and for the MSC therefore to sanction and recommend flexibility in the length and content of courses set up for them.

There were also general recommendations on providing language support for students on academic and vocational courses, on ensuring that teachers of all subjects across the curriculum were trained, and on colleges' developing cross-college language policies.

When the Swann Report finally appeared in 1985 it dealt exclusively with provision in schools, but its introduction identified the difficulties faced by school-leavers from ethnic minority groups (Swann, 1985, p vii). So, although the NATESLA report is included in the list of submissions (p. 791), the issues it raised relating specifically to the post-school sector were not addressed, although the fact that many pupils from ethnic minority backgrounds left school and went to college was noted by Swann (p. 168).

However, the Swann Report dealt at considerable length with language, and there were fundamental concerns and recommendations in common with the NATECLA submission. First, Swann cited the Bullock Report to reaffirm that the education system should provide 'education for all', that language has a central place across the curriculum, and that all teachers are language teachers – and therefore require training. It discussed the place of the language teacher and recommended the integration of specific language teaching into the mainstream curriculum, reflecting views similar to those that would be put forward in the Calderdale Report. It warned of the danger of equating no knowledge of English with low intellectual ability. The damaging effects of racism and stereotyping were tackled. The importance of the pupil's mother tongue was again reaffirmed, though how and when it should be drawn on and/or developed was left open to the further discussions which were taking place.[11]

The Eggleston Report

In the same year, a DES report on school-leavers from ethnic minorities appeared, complementing the Swann Report which had focused on schools. Its title, *Education for Some* (Eggleston, 1986), was the author's ironic commentary on Swann's hopeful *Education for All*.

As with Rampton's interim, and Swann's final, reports, the disadvantage faced by ethnic minorities in a racist society was again a central concern, but this time that disadvantage was supported by hard empirical evidence. This showed, for example, that for youngsters from ethnic minorities the levels of unemployment had risen from 11.4 per cent in October 1979 to 24.6 per cent in October 1982. The report, covering the school, FE and youth service sectors, and careers education, acknowledged that FE colleges offered some opportunity for second- and even first-chance education. However, in many colleges black and Asian students faced serious racist stereotyping as low achievers. The recommendation to FE colleges included the creation of access courses and the development of strategies to counter low expectations of young people from black and ethnic minority backgrounds living in the UK. These were contrasted with the high expectations of overseas students from similar ethnic and linguistic backgrounds (Eggleston, 1986, p. 288).

FE in Black and White

However, such stereotypical assumptions could not then (and cannot now) be confronted without properly organised teacher training programmes for all FE staff. *FE in Black and White* (FEU, 1987) reported on a survey of four colleges conducted by Celia Roberts and Val Yates of the National Centre for Industrial Language Training, with an agenda approved by the DES and HMI. This provided hard and disturbing evidence of the generally low expectations of ESOL students, and highlighted the tendency of staff to equate language difficulties with poor ability. It showed the inappropriateness of much of the material and many of the tasks given to such students. Quotations from interviews with vocational and academic staff ring with their frustration and incomprehension:

'It's a course for people of low ability, who haven't got the required grades or who have difficulty with English.'

'No, it hasn't changed [the course in relation to its 84 per cent ethnic minority intake]. *You see the white kids we had used to be either very poor education-wise or just hadn't got the knack of passing exams. So it hasn't changed the way it's taught.'* (FEU, 1987, p. 29)

The survey found that lecturers generally failed to understand that acquiring English was a core skill which must underpin all courses (FEU, 1987, p. 89). Some lecturers did try to cope but were ill-equipped:

'They have difficulty on the science side with lack of English. I try to explain more of the words but it really is a problem. It's not my field.' (FEU, 1987, p. 29)

Some teachers also expressed fear and resentment at students' using their own language to help each other. And – with the exception of ESOL and ILT lecturers and those teaching on the longer, specially adapted 21-hour courses (p. 17) – staff were also generally ill-informed about the backgrounds of their students.

The report makes for depressing reading, and the fact that, some 20 years later, many of the recommendations are still to be implemented is still more dispiriting. The survey recommended programmes of staff training to develop an understanding of the role of language in learning, create appropriate teaching and learning strategies, improve initial assessment procedures in order to avoid negative stereotyping, and 'tackle with confidence manifestations of racism in the college' (FEU, 1987, p. 37).

Language, Learning and Race

Aware of these difficulties in colleges, the FEU published *Language, Learning and Race: Developing Communication Skills for a Multicultural Society* (Robson, 1987). This offered colleges sound practical guidance on how to support students' language across the curriculum successfully by drawing on the work being developed at Shipley College. Again, the task of making proper provision for ESOL students was presented in the wider context of racism and disadvantage. Against this background there was:

> *...a recognition that the language needs of bilingual students are simply one aspect of their broader educational needs. Implicit in the work of the project, then, has been a rejection of the 'deficit model' of ESL provision, implying a linguistic deficiency on the part of the student which must be remedied before entry to the mainstream course can be deserved. The deficit model reinforces the notion of ESL as remedial education and assigns bilingual students and the staff who work with them a low status and marginal role 'outside' the main life of the institution.* (Robson, 1987, p 1)

Language in Education

Finally, in 1989 a summary of the consensus on good practice in FE appeared as *Language in Education* (FEU/NATECLA, 1989). This reflected the deliberations of three successive working parties representing HMI, the FEU, NATECLA, the LLU and practitioners across the country. It drew together the concerns and recommendation of the all earlier reports and studies noted here, consulted practitioners on good practice and how to implement it, and then provided an authoritative checklist against which colleges could evaluate their practice and procedures. These included ensuring access for bilingual learners, setting up good initial assessment and counselling systems, providing language support and running courses for staff on racism awareness and language across the curriculum. This report was very widely circulated. Many of the criteria and recommendations are as valid today as they were when they were published. They too have still to be fully implemented.

Other reports

The official reports noted so far have inevitably focused on one sector of education, but the needs of ESOL learners cut across such organisational divides, and it was left to other organisations, especially HMI, to report on this.

In 1982 the Council of Europe looked at the position in Coventry (Council of Europe, 1983a). In examining language provision, it reported favourably on the philosophy and approach of Industrial Language Training and on the Coventry home tuition and parental training schemes, which was part of its community education scheme. However, the difficult position of the isolated home tutor and the absence of appropriate teaching materials were noted. Another Council of Europe report looked at the ILEA's provision of ESOL in community, work-based and college courses (Council of Europe, 1983b). It found a great deal to commend, noting especially the 'linked skills' provision, but recommended increased opportunities for students to have access to accreditation and the development of more appropriate materials.

An HMI report on education provision for ethnic minority adults in the London Borough of Croydon (HMI, 1990) looked across the adult and further education provision. The strengths included a clear understanding of the barriers to access and good work preparation and employment training courses. Areas for improvement included more language support, but above all better communication between the adult education service and the college, possibly through a borough post-16 education plan to help student progression.

Such useful cross-sector evaluations would become very much more difficult after 1993, when colleges were removed from LEA control and separate inspectorates were set up. The same legislation would make cross-sector planning between schools, FE colleges and adult and community education increasingly difficult too (Chapter 6).

Conclusion

While the 1980s saw the establishment of a consensus on good practice and some valuable initiatives, especially in ESL/literacy and supporting language across the curriculum, concern grew over the quality and extent of ESOL provision nationally. The allocation to ALBSU of a limited, and changing, remit for ESOL for adults did very little to support its development. More significantly, the discussions on the place and funding of this provision revealed a deep official ambivalence, and sometimes even hostility. At the same time, there was a national struggle for resources for all education, and towards the end of the decade cuts in Section 11 were being planned.

During the same period, concern over the under-achievement of many young people from ethnic minorities, their growing alienation and disaffection and the racism they were experiencing led to urgent considerations of how FE provision could best meet their needs, and there was a major focus on language. Similar disaffection at the beginning of the next century, this time by fluent speakers of English, would evoke a different response, with the government then

189

concentrating on social cohesion. The focus on language would then be on what was spoken in the home, and attention would revert once more to how fluent wives and mothers were in English (Chapter 7).

The 1980s ended with the Education Reform Act 1989, but since its effects were felt only in the 1990s they will be dealt with in the next chapter, along with the other major piece of legislation, the 1992 FHE Act. This latter would launch a new world for ESOL in the post-16 sector, which for the first time would be funded centrally.

What would move from the centre ground would be the placing of ESOL within a commitment to sustaining a multicultural society and to combating racism and racial disadvantage. The big picture drawn in the Scarman, Swann and Eggleston Reports would be replaced by a concern with targets and an increasing emphasis on evaluation, accountability and monitoring. And under the new dispensation, the CRE would have a noticeably diminished role to play.

CHAPTER SIX

The 1990s: National funding and national concerns

The early years of the new decade continued to be difficult for ESOL provision. The situation improved with establishment of national funding for adult basic education in England and Wales, which for the first time included ESOL. However, there were still problems with accreditation for ESOL learners and training for ESOL teachers, and the waiting lists grew. National funding was followed by increasing scrutiny of provision and growing concern over its quality. In 1997 the OECD report *Literacy Skills for the Knowledge Society* alerted the British government to the low levels of literacy across the UK and this too affected ESOL learners.

At the same time, more immigrants, refugees and asylum-seekers were seeking to come to Britain, and further national legislation to control their arrival affected both learners and the teachers trying to support them.

The new legislation and post-16 education

Education Reform Act 1989

The 1989 Education Reform Act established a National Curriculum and set of standards for schools in England and Wales. These would have serious implications for the post-schools sector as the spotlight was turned, yet again, on national standards in reading, writing and mathematics. The Act also authorised the abolition of the ILEA. As a result, the Language and Literacy Unit, which had led the way nationally in many important developments in ESOL, and in literacy and numeracy, had for a time to struggle to maintain a precarious existence in a series of temporary homes (see p. 202). The Act also saw a change in the role of HMI, with the introduction of a new system of inspection under the Office for Standards in Education (Ofsted). This established a role for the inspectors that was less supportive and more systematic, and, many teachers felt, more critical.

Further and Higher Education Act 1992

The Further and Higher Education Act in 1992 removed control of the FE sector from local education authorities in England and Wales, and a new organisation, the Further Education Funding Council (FEFC), was set up to provide funding. A division was made between Schedule 2 and non-Schedule 2 provision. Schedule 2 provision covered all courses leading to nationally recognised qualifications. It also included access courses, adult literacy and numeracy courses, and any course 'to improve the knowledge of English of those for whom English is not the language spoken at home'. The breadth of this encompassing definition was more useful than the tortuous and constraining terms used in the successive Section 11 programmes. All other courses that did not lead to any form of qualification came into the Non-Schedule 2 category. Much of this was managed through very small grants made directly to LEAs. The ability of LEAs to run community-based adult ESOL provision was therefore contingent on grants from the Further Education Funding Council, and this meant there were new paths for managers and providers to negotiate.

The provision in the colleges, too, now depended increasingly on policy-making at a national level. ESOL courses were funded under Curriculum Area 10, which included provision for adult literacy and numeracy students, and for learners with disabilities and learning difficulties. Of all ten curriculum areas, only Curriculum Area 10 was characterised by the learners rather than by course objectives. So in Humanities (Area 9), for example, courses were funded in modern languages that were aiming for the GCSE qualification; in Curriculum Area 7 (Health and Community Care), courses were funded that were aiming for the BTEC National Diploma in Care. EFL provision was financed separately in the Humanities Programme area and prepared students for examinations such as those run by the University of Cambridge Local Examinations Syndicate (UCLES) and Trinity College. Colleges often experienced a conflict in deciding which course was most appropriate for a particular ESOL student. These decisions were then further complicated by the fact that the basic education courses received more favourable funding. Language support for students on academic and vocational courses was divorced from the discrete ESOL provision and was financed and managed under student support programmes. Funding for basic education also continued to be available through the Training and Enterprise Councils (TECs), the Single Regeneration Budget and smaller funding bodies.

The 1992 Act also changed the role of the HMI/Ofsted inspectorate, since further education was allocated to a new and separate inspectorate under the FEFC.

In Scotland the acquisition of devolved powers after the Scotland Act in 1998 opened the way for a more planned and coherent approach to the support of different communities, including refugees, asylum-seekers and immigrants, drawing on various departments of government and these are explored in Chapter 7.

ESOL learners

The different groups of ESOL learners increased and changed again during the 1990s. New refugees arrived, although it became even more difficult to gain entry to the UK legally other than through an official government programme with a quota. It was during the 1990s also that these new groups became known as 'asylum-seekers', to distinguish them from those who had already been granted refugee status. Citizens of the European Union had easier access, but more and more economic migrants from outside the EU were trying to enter, mostly illegally. The groups became conflated in a hostile public imagination which, ever ready to believe the worst, tended to label them all 'illegal immigrants' and 'bogus asylum-seekers'. Many of the new groups of refugees arrived from persecution and civil wars in Africa – from Algeria, Angola, Sierra Leone, Nigeria, Sudan, Somalia and Zaire.[1]

However, for the first time since the 1960s, refugees also began to flee from other parts of Europe, as conflicts broke out between the different ethnic and national groups after the breakup of the former Yugoslavia (Kushner and Knox, 2001, pp. 355–66). This presented a challenge to all European countries, which saw a refugee crisis 'the scale of which had not been seen in Europe since the Second World War' (p. 361), with an estimated three million people on the move. European governments were inevitably drawn into ascribing some measure of blame and responsibility for the situation, and there was constant coverage of the conflicts in the media and discussions on how to resolve them. The United Nations and NATO became involved in these efforts. These culminated in the Dayton Peace Accords which were agreed in November 1995. Meanwhile refuge had to be found for all those fleeing persecution. The UN High Commission for Refugees was active in discussion with individual governments, and there were intergovernmental agreements and policies.

The British government offered a programme of only limited entry, expressed a concern to pursue a policy of 'fair but firm controls' (Kushner and Knox, 2001, p. 362), and preferred to support programmes that kept refugees as close to their homes as possible, so that they could return more easily when it was safe to do so. However, in 1992 some 1,000 refugees and their dependants from the former Yugoslavia were given temporary admittance under the first quota programme (p. 366). Once again, the programme was managed by a voluntary organisation, Refugee Action, with support from the Red Cross, and the refugees were dispersed into camps across England and Scotland. In 1996, since hostilities were continuing, a further group arrived (p. 367). As the conflict developed further, special programmes were set up for the reception of Bosnian refugees, and a further 2,000 Bosnians came to Britain under their own initiative (p. 371).

The fact that refugees from all sides were arriving, and that some were in mixed marriages, complicated decisions on where and how to resettle them (p. 368), and the anxieties of the refugees were exacerbated by the temporary nature of their permission to stay.

Although there were some important and successful local initiatives to help these refugees, the 'response overall to the displaced people of Yugoslavia was fragmentary, helping only the fortunate few' (p. 372). But however small their numbers in relation to the overall refugee population, all wanted to learn English (p. 369), and teachers all over the country had to meet their needs.

Attempts at illegal entry
Asylum-seekers and economic migrants sought many different means of getting to the UK illegally, mainly using railways and the backs of lorries. Their desperate attempts to enter Britain from the Sangatte Red Cross holding centre near the French entrance to the Channel Tunnel led to some terrible deaths, which evoked horrified sympathy. However, the

banner headlines on illegal immigrants were normally extremely hostile.

The Sangatte centre, set up in 1999, was finally closed in November 2002 after prolonged negotiations between the French and UK governments which in effect led to the UK moving its border controls across the Channel. In the protracted debates on Sangatte, a Parliamentary Select Committee on Home Affairs Report admitted that the English language itself was a pull factor for immigrants (31 January 2001).

Legislation on immigration

To stem the flow of illegal immigrants and those claiming asylum, the government introduced further stringent, and often controversial, pieces of legislation. The Asylum and Immigration Appeals Act 1993 limited asylum-seekers' access to housing and introduced the policy of return to safe third countries. The Asylum and Immigration Act 1996 made it a criminal offence to employ a person not entitled to live or work in the UK, and denied benefits to those who had claimed asylum after their entry to the UK. The Immigration and Asylum Act 1999 set up the National Asylum Support Service (NASS) and introduced a voucher system of support, although this was subsequently abolished. A dispersal policy on a no-choice basis was introduced. The list of safe countries was abolished, though it was reintroduced later. The Carriers' Liability fine was increased to £2,000 per illegal entrant.

Effect of legislation on ESOL provision

The effect on ESOL practitioners and their work was considerable. Many illegal immigrants were hidden away in the black economy, but there were large numbers of asylum-seekers who enrolled in English classes, along with new arrivals from the European Union. There was insufficient funding to provide tuition for the new arrivals, and too few qualified teachers. Waiting lists lengthened again. The process of trying to manage a demand that it was impossible to meet became a real problem for providers (Rees and Sunderland, 1990; Sunderland, 1991).

Initially the impact of asylum-seekers was felt most strongly in the area of major immigrant settlement, in south-eastern England, but once the dispersal policy was in force teachers all over the UK were support-ing the asylum-seekers in their classes and faced the same difficulties.

Asylum-seekers could be moved on at short notice. Many teachers and Student Services Officers became involved in trying to sort out students' financial difficulties, which were exacerbated by the voucher system and denial of benefits. Particular difficulties were faced by teenagers who had arrived in the UK as unaccompanied minors. Under the terms of the 1989 Children's Act they were found accommodation in homes, bed and breakfast accommodation or foster care and were required to go to school. However, they were often unable to find a place in a school, and arrangements were sometimes made for them in further education classes. As soon as these young people turned 16, they were dropped into the adult asylum-seeking world and could even face deportation when they turned 18.

The Home Office was overwhelmed by the number of applications for asylum, and asylum-seekers often had to wait years to hear the outcome of their applications. Their situation would become even more difficult for those who arrived after February 2002, because then they were not permitted to work

ESOL teachers had always been aware of the situations facing their changing groups of students. *Language Issues* carried useful articles on the background and languages of the different groups as they arrived, and one whole issue was devoted to the history of refugees groups in the UK and biographical accounts of some of their experiences (*LI* 12.1).

However, the new situation demanded more than the acquisition of information. NATECLA members were urged to lobby their MPs on the effect of the new immigration Acts on their students, particularly the denial of benefits to those who claimed asylum after entry to the UK under the 1996 Act (*NN* no 50, p. 6), and they were concerned at the introduction of the voucher system and the dispersal policy under the 1999 Act. Several articles in *Language Issues* (vol. 13.1, pp. 4–15) described the damage that the dispersal policy, based solely on the availability of housing, had done to the educational opportunities for refugees and to community cohesion.

Home Office surveys

The Home Office itself knew, from a number of its own studies, that national ESOL provision was inadequate to meet the needs of refugees. What these Home Office reports had in common, and what differentiated them from DfES reports, was that they were not confined to the level of Basic Skills. The Home Office provided an analysis of the language and educational needs of refugees and immigrants that took into account the previous experience, qualifications and aspirations of the learners, and aimed to support them up to, and within, higher levels of academic and vocational training.

The first report, *The Settlement of Refugees in Britain* (Carey-Wood, 1995), is identified itself as 'the first systematic national assessment of the experience of asylum-seekers who have been recognised as refugees or granted exceptional leave to remain' (p. 1). Carey-Wood found that all refugees needed English language skills, and at differing levels, but that classes alone were insufficient. She recognised that very many refugees were already well qualified, and emphasised the importance of converting existing qualifications and enabling the refugees to gain employment, training and experience. In her second report, on the useful co-ordinating roles of refugee-specific initiatives (RSIs) (Carey-Wood, 1997), she again cited the vital importance of language courses at all levels. She also pointed out the dangers of short-term funding.

The third report, by David Griffiths (2003), looked specifically at language provision for refugees in Tower Hamlets, Newham, Haringey, Ealing and the East Midlands (Leicester, Nottingham, Derby), following the dispersal policy introduced by the 1999 Act. These findings too were unsurprising: there were too few classes, long waiting lists and a shortage of qualified ESOL teachers. Basic to higher levels of English were taught, but there was insufficient language support for professional and vocational development. More flexibility in provision was needed. Regular funding was essential, as was the existence of a good organisational infrastructure and co-ordination. Provision was better in areas such as London and Leicester, which had a long history of co-ordinated ESOL provision. Again, ESOL classes alone were not enough. Most tellingly, the Home Office document acknowledged the UK's national and international obligations:

> *The Consultation Paper on the Integration of Recognised Refugees in the UK (Home Office [1999]) states that language is the key to integration and that 'identification' of the different language needs of individuals, groups or age ranges will help in planning responses to actual needs. In a broader European perspective, the provision of adequate language training is regarded as one of the touchstones of effective integration policy (European Council on Refugees and Exiles 2000). Full economic and social participation of refugees in the UK depends partly on familiarity with the English language. It is*

crucial therefore for the integration of refugees into the local labour markets and communities in the UK that the provision of ESOL is adequate and appropriate. (Griffiths, 2003, p. 2)

There is no evidence that such obligations were accepted, or even recognised, by the DfES.

These Home Office reports confirmed what other reports found: that there were considerable weaknesses and inadequacies in the national provision of ESOL.

Attitudes and responses of learners

A further interesting exploration of the attitudes of learners came with the publication in 1998 of *Adult ESOL Learners in Great Britain. A Cross-Cultural Study* (Khanna *et al.*, 1998). This was based on a survey of 133 adult learners in ESOL classes: 90 women and 43 men. They came from Asia, Africa, the Near East and Europe, although the majority were from the Indian sub-continent. The group included both new arrivals and those who had lived in the UK for many years.

The whole report was interesting to ESOL practitioners and remains relevant today. It demonstrated how the attitudes of the learners towards learning English were much more 'instrumental' than 'integrative', i.e. geared towards work, education and training rather than social mixing. The survey found that learners viewed the host society positively only on those attributes that had an achievement orientation: 'successful', 'educated', 'efficient', 'confident'. Only 41 per cent of respondents related positive traits like 'sweet' or 'scientific' to the English language, and only 11 per cent judged English to be 'highly civilised', despite the influence of the Empire. The respondents' mother tongue was used extensively in the domain of the home and among family and friends, and adults expressed a strong wish that their children should maintain it. The survey found a discrepancy between the perceived and actual abilities in English of the respondents, who tended to think their abilities were better than they were. However, this also depended on the perceptions of the teachers, and the survey demonstrated how teachers' views of their learners' abilities were affected by their perceptions of the learners' educational backgrounds. What was encouraging, however, was that all the respondents were positive about learning English and their ESOL classes.

This survey was a useful reminder to practitioners that ESOL learners bring into class a complex range of emotions and motivations, and a need to maintain their own identity. NATECLA members were given several opportunities to reflect on this. The theme of the 1990 annual conference was 'Language and Identity: Threat or Crisis', and A L Khanna and Mahendra Verma presented their findings in a workshop that was reported on in *Language Issues* (vol 4.1, pp. 4–8). An interview with them was then published in *NATECLA News* (no 36, pp. 15–16).

ESOL provision

Practitioners continued to strive for good practice, still aided by organisations like the BBC and LLU and publishers like the NEC. Much of the new work was aimed at providing access to, and support in, further education and training, especially in the workplace.

The NEC moved further into the area of vocational training. In May 1992 it published a bank of resources, *Go to Work on your English* (NFER, 1992). Funded by the Department of Employment, and in conjunction with the National Foundation for Educational Research (NFER), this was identified as 'the biggest investment ever made in ESOL materials' using 'open learning to combine vocational training with English for speakers of other languages'.[2]

Trainees were introduced to open learning, in print and on tape, in English and in six community languages. The levels varied from basic literacy to advanced English, and the vocational areas included Hairdressing, Plumbing, Photography, and Painting and Decorating. The general areas covered Job Search, Information Technology and Health and Safety.

The series also included 'staff development modules in print and video forms for vocational trainers and tutors involved in ESOL provision, and full guidance on developing an open learning approach to English language teaching'.

Industrial Language Training

Although the central and local organisations had been abolished in 1989, the influence of Industrial Language Training continued. Films were made for the BBC – all of them influenced by *Crosstalk* (see p. 132).

Counselling and Advice across Cultures (plus booklet) appeared in 1990, and *Crosstalk at Work* (plus booklet) and *Recruitment Interviewing across Cultures* (plus booklet) in 1992. These were all part of the BBC Mosaic project (below, p. 000).

The consolidation of the ILT approach as it had developed since the 1970s was the publication in 1992 of *Language and Discrimination: A Study of Communication in Multi-ethnic Workplaces* (Roberts *et al.*, 1992). As Christopher Candlin said in his general introduction, 'One does not have to be an applied linguist to recognise that one key obstacle to the development of contemporary society is not the resources or infrastructure, but human interaction and communication' (p. ix).

It is regrettable that, in the publications and discussions on language in the workplace which followed the Skills for Life initiative, the major contributions of Industrial Language Training were rarely recognised and drawn on.

The BBC

In 1992 the BBC broadcast *Inside English* (reviewed in *Language Issues* by Usha Gupta: vol. 5.2, pp. 45–7). This series of eight 15-minute films was planned and developed by a team of experienced ESOL practitioners, including Europe Singh – a BBC education officer – and an HMI. The main consultant was Margaret Robson.[3] The series was targeted at learners whose language skills had progressed beyond 'survival level' and who were concerned to develop them in order to go on to further education or improve their job prospects. Each of the eight programmes focused on a different and useful language function: self-evaluation; making a case; negotiating; contributing to meetings; technical language; following instructions; organising information; dealing with complaints and giving a talk. The fact that the programmes were filmed on a series of different locations across the country, and with ESOL learners as participants, was widely welcomed by ESOL students and teachers.

However, since the target audience was so small, the BBC also aimed the programmes at native speakers of English. As a result, the actual language used in the content of the programmes was more complex than that identified in the planning, and ESOL learners found the pro-grammes quite difficult to follow on a first viewing. *Inside English* illustrated once again the dangers of trying to meet the needs of ESOL learners and native speakers simultaneously. However, since the series was accompanied by a teachers' book and video, it was possible to adapt the films for classroom use.

The BBC's Mosaic project started in 1989 with the aim of running for five years. An account by Rakesh Bhanot and Europe Singh, the BBC education officer involved, appeared in *Language Issues* (vol. 5.1, 1991/2, pp. 21–4). The project accepted and celebrated the reality of multi-lingual, multicultural Britain, while recognising the continuing discrimination faced by members of ethnic minority communities. It was concerned with:

- discrimination against members of the 'visible' minority groups, and what is needed to establish equal opportunities
- responses – both cultural and attitudinal to Britain's cultural diversity. (*LI* 5.1, p. 21)

The programmes were aimed at a general audience, but the specific targets were the trainers of professional groups, community groups and teachers in schools and colleges. Included were programmes on Housing, Law, Health, Employment and Education, and printed support material was provided for each programme.

The review in *Language Issues* pointed ESOL teachers towards the programmes specifically focusing on language, which included *Language for Life* (1980), as well as *Language is the Key* (1989), and *Mind Your Language* (1990); teachers were also directed to the films on cross-cultural communication (above). The review continued with yet another reminder of the continuing reality of institutionalised discrimination:

> However, as all the programmes looked at issues of inequality and dis-crimination, as well as providing examples of good practice in a variety of settings, the MOSAIC films can be used for a range of educational purposes when working with a range of multilingual adults.

> In many respects, education has not yet moved away from the 'deficit' model, whereby a lack of English language skills is equated with having no language at all, which in turn is often seen as a sign of low ability, and even low intelligence. These attitudes permeate all institutions and lead to bi/multi-lingual adults being denied access to education, training and employment. In addition, such notions of deficit can also hinder the equitable allocation of welfare benefits and other services. What the MOSAIC series has attempted

to do is to locate the institutionalised forms of discrimination rather than focusing on helplessness of the victims. (LI 5.1, p. 21)

Such an unambiguous commitment to multiculturalism by a major national institution would become increasingly difficult after 2000, as the concept itself began to be questioned (below).

London Language and Literacy Unit (LLU)

Under its new director Madeleine Held, who took over in 1990, the Language and Literacy Unit continued to provide training in numeracy, literacy and ESOL. During the tricky transition period after the abolition of the ILEA in 1989, it was first taken over by the London Borough of Southwark and housed in various buildings of Southwark College. The majority of its income at this time came from Section 11 funding. Some of this came directly to support the Afro-Caribbean Language and Literacy Project; the rest was claimed by the London boroughs, which then used it to subscribe to LLU programmes of in-service training. However, by the early 1990s the boroughs' training budgets were already stretched, and the tightening of the criteria for, and cash-limiting of, Section 11 funding put further strains on local authorities (p. 208). The LLU had therefore to seek other sources of funding, and the Unit successfully diversified its work through consultancy and customised training across the country, delivering accredited courses such as those leading to the RSA ESOL and adult literacy qualifications. In 1998 the LLU moved to London South Bank University as a free-standing, self-supporting unit. In January 2004 it changed its name to LLU+, thereby formally incorporating numeracy into its title, along with language and literacy.

Despite its difficulties, the LLU continued to make an important contribution to the development of ESOL, both in the London area and nationally. It reintroduced teacher networks across London, and charted the continuing shortfall in ESOL provision in London and the South-East with *Not Meeting the Demand* (Rees and Sunderland, 1990) and *Still Not Meeting the Demand* (Sunderland, 1991). The Unit played a major national role in teacher training; it represented the interests of the field in various national forums; it produced and published a considerable amount of valuable research and teaching materials. An example of the Unit's ability to work collaboratively and overcome problems of funding was the production by Helen Sunderland of the *ESOL Materials Database*

(1992a) (see p. 165).[4] This then formed the basis for Sunderland's *Tutor's Guide to ESOL Materials for Adult Learners* (1992b) (above, p. 165). In 1995 the LLU's assessment working party produced a useful handbook, *Working with the Criteria for the Assessment of English Language Skills: Examples of Current Practice* (LLU, 1995).

Issues of continuing concern to practitioners

Teacher training

In the early 1990s significant changes were occurring in the national systems for post-schools teacher training and its accreditation. These were affected by the adoption of national standards created by Training and Development Lead Bodies (TDLBs).

The Adult Literacy and Basic Skills Unit[5] announced in 1991 that it was sponsoring two new certificates to be offered by City and Guilds: an initial qualification (the one for ESOL was 9284), and the Certificate in Teaching Basic Communication Skills (9281, to become the 9285), which would be available for both ESOL and literacy and numeracy tutors and lecturers. The new certificates would become available nationally in 1992. ALBSU would fund LEAs £100 for each applicant for certificate accreditation, with some further funding 'to pay for training or support which addresses "gaps" in participants' competence in terms of the requirements of the Certificate' (*NN*, no 39, p. 5). The *ALBSU Standards for Basic Skills Tutors* was published in March 1992 (ALBSU, 1992), setting out the standards in detail and confirming that they were following the suggested TDLB guidelines.

ESOL teachers were concerned about these new developments, and NATECLA held a conference in November 1991 entitled 'Crisis in ESOL Teacher Training: Opportunities for Change' (*NN*, no 39, p. 4). Participants at the conference expressed considerable anxiety about the new schemes, particularly the omission of elements essential for effective ESOL teaching. These included ensuring that trainees had a strong foundation in linguistics and were trained to provide support for learners on other courses. The conference ended with resolutions that NATECLA should write to ALBSU saying that the new framework did not meet the needs of trainee ESOL teachers, and to the RSA urging it to continue its TESLA courses, which should be amended in terms of the new national development in teacher training. It also authorised

NATECLA to write to the DES expressing concern over cuts in money for teacher training, which meant that the only funding available would be for a course that was untested and did not cover training in many areas vital to ESOL teachers. Finally, the conference urged that a NATECLA teacher training working party should be established. This was set up and became increasingly influential in the next stages of the development of ESOL teacher training (below).

As it became possible to evaluate the new City and Guilds schemes in action, the concerns of NATECLA members increased. These were articulated at a special conference in Birmingham in March 1994. *Language Issues* (vol 6.1, 1994) carried a report of the conference, along with two articles exploring the issues in more detail. The report and articles got to the heart of the differences between teaching adult literacy to native speakers and teaching English to speakers of other languages.

In her report of the conference *(LI* 6.1, p. 5), Helen Sunderland summarised the concerns of the participants. ESOL practitioners believed there was an unbridgeable gap between the entry-level qualification (no 9284) and the full certificate (no 9285). However, their main criticism was that the 9285 qualification needed to be made more relevant to ESOL, 'especially in terms of linguistic rigour and attention to group needs'. The report concluded: 'The feeling from the con-ference, from all the workshops, was that, flawed though they may be, the RSA schemes best reflect ESOL good practice and should be fought for' (p 5).

In the same issue of *Language Issues*, an article by Christina Healey entitled 'Is 9285 [the City and Guilds Certificate in Teaching Basic Skills] an appropriate vehicle for training ESOL teachers?' (*LI* 6.1, pp. 10–12) summarised the judgements of teachers in a workshop run at the March conference to review the award in more detail. The article was fair and balanced in acknowledging that City and Guilds was using a new competency-based certification, and that teachers needed time to get used to it. ESOL teachers also acknowledged that the certificate represented a set of standards, 'not a map of how to get there'. The 9285 framework was also valuable in helping teachers to identify the needs of learners, to design learning programmes, to provide learning opportunities and to evaluate learning.

However, one major weakness for the many ESOL teachers and trainers working in many sites and situations across the country was that the 9285 framework was about accrediting people already working within a system of good practice, and was not really concerned with providing training to improve practice. Another difficulty for ESOL teachers was the focus on the individual learner. Though this was usual and appropriate practice in adult literacy schemes, it was not appropriate for teaching most language learners, who were usually best taught in groups. But the most significant criticism was that the generic nature of 9285 made it impossible to identify and accredit the essential knowledge, skills and understanding needed by the ESOL teacher, particularly in relation to knowledge *about* language – phonology, grammar, syntax, discourse systems. These were not required of the literacy teacher.

The article then summed up the ongoing dilemmas in assessing effective ESOL training:

1 *How far is it different from and how far is it similar to EFL training?*

2 *How far is it different from and how far is it similar to Adult Literacy and Basic Skills?* (*Language Issues*, vol 6.1, p. 12)

The article ended with a quote from a teacher: 'We have been trying for twenty years to professionalise ESOL teaching. If we embrace 9285 as it stands now, we will de-skill the tutors and we will disempower the learners' (p. 12).

The second article,[6] by Helen Waites, looked at the 9284 qualification from the experience and point of view of a teacher trainer helping new entrants into the profession. She too acknowledged the strengths of the new system in providing a clear framework of performance criteria and the value of regular assignments. However, important needs of inexperienced ESOL trainees were not being met. From Waites's experience, too little time was allocated to learning *about* language, and in any case this was not the same as 'language awareness' needed by adult literacy tutors. ESOL trainees needed to know about grammar, language functions, vocabulary, pronunciations and intonation, and it took more than the one two-hour session allocated to this in the training programme for trainees to acquire such knowledge and understanding. The emphasis on supporting the individual learner in a one-to-one situation was again seen as less helpful to ESOL trainees, who would most likely be supporting learners in classes. Waites also highlighted the unquestioned assumption behind the City and Guilds framework that basic education provision dealt with reluctant learners. This was sharply different from the experience of ESOL schemes, with long waiting lists of those eager to get into classes.

Concern among ESOL practitioners about the City and Guilds framework continued. The training video produced by ALBSU in 1992 to support the training for the 9284 course was severely criticised by the Language and Literacy Unit, and a report was sent to ALBSU.

However, these criticisms had no effect. Negotiations with City and Guilds and representations to ALBSU all failed to secure any changes in the training and accreditation.

NATECLA Teacher Training Working Party

From its inception, the membership of the NATECLA Teacher Training Working Party reflected a wide experience of ESOL training. It included those responsible for running the existing RSA course, the chief verifier for these courses, representatives from the Language and Literacy Unit and a number of experienced consultants.

Their work was based on the premise that effective language teaching demands a body of knowledge *about* language as well as knowledge *of* the target language. This had to be accompanied by an understanding of how learners – especially adults – learn, and of the position of the different groups of ESOL students. The ESOL practitioner had then to know how to develop appropriate methodologies, curricula and materials to meet the needs of these learners. The Working Party was determined to preserve an initial and post-experience teacher training programme, as well as programmes of continuing professional development that included all these elements. It would also incorporate aspects of the successful training of teachers of overseas students of English.

The first task of the Working Party was to sustain the RSA teacher training scheme after the main EFL certificate moved to the University of Cambridge Local Examinations Syndicate (UCLES) in 1988 and became known as the RSA Cambridge Certificate.

The RSA certificates and diplomas for teaching children and adults resident in the UK stayed with the RSA. NATECLA members were involved, in the early 1990s, in the RSA's plans to reorganise their ESL schemes in accordance with National Vocational Qualification (NVQ) requirements. However, by 1994 the RSA found that the ESL schemes were becoming unviable. During 1995 the NATECLA Teacher Training Working Party worked closely with the RSA to sustain its language teaching schemes, which were found temporary homes under the RSA's

'Customized Qualification' arrangements. The adult certificate (Dip TESLFACE) was taken over by NATECLA, and managed from Birmingham (*NN*, nos 44, p. 2; 45, p. 11; 47, p. 3).

Meanwhile, the NATECLA Teacher Training Working Party approached other awarding bodies about possible accreditation, finally working with UCLES on its new TESLA certificate, which was aimed at ESOL teachers of both overseas learners and those resident in the UK. The role of the Working Party was to ensure that the new certificate reflected the needs of teachers of adults resident in the UK as well as teachers of EFL overseas. In 1996 UCLES established the Certificate in English Language Teaching to Adults (CELTA), bringing together the best practice of both EFL and ESL – a shared emphasis on practical teaching skills, a focus on the needs of the students, and a requirement that teachers master a basic knowledge of language – thereby producing what was generally felt to be a more rigorous training and qualification. The scheme quite quickly gained credibility with NATECLA members. A workshop run at the annual conference at Salford in June 1998 was well received (*NN*, no 58, pp. 6–7). The gulf between EFL and ESL had been bridged – at least for the time being.

The next task would be to influence the development of teacher training under the Skills for Life initiative (p. 222).

Accreditation of student learning

ESOL practitioners continued to look for qualifications that recorded student achievement on appropriate and relevant programmes of learning but also had currency nationally and enabled learners to progress further in their education and training and into employment. The British Council's IELTS examination, pioneered in the early 1990s as a test of English for academic study, was becoming increasingly useful for ESOL learners aiming to enter university, but it was at a high level. The RSA developed an NVQ in English aimed at second-language speakers and in line with NVQ qualifications in foreign languages; but, since it was not the equivalent of a grade A–C in GCSE English (started in 1986), it had little currency in the UK.

The development by ALBSU of Wordpower in 1992 had a particular impact on ESOL learners. Aimed at assessing the overall communication skills of adult literacy students, Wordpower was promoted for ESOL students too. On some externally funded courses it was the only form of accreditation available, and was the required accreditation for Job Centre programmes of basic education. Practitioners applying to ALBSU for its kite-mark were strongly urged to use the accreditation.

However, even within ALBSU itself, there was an acknowledgement that the accreditation was not appropriate for most ESOL learners. A review of Wordpower in *ALBSU Newsletter* (no 44, p. 13) demonstrated this. The reviewer compared Wordpower with the RSA Profile Certificate. The latter was developed in 1983 to assess students' achievement in all four language skills, whereas Wordpower assumed native speaking competence in listening and speaking. The review further pointed out that ESOL students might have better levels of reading than speaking. Finally, the reviewer emphasised that Wordpower was an assessment of competence and did not replace programmes of learning.

Funding

Section 11

The incremental changes in Section 11 funding between 1990 and 1994 raised new difficulties for all ESOL managers and organisers. From 1990–91 onwards, the Home Office had to bid to the Treasury for Section 11 funding, justifying the expenditure in terms of value for money. As a result, local authorities had to identify block grants and specific grants separately. There were also government plans for privatisation and deregulation, which meant that local authorities had to compete with voluntary and private organisations for the same resources. Most important were the new cash limits that were planned to take effect in 1994 and would reduce Section 11 funding over six years, with education grants carrying the full cuts, while other services were cut proportionately less.

In the summer of 1990, *NATECLA News* (no 35, p. 14) alerted its readers to the impending changes following the 1989 Scrutiny. These changes did not always follow the recommendations in the Scrutiny (above, Chapter 5), and NATECLA members were dismayed to note that support for mother-tongue maintenance had been removed, and that the funding was still restricted to New Commonwealth immigrants.

The emphasis was now on funding courses that provided access to further and higher education for people from ethnic minority backgrounds, and to encourage them to enter the professions, especially teaching. There was still support for 'adults from ethnic minorities who have an inadequate command of English or who lack other skills in numeracy or literacy, sufficient knowledge of English and other basic skills to compete for jobs and to participate fully in society'(*NN*, no 35, p. 14). The grant was cash-limited, bids had to be project-based as opposed to post-based, and each year local authorities had to provide details of performance against approved targets and objectives. Applicants also had to show in their bids that they had consulted representatives from a cross-section of the intended beneficiaries of special provision.

As recommended in the *Scrutiny*, the money was no longer earmarked for use by local authorities alone. The voluntary sector was now included, either in partnership bids with local authorities or in direct funding from government agencies. The Circular also gave guidance on how Section 11 money could be used in employment training enterprises.

ESOL practitioners found many difficulties with the new system. In spring 1992 *NATECLA News* (no 39, p. 1) carried a lead article entitled 'The Great Section XI Lottery', reflecting the anger and frustrations of practitioners at the anomalies in the way the funding had been allocated. This had also been affected by a clear shift away from funding community education provision to providing language support in further and higher education, in line with the government's policy of widening participation. However, the article reported that there had been some useful developments. One was Shipley College's Language Network Development project, which had received £40,000 from the National Development Fund – via their local Training and Enterprise Council (TEC) – for materials development.

In 1992 the government announced the further changes to Section 11 that would take effect from April 1994 and would involve major cuts in funding. ESOL practitioners were forewarned of these in an article by Peter Wardle entitled 'Section 11 funding crisis' in *Language Issues* (vol 6.1, pp. 17–18). Wardle reported that in 1993 Section 11 funding had amounted to £174 million and had funded the employment of more than 10,000 people Almost 90 per cent of the money had been spent on education, the lion's share going to pay teachers of ESOL schools and colleges. From April 1994 onwards, the government would progressively reduce its contribution from 75 to 57 per cent and then from 57 to 50 per cent. Local authorities would be expected to make up the deficit, though very few had the resources to do so and there would therefore be cuts. The article reported that opposition to these cuts had erupted on a national scale. It came from the NUT (which was going to demonstrate against them), the All Party Parliamentary Group on Race and Community and the Runnymede Trust. The article quoted from the latter:

> ...*it is increasingly difficult to believe that the government really does want black and ethnic minority people 'to participate fully and freely in the economic, social and public life of the country (from The Future of Section 11 Funding, Runnymede Trust, 1993)* (*Language Issues*, vol 6.1, p. 18)

However, as a result of a Private Member's bill, sponsored by the MP for Waltham Forest and passed in the autumn of 1993, the anomalous New Commonwealth restriction on eligibility for the funding was finally lifted. Refugees could now be included, but this only meant that decreasing resources would have to be spread even more thinly.

Finally, in 1998, with a new government in place, Section 11 was abolished, and the educational element was replaced by the Ethnic Minority Achievement Grant (EMAG), processed by the DfES for schools, and by the Ethnic Minority Students Achievement Grant (EMSAG), processed by the Learning and Skills Council (LSC) for colleges. Responsibility for ESOL and EAL had finally been passed from the Home Office to education.

At the point of handover, the Adult and Basic Skills Strategy Unit (ABSSU) at the DfES did not realise, until approached by Manchester LEA, that LEAs had been claiming Section 11 money for adult education, mainly ESOL. ABSSU estimated that this had amounted to one per cent of the total budget, and so that amount was set aside for LEAs to continue to claim via the Learning and Skills Council. The non-educational element of Section 11 funding remained with the Home Office as 'Core Funding for the Voluntary Sector'. When the National Asylum Support Service (UK Immigration Service and Department for Work and Pensions) was set up, it acquired the element that related to asylum-seekers. As a result, the Home Office was left with the core funding for voluntary organisations dealing with refugees.

Other funding
Other funding for ESOL courses continued to be available, particularly under the Training Services Division (TSD) but also through programmes such as the Single Regeneration Budget. However, these

210

were not aimed specifically at ESOL learners and were in any case short-term and project-based. The TSD's dissatisfaction with the quality of the training it was funding is described below

National concerns

ALBSU

ALBSU's continuing concern over ESOL was expressed in its annual report for 1990–1 (ALBSU, 1991). The UK's failure was contrasted unfavourably with practice elsewhere in the English-speaking world:

> *The scale of provision and the priority given to the development of ESOL is disappointing in comparison with other industrialised countries, such as the US, Canada and Australia; and, although Section 11 of the Local government Act 1966 provides financial support, recent changes in Section 11 are not likely to improve ESOL for adults. ALBSU believes that it is time to cease funding ESOL through Section 11, particularly as this part of the Local Government Act 1966 was based on the concept of assimilation, rather than meeting the language needs of a diverse and multicultural society such as exists in the 1990s.* (ALBSU. 1991, p. 20)

In fact, in its implementation the 1966 Act was not totally assimilationist, as its respect for cultural identities and support for the maintenance and use of the learners' mother tongue demonstrated. However, the rest of the ALBSU analysis was to be welcomed. The report continued:

> *We still have not managed to convince the central government that there is a need for some development funding for English as a Second Language work with adults, and 1990–1 has been a frustrating year for our efforts in ESOL. We believe that there is convincing evidence of need for help with English for a substantial number of people, many of whom have permanent residents [sic] in the UK for decades rather then years. We also believe that some central initiative is necessary if the scale of ESOL provision is to be increased and if the quality of the learning opportunities available is to be of a high standard. We will continue to promote the need for greater effort and increased resources for ESOL in the years ahead.* (ALBSU 1991, p. 20)

Any efforts made by ALBSU were clearly ineffective, for in 1994 a further admission of failure appeared in the spring *Newsletter*. The hopeful headlines for a two-page review of ESOL (pp. 2–3) announced

'ESOL: Time for a New Beginning'. After reflecting back on practice and provision, the piece concluded:

> *In the UK we have made a very poor job of providing opportunities for people who don't speak English as their mother tongue, to learn English. The history of ESOL has been a history of short-term expedient turned into long-term inadequacy; lack of any discernible policy has been reflected in a lack of strategy, poor co-ordination and a waste of human potential. (ALBSU Newsletter, Spring, p. 2)*

Practitioners themselves were not blamed, but ALBSU was:

> *Too often ESOL has followed behind our longer established involvement with literacy and numeracy and the need has become submerged. (p. 2)*

The piece went on to recognise what all ESOL practitioners knew very well indeed, and had long been saying:

> *Sometimes we have got it wrong, and for all our efforts, we have not established the same level of government commitment to ESOL as we have to other basic skills work. (p. 2)*

The article maintained that the fault had been to assume that all ESOL learners had the same needs, and not to recognise that over the previous thirty years the client group had changed. But ALBSU's own pronouncements over the previous decade had already identified this fact (Chapter 5, p. 169). The article then quoted again from the 1989 survey, which concluded that the three million members of ethnic minority communities in England and Wales were not spread evenly across the country, that they included refugees and settlers from the EEC, and – once again – that half a million needed very basic ESOL. There was no mention of the needs of other groups of ESOL learners. The article noted that ESOL provision had grown but there were still long waiting lists.

To deal with this situation, ALBSU proposed to commission research at the University of London Institute of Education into student dropouts and progression. Why these were the foci is not made clear. ALBSU had identified the need for more information on good practice – but the article did not indicate how this would be collected. Finally, ALBSU proposed to urge the government to agree on the entitlement of new settlers to learn English, following similar practice in other developed countries – a welcome repeat of its view in the 1990–1 report.

The research at the Institute of Education was published in 1996 by the Basic Skills Agency[7] as *Lost Opportunities: The Language Skills of Linguistic Minorities in England and Wales* (Carr-Hill et al., 1996). This study found that there was a correlation between interviewees' level of English and their previous education, their previous knowledge of English and their current exposure to it. Refugees tended to have the highest levels of English, and women from certain minority groups and the elderly had the lowest. Following its brief from the BSA, the study concentrated on those with lower levels of competence as measured against the BSA's own Communication Skills Standards for native speakers, once again yoking ESOL learners with English-speaking adult literacy students. This perpetuated the arbitrary division of the ESOL client group and, in particular, failed to deal with the specific problems faced by refugees who, though they tended to be more able, were less likely to be living here in settled communities and with existing ESOL provision. However, even within the restricted coverage that had been imposed on it, the survey's finding were 'startling' to those who had conducted it:

> In the South Asian and Chinese populations, nearly 150,000 people score zero. 450,000 fail to reach a 'survival' level. There are many more thousands of people, both outside and inside London, who are functionally illiterate in English. They cannot participate fully in English society, nor can they make the full contribution of which they are capable. The picture is indeed one of opportunities lost. (Carr-Hill et al., 1996, p. 113)

ESOL practitioners noted wryly that the 'official' estimate of those needing ESOL support had increased by only 100,000 (from 500,000 to 600,000) over the 13 years since the NATESLA survey in 1981 (p. 166).

The concerns of ESOL practitioners were expressed in *NATECLA News* (no 53, 1997, p 1) and in a review of *Lost Opportunities* by Phillida Schellekens in *Language Issues* (vol, 10.2, 1998, pp. 38–9). Schellekens was critical of some of the methodology used in the survey and of the absence of recommendations on how to achieve local or national improvement. Her greatest concern, however, was that the groups surveyed were deliberately chosen to represent those with lower levels of English, and that even for this group the survey failed to differentiate effectively among different skills in listening, speaking, reading and writing (p. 38). Noting the danger of arbitrarily dividing the ESOL client group into the elite and the less proficient, she cited as much more accurate the picture presented by the Home Office 1995 study, *The Settlement of Refugees in Britain* (Carey-Wood, 1995 and p. 197) which, she believed, 'depicts much more diverse achievement in terms of English language as well as education and employment' (p. 39). She challenged the assumptions of the *Lost Opportunities* report that an overall estimate of national need could be extrapolated from it. However, she agreed with the survey's finding that 'there is a substantial need out there' (p. 39).

The *Lost Opportunities* report was to prove very influential, in that its findings were drawn on in *A Fresh Start* (DfEE, 1999a, p. 19) and were quoted in *Breaking the Language Barriers* (DfEE, 2000, p. 10) (see below).

NATECLA

ALBSU's statements on ESOL always made reference to the importance of NATECLA. However, even when both organisations were working towards the same end, their efforts met with very little success – at least before the implementation of the FHE Act.

NATECLA made several representations on behalf of ESOL[8] in the period 1993–5. The first was to William Stubbs on the setting up of the Further Education Funding Council in 1993. A deputation, including the then current chair and a previous chair from a community language background, attended a meeting at the FEFC headquarters in Coventry. The delegation presented the needs of ESOL learners and asked that they be taken into account under the new funding arrangements. The delegation was referred to the DfEE.

In the event, of course, a considerable amount of ESOL provision for adults was funded by the Further Education Funding Council as part of Adult Basic Education (above). However, NATECLA was still concerned about teacher training and qualification, and also about how to make appropriate ESOL provision available to the wider constituency of learners. Correspondence between the DfEE and NATECLA, including a report on a meeting in February 1995, shows NATECLA yet again representing the complexity of the ESOL population and its learning needs. This population included people with high levels of previous education and qualifications who did not fit easily into the philosophy and framework of Basic Education. The majority of ESOL learners needed progression routes into further education, training and work, and support while they were on academic, technical and vocational courses.

NATECLA's main concerns were with funding, quality and access. The continuing labyrinth of funding, including the TEC-funded courses, was described. Quality was seen primarily as the need for good initial teacher training and continuing professional development, which should include the acquisition of solid subject knowledge as well an appropriate methodology. This was not provided in courses leading to the qualifications supported by the Basic Skills Agency. There were insufficient opportunities for ESOL learners to gain access to further education and training (letter, 24 October 1994). The DfEE official's answer expressed doubt that his department – the Further Education Branch – could help (letter, 23 November 1994).[9]

Finally, on 23 February 1995, a meeting did take place at the DfEE between the official and the then current and two previous chairs of NATECLA. During the course of the interview, the DfEE official felt able to offer his belief that 'there's no need; we are not a nation of immigrants'. He wrote on the same day, expressing some disapproval of those ESOL speakers who, despite years of residence in the UK, had not yet mastered fluency and literacy in English, compared with those he described as 'able incomers', and was surprised that much teacher training was inappropriate:

> I had appreciated, for example, that ALBSU's work, which focuses upon teaching literacy and numeracy to those who have failed to acquire those skills, despite prolonged residence in this country and [which] reflects government's priorities in this area, is not designed to cope with the needs of able incomers. I had not appreciated, however, its impact on the RSA courses which are NATECLA's concern. (letter to NATECLA, 23 February 1995)

The delegation was referred back to the FEFC for basic skills provision, to ALBSU and the Teacher Training Agency for teacher training, and to NIACE for moral support, so meeting none of NATECLA's immediate concerns.

Widening participation

There was growing government concern in the 1990s that only a small proportion of adults who had few or no existing qualifications were taking part in education and training programmes.

The situation was highlighted in 1997 in *Learning Matters,* the Kennedy Report (Kennedy, 1997). In many ways this was an excellent report, thoughtful, well informed and useful to ESOL practitioners. Kennedy supported the entitlement of the individual learner to basic education, and the view that this empowered him or her as an adult. There was a useful analysis of the barriers to learning, particularly the way in which the benefit system impeded learning by restricting the number of hours permitted for study; this had recently been reduced from 21 hours a week to 16. There was a clear account of the vagaries of funding available for courses, including the effect of the non-Schedule 2 ruling. The report offered suggestions and made recommendations on how to overcome these difficulties

However, *Learning Matters* also raised problems for ESOL practitioners. Once again, ESOL learners were grouped together with unqualified adults needing basic education. There were of course similarities. Many ESOL learners were stuck in low-income occupations and lived in poor areas; many had few UK qualifications and needed to learn English. However, many others were already qualified, and simply needed language to help them transfer their existing skills and knowledge. Above all, with the exception of some very particular groups, such as the Asian women Kennedy identified as being under-represented in training and education, ESOL learners were not difficult to reach. On the contrary, there were far more aspiring ESOL learners queuing to enrol than there were learners in classes, and the waiting lists continued to grow. It was unfortunate that so important a piece of work should again perpetuate some of the ESOL/basic skills misconceptions and confusions.

HMI and other reports and critical evaluations

HMI/Ofsted evaluations
In the early 1990s HMI and Ofsted inspectors still had the advantage of being able to evaluate the opportunities provided for bilingual learners across the education sectors. Two reports supported the concerns of ESOL practitioners, while at the same time identifying some strengths in the provision.

Bilingual Adults in Education and Training (HMI, 1991) reported on an ambitious and wide-ranging HMI survey. It looked in the main at provision in five education authorities in the London and Bradford

216

areas, but also drew evidence from other LEAs in the Midlands, the South-West and other parts of London. It was a cross-sector exercise, covering not only adult institutes and colleges of FE, but also a polytechnic.

The report acknowledged the challenge facing hard-pressed institutions in areas of high and increasing refugee settlement. It described how complex the group of learners was and identified their very diverse needs. It cited many aspects of good practice, including good analyses of local labour market trends and the consequent development of appropriate courses, which included access courses to teaching, a range of linked skills courses and the effective use of Technical and Vocational Education Initiative (TVEI) money. Identifying weaknesses, the report called for more support for progression, more vocational provision with language support, better initial guidance, counselling and record-keeping and more bilingual approaches. It also argued for more development in Open Learning and self-study approaches and for increased learning support to improve access and develop student autonomy

Acknowledging the high demand for provision and pressures on institutions, it gave a timely warning of the need 'to balance carefully the value of short term responses against the necessity to plan and develop a provision which guarantees students a reasonable chance of success' (HMI, 1991, p 10).

Section 11 and Further Education for Adults (Ofsted, 1993) surveyed provision in five LEAs, looking mainly at provision based in the community, although some language support in colleges was also observed. The main focus of the report was on ESOL, with passing references to literacy and only one reference to numeracy. The report was reassuring in that it identified good practice across a range of provision (return to study, linked skills, some literacy courses) and was supportive of the employment of bilingual approaches and use of the mother tongue. However, it also identified poor practice in the often low expectations of students, poor record-keeping and monitoring, inadequate initial assessment and, above all, universally poor management information systems.

The report identified the problems of disaggregating the various forms of funding (Section 11, YOPs, TOPs and others) and warned of the dangers of duplication. It ended with concern for the future of Section 11 funding for the further education sector after the incorporation of colleges, and was especially anxious about the loss of local cross-sector and community links. It suggested that, in any future measurement of success, the main criterion should be how far provision effectively removed barriers to access.

In 1994 the newly-established Ofsted produced *Educational Support for Minority Ethnic Communities* (Ofsted, 1994). Referring to the new regulations in Section 11 funding relating to refugees and other groups, it dealt mainly with schools, with passing reference to language classes for mothers. The value of the funding to support teacher training was emphasised. The report identified the need for clear targets, record-keeping and monitoring. The use of the learners' mother tongue was encouraged, along with effective partnership teaching between the class teacher and the EAL teacher, the strategy used by schools to incorporate language support into the curriculum.

An Ofsted survey in 1999 of 16–19 provision in Hackney and Islington (Ofsted, 2000) noted that more than 90 languages were spoken at home by the students in the sixth forms, in colleges and on training courses. A main finding was that some students 'have weaknesses in written expression and accuracy, often related to the fact that English is not their first language'. The report did not indicate how many of these had been born in the UK.

Training Services Agency
With the abolition of Industrial Language Training in 1989, the major responsibility for meeting the needs of ESOL learners in the workplace and employment market fell directly on the government department dealing with employment, which was also the department responsible for monitoring the quality of the provision.

In 1991 an unpublished Training Standards Advisory Service (TSAS) report[10] identified even more weaknesses in the courses it funded than those funded by HMI and Ofsted in LEA provision. The TSAS reported that

> *the quality, extent and content of the programmes providing ESOL training and language support do not meet the needs of the trainees being submitted for entry to occupational training programmes* (Janssen, 1992, p. 105)

and that many training providers in London

have little or no understanding about the concept of ESOL with an occupa-
tional focus, and the need for language support for trainees from ethnic
minority groups, with moderate language difficulties, who are working towards
national vocational qualifications. (ibid.)

The recommendations were to improve procedures for recruitment, assessment, programme design, staffing and progression.

Ann Janssen reported that some similar failures in training emerged in her own review of 15 ESOL projects in the public, private and voluntary sectors, funded under the National Development Funding of the Employment Department in 1991–2 (Janssen, 1992, pp. 110–28). However, a number of positive outcomes were noted, including some increased understanding of the weaknesses in provision and how to overcome them and improve practice.

The Department for Education and Employment was so concerned about the weaknesses of much of the provision it was funding that it in 1996 it commissioned Phillida Schellekens to produce some good practice guidelines. *TEC Provision for English as a Second Language* (Schellekens, 1996) offered practical guidance on how to identify the wide range of needs of ESOL speakers, and described the best way to provide appropriate, embedded provision. She also emphasised that 'second language speakers often have valuable skills which are transferable to the UK environment' (p. 2).

What emerges clearly from all these surveys is that the quality and quantity of ESOL provision were endangered by lack of staff training, piecemeal development and forms of funding that were short-term, unclear or ill-judged.

FEFC reports
From its inception in 1993, the FEFC inspectorate reported on the new centrally-funded Programme Area 10, comprising adult literacy, numeracy, provision for students with learning difficulties and disabilities (SLDD) and ESOL. However, these areas were not systematically disaggregated in the final reports (except for SLDD, following the Tomlinson Report), although colleges often knew the balance of strengths and weaknesses across the various sections. The reports for 1994–5 (FEFC, 1995) noted grades in line with the previous year, with strengths outweighing weaknesses. The weaknesses lay in schemes of work, record-keeping and assessment and continuing professional development. The report for 1995–6 (FEFC, 1996) noted worsening

grades, and the weaknesses included the high number of staff who were teaching both basic skills and ESOL without appropriate qualifications, particularly in ESOL.

In April 1998 a separate FEFC Curriculum Area survey, *Basic Education* (FEFC 1998), reported that, while more than half the courses inspected had more strengths than weaknesses, there were causes for concern. There were weaknesses in assessment, accreditation, achievement, progression, management and quality assurance. Once again, too many staff were not suitably qualified. ESOL was not identified separately. This report influenced the thinking of the Moser Committee, which had already started its deliberations and would later publish *A Fresh Start* (DfEE, 1999a, p. 29).

The Curriculum Area Survey led to the FEFC good practice guidelines *Basic Education*, which appeared in September 1999 (FEFC, 1999). The recommendations in these guidelines were applicable across the whole basic skills sector. Literacy and numeracy were referred to in the context of the work of the Moser Committee, and SLDD was reported on separately on a number of occasions. However, despite the wealth of evidence to support considerable national need, ESOL was not identified separately. The analysis of the specific needs of ESOL teachers and learners, and how to meet them, would have to wait until the Moser Committee had reported, and its recommendations been implemented (see Chapter 7).

What is clear from these evaluations is that by the end of the 1990s ESOL provision nationally was still piecemeal and fragmented, too many teachers were untrained and the quality was variable.

The Moser Committee

The publication in 1997 of the OECD report, *Literacy Skills for the Knowledge Society* (OECD, 1997), highlighted for the British government the low levels of literacy in the UK. Its concern was further fuelled in England, in particular, by the critical FEFC inspectorate report on the standards of teaching and learning in Programme Area 10 (above).

In June 1998 a working group on adult basic skills was appointed by the Secretary of State for Education, chaired by Sir Claus Moser, chairman of the Basic Skills Agency, eminent academic and social statistician, and adviser to successive governments. It began work 'to advise on ways in which the government's plans for basic skills provision for adults can be supported and developed to achieve the target to help 500,000 adults a year by 2002' (DfEE, 1999a, p. 6). Although the group included a distinguished principal with a background in and commitment to ESOL, there was no focus in its remit on the specific needs of ESOL speakers. Furthermore, the groups and individuals consulted did not include those with a specific ESOL experience, although NATECLA made a submission on behalf of ESOL learners.

However, the Moser Report did quote directly from the 1998 FEFC *Curriculum Area Survey Report* and from the BSA *Lost Opportunities* report (Carr-Hill *et al.*, 1996). In this way, it prepared the way for the debates and decisions which resulted in the inclusion of ESOL in the Skills for Life framework in England and Wales (Chapter 7). The position of ESOL in Scotland and Northern Ireland would remain entirely different.

Conclusion

The 1990s saw the allocation, at last, of some of national funding for ESOL provision. This was welcomed. However, this funding was accompanied by increased concern over the quality of the provision, and in any case it was still insufficient to meet the full range of the needs of the learners. The Home Office itself began to be concerned about the language needs of refugees. It remained to be seen how ESOL learners would be affected by the government's response to the Moser Report.

Government efforts to control immigration would continue after 2000 but would be accompanied by concern to counter racism and by preoccupations with social cohesion, national security and citizenship. ESOL learners and ESOL provision would be directly affected by all these.

CHAPTER SEVEN

Skills for Life and after

The Moser Report

In June 1998 the working group on adult basic skills, chaired by Sir Claus Moser (see p. 220), began its deliberations. Its terms of reference were broad: to look at the effectiveness of different forms of provision, models of good practice and ways of increasing volume and effectiveness.

The final report, *Improving Literacy and Numeracy: A Fresh Start* (DfEE, 1999), proposed the development of a national strategy for adult basic skills which would encompass: national targets; an entitlement to learn; guidance, assessment and publicity; better opportunities for learning; quality; a new curriculum; a new system of qualifications; teacher training and improved inspection; the benefit of new technology; and planning of delivery. It identified the needs of half a million ESOL speakers, drawing on the Lost Opportunities report (Carr-Hill *et al.*, 1996), but made no specific recommendations. However, it noted:

> Most of our proposals are appropriate for teaching English as an additional language (EAL) and certainly we have kept this in mind throughout. At certain points we refer to special EAL aspects. But it would be sensible if a separate effort is made, following this report, to review its special implications in the EAL context. (DfEE, 1999, p. 4)

NATECLA members were urged to lobby their MPs on the failure of the committee's report to address the position of ESOL teachers and learners (*NATECLA News*, no 59, p. 5). The July 2000 NATECLA conference theme was 'Moser: The Way Forward'.

Breaking the Language Barriers

The recommendation 'to review [the report's] special implications in the EAL context' led to the setting-up of a working group on English for speakers of other languages. This was chaired by the director of Skills and Lifelong Learning at the DfEE and with representatives from the BSA, LLU, NATECLA, FEDA, NIACE and the Refugee Council, as well as representatives from FE and AE institutions. Their report, *Breaking the Language Barriers* (DfEE 2000), came to some important conclusions.

The report stated that ESOL learners, in common with other basic skills learners, required a clear framework of standards: a national curriculum framework that identified the skills to be learned; sound assessment; qualifications mapped against nationally agreed standards; and high-quality teaching (p. 1). However, the needs of ESOL learners differed in a number of significant ways from those of native speakers who needed help with literacy. ESOL learners in general required more attention to speaking and listening skills. Many learners were also already highly literate and numerate, albeit often in a different script.

There was an extensive debate within NATECLA, and among practitioners in general, about whether ESOL provision, ESOL teachers and ESOL learners should – and could – be included in the new national strategy (DfEE, 2001). It was finally agreed that, in order to ensure parity of esteem and equal access and opportunities for ESOL learners, practitioners should seize this opportunity to be part of the national framework. However, it was crucial that the specific needs and strengths of ESOL learners were fully taken into account in implementing the strategy. This applied in particular to the development of speaking and listening skills, but also to other areas of teaching and learning. A recognition of the special position of ESOL learners should extend to curriculum development, teacher training, the mapping of qualifications and inspection.

The report itself was sensitive and thoughtful in detailing the diversity and complexity of the needs of ESOL learners. It accepted that students encountered racism, particularly if they were refugees or asylum-seekers. There was some recognition of the value of a rich cultural diversity. However, the general focus was still problem-centred. ESOL learners brought 'a wealth of cultural experience and diversity to this country but this very diversity presents challenges to planning and offering appropriate learning provision' (DfEE 1999, p. 7). Perhaps inevitably, the report was only a little less problem-centred than those of 1963 and 1965 (above, Chapter 3). In contrast to initiatives in earlier decades, the CRE had had no part to play, although the Refugee Council was represented on the working group.

Practitioners noted with concern, and some surprise, that there was no recognition in the document of the good practice that had been developed since the early 1960s. The section dealing with 'The Impact of Lack of Fluency in English' was very clear (DfEE, 1999, p. 12). It cited the price paid by the learner in seeking employment and education, and in participating in the community; the price paid by society in economic costs; and the price paid by the nation in lost potential in terms of skilled workers and professionals. However, little attention was paid to strategies to help native speakers of English contribute from their side of the communication barrier, which had been the approach of Industrial Language Training. In the sections in the report on cross-cultural understanding (§6.9, p. 18) there was no reference to the good practice models, going back to the 1970s, that existed to tackle this; and, although the findings of *Language and Discrimination* were published in 1992 (Roberts *et al.*, 1992), they were not referred to. The section on the development of work-based learning failed to recognise and draw on 15 years of pioneering work in Industrial Language Training – including the education of employers. The actual wording of this section (§6.5, p. 17) used to encourage employers to release their workers for language tuition was uncomfortably close to that of the Ministry of Education (1963) pamphlet. In the same way, although there was much encouragement for the idea of language support (§5.2, p. 14) in the sections on embedded learning, the report did not cite the work that had already been done in the ILEA, at Shipley College and elsewhere.

All this being said, the working group was commendably successful in safeguarding the interests of ESOL learners in the first nationally-funded basic skills strategy, and in ensuring that ESOL practitioners would be involved in all the developments of ESOL within the Skills for Life framework.

Government responses

The Learning and Skills Act of 2000 established the Learning and Skills Council for England, replacing the Further Education Funding Council. In Wales it was replaced by Education and Learning Wales (ELWa), a public body sponsored by the Welsh Assembly, which in 2006 was incorporated into the Department of Education, Lifelong Learning and Skills (DELLS). These took on the responsibility for the Skills for Life initiative in Wales (p. 239).

In England, the Department for Education and Skills (DfES) responded to the scale of the problems outlined in the Moser Report by setting up a new unit, the Adult Basic Skills Strategy Unit. This was replaced by the Basic Skills Strategy Unit and then the Skills for Life Strategy Unit. Although the names changed, the overall remit and aims remained very much the same: to implement the Skills for Life national strategy, and in this to include ESOL. Most important of all, the unit had funding to carry this through. This was the first time that central government had committed itself directly and overtly to funding the development of curriculum material and teacher training for ESOL.

A series of Pathfinder Projects in ESOL was funded to encourage the integration of the Skills for Life strategy into teaching and learning. In 2002 the Strategy Unit funded the establishment of the National Research and Development Centre (NRDC) for adult literacy and numeracy, a consortium representing the University of London Institute of Education, the University of Lancaster, Kings College London, the Basic Skills Agency, the Learning and Skills Development Agency, LLU+ at London South Bank University and NIACE. The NRDC sponsored a number of useful initiatives in ESOL (see p. 233), in spite of the fact that its title omitted the word 'language', let alone the acronym 'ESOL'.

This omission was in line with the government's characterisation of the Skills for Life strategy as 'Delivering Skills for Life: the national strategy for improving adult literacy and numeracy skills'. However, a very great deal of government effort and funding went to support ESOL in the Skills for Life programme, and ESOL learners in the programmes far outnumbered literacy and numeracy students. Unlike the situation obtaining in the 1980s, therefore, the inclusion of ESOL under the broad umbrella of 'adult literacy' was not to do with saving money. It did, however, perhaps reveal a continuing government unease at publicising too widely its funding of minority ethnic communities.

The Skills for Life strategy and ESOL

There were many advantages for ESOL learners in being incorporated into the Skills for Life strategy. However, the systems which were already being developed for adult literacy and numeracy had to be adapted for them. The first challenge was to draw up a curriculum tailored specifically to meet the needs of ESOL learners while retaining the national standards established for adult literacy learners. Commissioned by the Basic Skills Agency, the London Language and Literacy Unit (now LLU+) had to work swiftly to develop the *Adult ESOL Core Curriculum*, so that it could be published by the DfES in November 2001 (DfES, 2001b), the same year as the *Adult Literacy Core Curriculum* appeared (DfES, 2001a).

Consultation on the curriculum had been extensive and had included regional training sessions and workshops for nearly 200 participants at the NATECLA 2000 national conference. These had prepared ESOL practitioners for what was to come.

Once the *Adult ESOL Core Curriculum* had been published, teachers had to be trained to use the new system. LLU+ won the national contract to run the National ESOL Training and Development Project between 2001and 2003. The project partners were NATECLA, the Learning and Skills Development Agency (LSDA) and NIACE. Providers were now expected to ensure that all ESOL provision was aligned to the national standards. The next task was to ensure the establishment of a teacher training programme appropriate to the specialist needs of the sector. This involved the development of subject specifications at levels 3 and 4 of the National Qualification Framework (NQF). These would be used in conjunction with the Further Education National Training Organisation (FENTO)-approved generic teaching standards, which were designed to implement the government policy to ensure that all FE teachers were appropriately trained and qualified. Awarding bodies such as Trinity College, City and Guilds and the University of Cambridge Local Examinations Syndicate (UCLES) had to ensure that their qualifications[1] conformed to these standards. A further task for ESOL trainers and managers was to help experienced practitioners, already in service with a range of previous qualifications, to assess how far these conformed to the new system. Alongside these major training initiatives, NATECLA, LLU+, NIACE and the NRDC provided national forums for continuing professional development on a wide range of topics.

Diagnostic materials were developed by the DfES to help tutors working with Skills for Life learners, including a quite detailed pack for ESOL tutors.[2] ESOL practitioners were also involved in the development of the *ESOL Exemplars* (DfES, 2004). Both were aimed to help teachers assess the levels of their students and their learning needs. Practitioners created ESOL learner materials and teachers' guides (led by the Centre for British Teachers) and monitored the development by the different examination boards of learner qualifications which conformed to the national standards.

National targets

The original Learning and Skills Council targets for the Skills for Life initiative were for 750,000 adults to attain a qualification by 2004. This was met. The next target was for 1.5 million adults to attain a qualification by 2007, and for 2.25 million to do so by 2010.

The Skills for Life accreditation fitted within the levels of the National Qualifications Framework (NQF), in which Level 2 was equivalent to achieving Grade A–C in GCSE. The four lower Skills for Life levels – Entry Levels 1, 2 and 3 and Level 1 – were seen as stages leading up to Level 2. The qualification was criterion-referenced and separated out reading and writing as two modes, with listening and speaking combined into one mode.

The qualifications which counted towards the government's national targets were broad. In addition to GCSE passes in English at grades A–C, they included those at grades D–G, as well as equivalent Key Skills qualifications and the Skills for Life qualifications gained at Entry Level 3 and Levels 1 and 2.

For Skills for Life ESOL learners, only the full Skills for Life qualification at each level (covering assessments of reading and writing and listening/speaking) counted as a full qualification. Adult literacy learners could achieve the full qualification at Levels 1 or 2 by successfully completing the single-mode, online reading test; they did not have to demonstrate competence in writing or in listening and speaking. However, the Qualifications and Curriculum Authority (QCA) did accredit some full qualifications in listening and speaking, which, although they did not count towards the national targets, could be used to demonstrate the language levels of those who were applying for citizenship and who were at Entry Level 3 and below.

From 2004, when the new Skills for Life qualifications became available, the Learning and Skills Council insisted that all providers should ensure that 80 per cent of their provision was leading to qualifications and only 20 per cent was non-accredited, although it must be aligned to the national standards. However, the achievement of qualifications at lower levels did count towards the 80 per cent of an institution's provision, which must be aimed at securing some national qualifications for learners. This was because learners at Entry Levels 1 and 2 were regarded as having embarked on an accredited progression route leading towards the higher-level accreditation at Entry Level 3 to Level 2, which then counted towards the national target. The remaining 20 per cent of an institution's provision could include non-accredited courses, for example short summer courses or courses for learners not yet ready to work towards Entry Level 1.

The interpretation of these rulings led at times to tensions between practitioners putting on ESOL courses to meet learners' needs and college managers anxious to meet overall government targets for the numbers of students achieving qualifications.

Implications for ESOL learners and teachers

The new Skills for Life accreditation meant that, for the first time, ESOL learners had direct access to a marketable qualification with national currency, and this was a positive development. The fact that learners could be assessed separately in oral skills, as well as in reading and writing, was an advantage for those with different levels of ability in the different skills (often referred to as learners with 'spiky profiles').

The level descriptors (standards) for ESOL were the same as for adult literacy, but for ESOL learners each descriptor was accompanied by a much more detailed breakdown of the elements necessary to achieve the level successfully. So, for example, at Entry Level 1 in speaking and listening, a student was able to 'make simple statements of fact', and the breakdown covered the basic grammar necessary for this. At Level 2 the learner could 'express clearly statements of fact, explanations, instructions, accounts, descriptions using appropriate style and vocabulary', and the breakdown listed the complex range of grammatical forms, as well as an understanding of register, essential for this. This helped ESOL teachers to assess the achievement of their students.

However, there was a significant difference between the learning journeys taken by adult literacy students and those taken by ESOL learners to reach the different levels and meet the government's national targets – the difference between operating in one's mother tongue and operating in a foreign language. Level 2 was difficult for even advanced ESOL learners, while some absolute beginners found working towards even Entry Level 1 was very challenging.

The Qualifications and Curriculum Authority estimated that on average it took an ESOL student 300 hours of tuition to progress from one level to another. The jump from Level 1 to Level 2 in particular was considerable, especially if the full qualification at Level 2 was taken, involving listening/speaking and writing, in addition to the on-line reading test. (Another estimate of the time taken to acquire English (Schellekens, 2001, p. ix) was based on the Australian experience, which suggested that it took a full-time FE student four years to progress from 'no level to the level of competence required for further study or a job'.)

For ESOL students, it was also useful to compare the time taken for them to acquire English with estimates for learners in general seeking to acquire a foreign language. Using this comparison, the jump from Entry Level 1 to Level 2 was considerable – equivalent in EFL terms to progressing from beginners to the Cambridge Certificate in Advanced English (assessed as being at NQF level 2 using the Common European Framework, CEF[3]). The Cambridge ESOL website stated that this required approximately 700–800 guided learning hours. It did not add that this could be over a considerable period of time, that the learners started with a good level of education, and that in any case relatively few even able learners reached that level.

Comparisons between various language qualifications became possible only because of recent attempts to map all language qualifications, first against in-country internal assessments and then alongside those in other European countries, using the Common European Framework (CEF). The Skills for Life standards in England and Wales were mapped against the National Qualifications Framework (NQF), against the National Curriculum levels for English in schools, against the Key Skills Communication Specifications, against the National Language Standards for foreign language learning and against the CEF (DfES, 2003a).

These exercises were useful to governments and examining bodies aspiring to establish some common standards, but they also highlighted some obvious anomalies to ESOL practitioners, especially that, in the case of native speakers and foreign language learners, like was not being compared with like. Mapping could also remind them of the sometimes contradictory global and national contexts in which second language learning took place and was evaluated. It remained to be seen whether, and how, such mapping might be used in the developing debates about the kind of English language tuition and accreditation that it was believed workers from the new Accession states of the EU needed and asked for: whether these should be aligned to Skills for Life standards, and so in line with language used by native speakers, or in line with the needs of students of English as a foreign language.

So, although it was valuable to ESOL students that they were being assessed against the same standards as native speakers, the challenge involved in reaching those standards was considerable. It was hardly surprising, therefore, that ESOL learners on the whole achieved the government targets at the lower levels and that, since achievement in individual elements did not count as full achievements, only 30 per cent were meeting those targets.[4]

It is perhaps ironical, therefore, that, even with access to national qualifications, ESOL learners were again at a disadvantage in a system designed primarily for native speakers. The reason this time was not the curriculum, or the materials or the teaching methodologies. It was the fact that the timetable and targets set by central government had not been designed with ESOL learners in mind.

Such mapping and comparisons relating to foreign language learning were largely irrelevant for adult literacy practitioners. But even for adult literacy students who were native speakers of English – as distinct from school-leavers trying to improve their GCSE grade – the progress from one level to another was difficult and involved, in the estimation of NRDC, 150–200 guided learning hours.

Examinations for students

There was a brief interim period during which some EFL qualifications[5] were used as 'proxy' qualifications to assess achievement against the Skills for Life framework. By the summer of 2004, new ESOL Skills for Life qualifications were available, accredited through the Qualifications and Curriculum Authority (QCA). From January 2005 these new qualifications were the only ones fundable under the Skills for Life Framework.

This caused problems for Skills for Life learners who were at a more advanced level and were aiming to enter higher education or seeking to practise as doctors. For them, the IELTS (International English Language Testing Service) examination was an appropriate examination because it was recognised by universities and professional bodies as an entrance qualification. However, IELTS was designed as an international EFL qualification, and this raised funding problems. The DfES eventually granted interim approval (January–December 2006) for both the IELTS and Level 3 qualifications (from UCLES, Trinity and the City and Guilds of London Institute) to be funded by the LSC, but not as basic skills qualifications. At the time of writing, the challenge remained of enabling students resident in the UK to demonstrate their achievement of higher levels of language skills, in order to progress into higher education and training.

Meanwhile the QCA was working to accredit EFL qualifications as ESOL International qualifications. These would probably not receive any public funding at all, apart from IELTS. At the same time, there were also ESOL for Work qualifications under development for September 2007. These were likely to be targeted in particular at the needs of migrant workers and their employers.

The debates over appropriate qualifications highlighted yet again the problems that could arise when the heterogeneous community of ESOL learners was divided into groups by accreditation and funding, rather than by their learning and training needs and educational aspirations.

Curriculum and materials

There was a general welcome for the ESOL curriculum and materials developed under the Skills for Life framework. Some practitioners found the minutiae of the level descriptors in the curriculum tedious to follow and use; and, even with the breakdown of each standard into constituent elements, there was some anxiety over the assessment of levels. However, the guidance materials and exemplars produced to help with these were useful. Practitioners also had to adjust to the fact that the curriculum was a *framework* against which to assess learners' achievements, not a scheme of work. A scheme of work has to be created to meet the specific needs of each particular group of learners.

Practitioners on the whole welcomed the teaching materials, which were attractively produced and used different media. The fact that these were centrally financed and published, and were readily available throughout England, and to some extent in Wales, represented a marked improvement on the past, when materials – many locally produced – were advertised and circulated through the NATECLA Catalogues and travelling exhibition (above, Chapters 4 and 5).

Teacher training

The NATECLA Teacher Training Working Party, LLU+ and other ESOL practitioners worked particularly hard to develop an ESOL teaching qualification which ensured that teachers had the necessary knowledge and understanding to operate effectively. The ESOL 2002 *Subject Specifications* (DfES 2002) at Levels 3 and 4 of the National Qualifications Framework were generally felt to be appropriate and stringent. They required the trainees – as relevant to their particular level – to have a sound theoretical knowledge, including of grammar and linguistic features such as phonology; to understand the personal, social and historical factors affecting language learning; and to have some understanding of the appropriate pedagogy. So the concerns of ESOL teacher trainers in the 1980s and 1990s to establish an appropriate qualification were generally met. However, trainers believed that trainees still required a stronger grounding in a specific ESOL pedagogy. This would be achieved with the revised standards for Initial Teacher Training and the updated Subject Specifications, due to be implemented in September 2007.

Research, development and publications, 2000–2006

In addition to the development of a considerable amount of material for the Skills for Life initiative, and for ESOL learners applying for citizenship (see p. 246), the period 2000–2006 saw increased activity in ESOL publications in general, including research reports, guidelines for good practice and support for teacher training.

The LLU+ developed online modules to support the delivery of ESOL teacher training and build on its existing programmes of support for ESOL teachers dealing with dyslexic learners. They then produced a training course on teaching basic literacy to ESOL learners (Spiegel and Sunderland, 2006) and banks of materials, including videos and a handbook.[6] A particularly important contribution of LLU+ was its key role in developing an ESOL version of 'Access for All', to support practitioners working with ESOL learners with learning difficulties and disabilities.

In addition to its substantial and important report on ESOL, *More than a Language...?* (NIACE, 2006a) (see p. 253), NIACE published a useful handbook for the inexperienced teacher (Windsor and Healey, 2006), a work on e-learning and ESOL (Moss and Southwood, 2006) and a good practice guide for developing ESOL in the community (Grief *et al.*, 2002).

The NRDC focused considerable attention and resources on identifying good classroom practice in literacy, numeracy, ESOL and ICT and how to achieve it. This involved classroom observation, reviews of research and investigations of teacher training, and included a focus on the experience and responses of the learners.

Of particular interest to practitioners were the effective practice studies, involving evaluative visits by trained researchers looking at number of classes (40 in the case of ESOL). There were three observations of each class, using a detailed observation schedule, plus in-depth interviews with students and teachers. The ESOL report (Baynham, Roberts *et al.*, 2007) reinforced the importance of good teacher training and found much practice that was good. However, it emphasised the need for teachers and learners to recognise and accept that 'talk is work' in the ESOL classroom, and it found that teachers did not draw sufficiently on students' own experiences and contributions. The report recognised the difficulties of supporting off-site classes effectively and the challenge faced by teachers in trying to help trauma-tised refugees. It also advocated more differentiation in the types of ESOL classes on offer, rather than relying on ESOL teachers to deal with the often extremely heterogeneous groups of learners in their classes. The enormous demand for ESOL was recorded, and the 'hyper-diversity' of ESOL learners described. The findings that more recent arrivals made greater progress than those who had been in the UK for some years were in line with the findings of other studies.

Learners' attitudes, responses and motivations
The other large project was the collection by the NRDC of student case studies covering literacy, numeracy and ESOL. The report on ESOL learners[7] (Roberts, Baynham *et al.*, 2004) gave an account of student responses to different teaching and learning strategies, the barriers to learning they found and their main motivations for coming to class.

The studies confirmed again what experienced ESOL practitioners knew about their learners. The main reasons for learning English were to gain access to education and work and to acquire an understanding of the UK society and systems. The learners were diverse. Refugees and asylum-seekers needed support negotiating bureaucratic structures at a time when they were also often coping with extreme personal distress. The case studies of asylum-seekers dispersed to Blackburn (Roberts, Baynham *et al.*, 2004, pp. 20–50) reinforced other pressing motives for learning English. When your main social contacts are your fellow multi-lingual students, English becomes an essential lingua franca. When you do not have access to a settled community whose language you share, and on which you can draw for information and support, English once again becomes an essential tool for survival, as it did for earlier refugees and the first waves of immigrants.

There was an ESOL focus also in other NRDC studies, and David Mallows drew all these together in his *Insights: What Research Can Tell us about ESOL: Review of NRDC Studies on English for Speakers of Other* Languages (Mallows, 2007, forthcoming). A number of these works appeared after the NRDC's publication in 2003 of *Adult ESOL Pedagogy: A Review of Research* (Barton and Pitt, 2003) This found that the literature specifically relating to the pedagogy of ESOL 'has been fairly small scale or not directly concerned with pedagogy', and as a result the critical bibliography included research carried out in the USA, Canada, Australia and Europe (p. 7). In an article in *Language Issues*, Mike Baynham said he believed that the reason there was so little UK-based research on a specific ESOL pedagogy was that ESOL in the UK had relied on the 'strong research base to English Language Teaching and Applied Linguistics worldwide' (*LI*, vol. 18.1, p. 10). This history has demonstrated such a reliance, but it has also shown that the particular challenges faced by ESOL teachers had always demanded new under-standings and the exploration of new approaches and methodologies, but that there that there had never been the funding to support this before the Skills for Life initiative.

Quality of ESOL provision

Despite the best endeavours of the NRDC, NIACE, LLU+ and others, the quality of ESOL provision continued to cause concern.

In April 2001 the Adult Learning Inspectorate (ALI) and Ofsted produced a Common Inspection Framework. This allowed the two inspectorates to use the same set of criteria to report on the quality of education across all post-16 sectors. This framework was used in 2003 and 2005 to report on literacy, numeracy and ESOL in post-16 provision.

In September 2003 Ofsted published *Literacy, Numeracy and English for Speakers of Other Languages: A Survey of Current Practice in the Post-16 and Adult Provision*. This was a wide-ranging report, drawing on 650 full inspections and the examination of the delivery plans of the 47 local Learning and Skills Councils. Inspections covered colleges, prisons, Jobcentre Plus and work-based learning providers, along with provision made through adult and community education. The report noted some positive developments in the government's Skills for Life strategy, but that there were many causes for very considerable concern. The opening sentence of the Executive Summary was unambiguous:

> *The Skills for Life initiative has been highly successful in increasing the number of literacy, numeracy and ESOL learners...but there needs to be a sharper focus on the quality of the education and training that is available.* (Ofsted, 2003, p. 3)

The survey found that provision in literacy, numeracy and ESOL was weaker than in other areas of post-16 and adult education. Above all there was a shortage of qualified staff, and this had been exacerbated by the rapid increase in the numbers of learners, and in the delay in introducing the new teaching qualifications.

The detailed list of weaknesses included poor-quality initial assessment procedures and individual learning plans (ILPs) and a continuing shortage of good learning materials. Support for students who were studying on other courses was often weak, with vocational tutors ill-prepared to provide the necessary language, literacy and numeracy support which many students needed. 'Most providers do not effectively promote equality of opportunity to learners' (Ofsted, 2003, p. 7). Accommodation in the main college sites was good, but there were instances where both resources and accommodation for ESOL was poorer than for literacy and numeracy.

The finding on ESOL noted some good teaching in discrete provision, though this was matched by poor teaching elsewhere. Language support was still often poorly planned and delivered. One of the main findings pointed to the 'high levels of absenteeism and persistent lateness of many ESOL learners' (Ofsted, 2003, p. 5). However, the body of the report acknowledged the particular problems faced by asylum-seekers in keeping appointments with lawyers and attending court hearings, and also the fact that they could be sent to other parts of the country (p. 12). On the other hand, the report noted that some colleges dealt with these difficulties better than others. Again, the major weakness was the severe shortage of trained ESOL teachers, especially in London.

This ALI/Ofsted report was reviewed for ESOL practitioners by Pam Frame (herself an ALI inspector) in *Language Issues* (vol. 16.1, 2004, pp. 30–2). She welcomed the broad conspectus offered in the report and was pleased that good practice had been identified, but she acknowledged that there was still much to do. She was, however, able to point to the many initiatives that had been put in place since the inspections were carried out: developments on assessment, on ILPs, on embedding support and on new teacher training programmes. These developments had been carried out by dedicated and competent professionals.

It was all the more disappointing, therefore, that the next report, *Skills for Life in Colleges: One Year On* (Ofsted, 2005) found that, although there were some notable improvements, many weaknesses persisted. The quality of the new teacher training was praised. Resources had improved. Personal support for students was generally good. But the greatest weakness was still that too many staff members were unqualified to provide the appropriate support; this was often the case with vocational tutors, because their own literacy and numeracy skills were inadequate:

> The lack of skilled teachers is at the heart of the continuing difficulties with effective implementation of the Skills for Life Strategy. This is exacerbated by the short-term and uncertain funding arrangements to support the necessary teacher training. (Ofsted, 2005, pp. 1–2)

This bleak picture was redeemed by the fact that, where teachers *had* been trained, the quality was better. However, as the report noted, insufficient training was available. What the report did not add was that managers releasing staff to undertake training had difficulty finding qualified teachers to cover their lessons.

The report's findings on ESOL in particular were worrying to practitioners. The quality of teaching had deteriorated since the 2003 survey, with nearly one-third of ESOL provision in general education colleges being unsatisfactory:

> *There is often an over-emphasis on the completion of written tasks: students copy text without understanding the language content. There are too few opportunities for them to develop their listening and speaking skills. Teachers fail to take enough account of students' prior learning and do not meet their individual needs.* (Ofsted, 2005, p. 8)

But again, there was evidence that training could remedy such deficiencies.

ESOL provision across the UK

At this point it is important to remember that ESOL learners were to be found throughout the United Kingdom, and increasingly so as a result of the Home Office policy of dispersal for asylum-seekers and the local recruitment of migrant workers. However, the educational provision for them was different in England, Wales, Scotland and Northern Ireland, and differences increased after devolution. Any attempt to identify and describe these differences must be accompanied by a caution that, at the time of writing, the situation had become fluid and ever-changing. The situation in the first years of the new millennium, however, was easier to describe. Understanding these national differences could be difficult for learners if they moved around the UK, and this could affect their access to provision.

Scotland

As has already been seen, Scotland too had a long history of ESOL provision, and the problems of under-funding have already been noted (see p. 167). There had been no programmes equivalent to those in England and Wales funded by the Further Education Funding Council or the Skills for Life initiative.

From October 2001, a major decision was taken in Scotland which broke with practice in the other three countries of the UK. That was to waive the three-year residence rule for refugees, asylum-seekers and other ESOL students, but not for 'students whose main purpose for being in the EU was to receive education' (Scottish Further Education Funding Council, 2001, para 5). Fees were charged for ESOL courses, but they were automatically waived for asylum-seekers (para 7). Other ESOL students – excluding those identified as being in the EU to receive education – had to show evidence of poverty (para 8). ESOL learners also had access to ESOL literacy classes funded by the Adult Literacy and Numeracy Programme, but only if they were illiterate in their mother tongue.[8]

The Scottish Executive, through the Enterprise, Transport and Lifelong Learning Department, next conducted a consultation exercise to develop a revised Adult ESOL Strategy for Scotland (Scottish Executive, 2006). The consultation took a 'holistic, inclusive, flexible and learner-centred approach' (p. 4), which was welcomed. A wide range of organisations, including NATECLA Scotland, was consulted. Meanwhile a mapping exercise and scoping study was carried out on behalf of the Scottish Executive (Rice *et al.*, 2005). This provided a profile of ESOL learners, identified the need (there were waiting lists) and described the funding mechanisms. This exercise found that ESOL was funded mainly through Adult Literacy and Numeracy (ALN) partnerships, the Scottish Further Education Funding Council and international student fees. The study recorded:

> *There is some concern amongst ESOL practitioners that ALN partnership funding cannot always provide appropriate tuition for ESOL students, with their wider range of educational qualifications and communicative needs, compared to native speaker literacy students.* (Rice et al., 2005, p. 2)

In March 2007 the Scottish Executive published the final report (see p. 256).

Wales

In Wales there had been funded tuition for ESOL learners going back to the 1960s. It was provided by the adult education service, through community relations councils and through charitable organisations, in a combination similar to that found in England. As in England, there was access to Section 11 funding for some of the provision in areas of New

Commonwealth settlement. There was also the same problem of too little provision and student waiting lists.

A difference between Wales and other parts of the UK was that it was already officially a bilingual country, with two national languages. Dispersed linguistic minority communities were to be found across the principality, including in predominantly Welsh-speaking areas. In these areas ESOL learners faced a further linguistic challenge. A growing number of ESOL teachers were also Welsh-speakers, accustomed to operating in more than one language. Indeed, some could have learned Welsh as a second language themselves as adults, after moving into a Welsh-speaking area. These teachers were able to incorporate some Welsh as a second language into their ESOL classes, where appropriate.

In 2001 the Welsh Assembly awarded the Basic Skills Agency the responsibility for managing the *National Basic Skills Strategy for Wales* (Wales National Assembly, 2001). This aimed to raise achievement in numeracy, reading, writing, speaking and understanding in both English and Welsh, and it included ESOL. Wales had the same basic core curricula (plus Welsh literacy and numeracy for people whose main language was Welsh) and used the same range of Skills for Life qualifications as England. Although targets appeared to have less of a profile than in England, there was a national target in the strategy – by 2010, 80 per cent of working-age adults would have at least Level 1 in literacy skills and 55 per cent would have at least Level 1 in numeracy skills. There was access in Wales to some of the Skills for Life materials produced in England.

The BSA convened an 'ESOL/EAL' advisory group in 2002/03 to support the development of the ESOL/EAL strand of the National Strategy. During the first phase the focus was on supporting ESOL programmes to achieve the Post-16 Quality Mark; trialling and developing Levels 2 and 3 qualifications for adult learning support staff and for staff delivering ESOL; developing family language programmes; working with asylum-seekers; and producing teaching and learning resources. Some of these developments were showcased at the first national conference on ESOL with Citizenship as the theme in March 2005.

Northern Ireland

Historically, Northern Ireland had had fewer resident adults who were learning English than the rest of the UK. However, there was a tradition of providing some English language tuition for overseas students. From the late 1990s the client group of ESOL learners changed, with the arrival of refugees, asylum-seekers and migrant workers. An adult literacy and numeracy programme was funded through the Department of Employment and Learning, but this did not cover ESOL. Most of the ESOL classes were run in further and higher education colleges, such as at the Belfast Institute, but some were run by community organisations. Fees were payable, but there was some support from charities.

To access tuition, students had to have been resident for three years and/or been granted indefinite leave to remain. However, asylum-seekers could join classes immediately upon arrival. Although the fees set were at the discretion of the providers, asylum-seekers were generally charged a concessionary fee which was usually half the full fee. The balance was picked up by the Northern Ireland Council for Ethnic Minorities, which cared for asylum-seekers.

Growing concerns about racism, social cohesion and citizenship

The new learners

The opening years of the new century saw a further and considerable increase in the numbers of adults wanting ESOL tuition. Waiting lists continued to grow across the UK and there were still too few qualified teachers. In the first four years the demand was from immigrants and refugees already here. After the enlargement of the European Union in 2004 to admit the citizens of ten more countries, the numbers grew again, and ESOL practitioners found that they were catering for Polish bus drivers in addition to newly-arrived brides from Bangladesh. As numbers increased, so did the pressure on provision, and racist incidents continued to occur.

Anti-racist legislation

In response to a number of high-profile racist attacks, including the murder of the young black man Stephen Lawrence, the government enacted further legislation. The 2000 Race Relations (Amendment) Act made it unlawful to discriminate against anyone on the grounds of race, colour, nationality (including citizenship) or ethnic or national origin. It imposed a duty on many public authorities to promote racial equality. Incitement to racial hatred and racist incidents – which could range from harassment and abuse to actual physical violence – were already criminal offences under the Crime and Disorder Act of 1998. In 2006 the Racial and Religious Hatred Act was passed. However, despite these pieces of legislation, incidents of racism still occurred, and the demonisation of asylum-seekers and refugees continued.

Social cohesion

The period 1999–2003 also saw renewed government concern over civil unrest and the fragmentation and alienation of communities. An increasing focus on social cohesion and responsible behaviour, and the belief that these might be fostered through citizenship education in schools, led to government-sponsored research at the Department for Education and Skills, under Sir Bernard Crick. The results of the research, and recommendations to government, had been published by the Qualifications and Curriculum Authority (QCA) as *Education for Citizenship and the Teaching of Democracy in Schools* (DfEE, 1998). This outlined three basic themes for education for citizenship: social and moral responsibility, community involvement, and political literacy. In its review of the National Curriculum in 1999, the government announced that citizenship education would be mandatory in the curriculum for schools from 2002. So there was already a national policy context for discussing citizenship *before* the 2002 Nationality, Immigration and Asylum Act made it a requirement for those applying for citizenship to demonstrate knowledge of life in the United Kingdom (see p. 246).

Incandescent youth – again

In 2001, before the changes in the National Curriculum could be implemented, riots occurred in Oldham, Bradford and Burnley. These

241

demonstrated the alienation and frustration of some second- and third-generation members of ethnic minorities and reinforced the government's anxiety about social cohesion.

The Cantle Report

In response to the unrest in the northern towns, the government set up a committee of inquiry under Ted Cantle. The report it produced, the 'Cantle Report' (Home Office, 2001), gave a very different view of communities who spoke English as a second or other language from that given in the Scarman, Swann and Eggleston Reports in the 1980s (above). The focus in the Cantle Report was on the fracturing of communities and the confrontations between them. Reference was made to disadvantages in employment among certain minority ethnic groups, and to the fact that certain groups did not stay on in education after the age of 16, but there was none of the hard empirical evidence of disadvantage given in the Eggleston Report – though clear evidence was available.[9]

In the Cantle Report the primacy of English was unquestioned, and 'a universal acceptance of the English language' was called for (Home Office, 2001, p. 19). Describing the new values to be developed, the report adopted an admonitory tone and the sentence structure became opaque – perhaps betraying an unease on the part of the committee? Those who were identified as needing to learn English included applicants for citizenship and, by implication, parents. For the latter, the main reasons seemed to be to bridge the intergenerational gap and to prevent their children needing expensive EAL provision in school. The support for the use of the mother tongue was at best token:

> *we would expect the new values to contain statements about the expectation that the use of the English language, which is already a pre-condition of citizenship (or a commitment to become fluent within a period of time), will become more rigorously pursued, with appropriate support. This will ensure that subsequent generations do not bear the burden of remedial programmes, and, more importantly, that the full participation of all individuals in society can be achieved much more easily. This is not to diminish the value and role of second and minority languages, which reinforce sub cultural communities.*
> (Home Office, 2001, p. 19)

The levels of English needed to claim citizenship, and how these were to be taught and tested, are dealt with below.

A long piece by Arun Kundnani on the Cantle Report appeared on the Institute for Race Relations website of 1 April 2002. Entitled 'The Death of Multiculturalism', it pointed out the racism inherent in blaming the victims for their disadvantages and claimed that it was irrelevant to raise the question of ability in English, since the young people who rioted were fluent speakers of the language.

Kundnani's title itself indicated how the general consensus on multiculturalism established in the1980s was being challenged. A debate was now launched which would be further ignited after the bombings of 7 July 2005, when Trevor Phillips, chair of the Commission for Racial Equality, courted further controversy with his article in the *Sunday Times* of 18 September 2005, in which he saw the country 'sleepwalking to segregation.'

Integration with diversity

The Home Secretary, David Blunkett, had himself entered the debate in 2002 with his 'Integration with Diversity in Modern Britain: Globalisation and the Renewal of Democracy and Civil Society' (Blunkett, 2002), published in *Reclaiming Britishness* (Griffiths and Leonard, 2002) by the Foreign Policy Centre and also printed in *The Observer* of 15 September 2002. The article was a long piece, dealing with global politics and the 11 September attack on the World Trade Center, as well as crime and disorder at home. It was in the section entitled 'Giving Meaning to Citizenship' that he tackled both multiculturalism and the place of the English language, and raised the controversial issue of which language should be spoken in the home:

> *An active concept of citizenship can articulate shared ground between diverse communities. It offers a shared identity based on membership to [sic] a political community, rather than forced assimilation into a monoculture, or an unbridled multiculturalism which privileges difference over community cohesion. It is what the White Paper Secure Borders, Safe Haven called 'integration with diversity'.* (Blunkett, 2002, p. 76)

This aroused some considerable discussion, and commentators and observers were left to guess what else Blunkett thought should be reined in, besides the forced marriages and female genital mutilation that he cited. The passage on language led to some heated opposition:

243

Citizenship should be about shared participation, from the neighbourhood to national elections. That is why we must strive to connect people from different backgrounds, tackle segregation, and overcome mutual hostility and ignorance. Of course, one factor in this is the ability of new migrants to speak English – otherwise they cannot get good jobs, or share in wider social debate. But for those long settled in the UK, it is about social class issues of education, housing, jobs and regeneration and tackling racism.

I have never said, or implied, that lack of fluency in English was in any way directly responsible for the disturbances in Bradford, Burnley and Oldham in the summer of 2001. However, speaking English enables parents to converse with their children in English, as well as in their historic mother tongue, at home and to participate in wider modern culture. It helps overcome the schizophrenia which bedevils generational relationships. In as many as 30% of British Asian households, according to the recent citizenship survey, English is not spoken at home. But let us be clear that lack of English fluency did not cause the riots. (Blunkett, 2002, pp. 76–7)

David Blunkett's suggestion that it was the business of governments to decide which language should be spoken in the home created a furore.

With the benefit of five years' hindsight, and with the 7 July 2005 London bombings having been carried out by British nationals fluent in English, it is interesting to consider David Blunkett's statement again, and examine the assumptions behind them. First, research for this history revealed very few instances of anyone actually denying the usefulness of learning the language of the country of settlement. The work of the Linguistic Minorities Project in the 1980s and of Khanna *et al.* (1998) in the 1990s confirm this, especially in terms of giving settlers access to training and work. There was also little resistance to the requirement to have mastered some levels of English in order to apply for citizenship. Second, both David Blunkett himself and other writers in *Reclaiming Britishness* pointed to economic factors and difficulties in employment and housing as important triggers for dissatisfaction and unrest, and stated that these usually now had little to do directly with language.

What was new in Blunkett's statement was the drawing of a direct relationship between social responsibility and not speaking English. This had never before been voiced in this way. It had barely been applied to the Yiddish speakers, overcrowded and impoverished in London's East End, whose children had still achieved well in monolingual schools. *Pace* the suspicion that they were spies, which some German-speakers faced in the First World War and in the 1930s and early 1940s, it had never been applied to subsequent groups of refugees and immigrants: not to the Poles in the 1950s, the Italians in the brickfields of Bedfordshire, the Vietnamese boat people, the Ugandan Asians fleeing from Idi Amin, the Greek Cypriots and many more.

Furthermore, the evidence quoted in this history has shown how each succeeding group had spoken the mother tongue at home and that sometimes children had mocked their parent's English: 'my mother spoke English in twenty-six different languages' (see p. 10). However, research has shown that the use of the mother tongue can be a stabilising force and can strengthen family bonds, and that its loss by the second and third generations is often mourned.

David Blunkett's injunction to mothers to learn English echoed that in the 1963 Ministry of Education Pamphlet (see p. 98). In the 1960s the Ministry of Education was dealing with very newly-established communities and was concerned that children would start school at a disadvantage. Subsequent LEA league tables (especially in the ILEA and London boroughs) showed that children from some groups with homes where English was a second or other language were among the highest achievers nationally. However, experienced ESOL practitioners also knew that at the beginning of the twenty-first century some of these communities in northern towns like Bradford (and others such as the Bangladeshi community in the East End of London) differed from other groups of settlers in that they were regularly renewed by fresh arrivals of early-stage learners of English, as spouses and other family members came quite legally to the UK. So in some ways drawing analogies with the 1960s might not be so inapt.

There is another possible inference to be drawn from the Home Secretary's focus on women. As this history has shown, Asian women have long been identified as having the least knowledge of English and as being significantly under-represented in further education and training; and such perceptions of Bangladeshi and Pakistani women continued in departments across the government after 2000 (see below). Could it be that these women were now being blamed for the disaffection of their English-speaking sons and grandsons? There may be a subtext here combining gender, class, culture and religion. These issues are not easy to grapple with, let alone explain, and oversimplifications are dangerous. Class and economic disadvantage could lead to alienation and disaffection, as they did in the 1980s. Continuing racism, global politics and ethnic and religious identity played an increasingly important role, too.

What was true was that by 2002 the teaching and learning of English had become highly politicised, closely associated with cultural identity, social responsibility, citizenship and, later, even with eligibility for settlement.[10]

Citizenship

In February 2002 David Blunkett published his White Paper *Secure Borders, Safe Havens: Integration with Diversity in Modern Britain* (Home Office, 2002), noting the government's intention to underline the importance of British citizenship by 'preparing people for citizenship by promoting language training and education for citizenship' (p. 31). This White Paper paved the way for the 2002 Nationality, Immigration and Asylum Act, which required 'those seeking naturalisation as British citizens to demonstrate that they have a sufficient understanding of English (or Welsh, or Scottish Gaelic) and a sufficient knowledge of life in the UK.'

Sir Bernard Crick was again called upon to advise on the implementation of this policy and was appointed chair of the 'Life in the United Kingdom' Independent Advisory Group. This commissioned research, which resulted in the Home Office report *The New and the Old: The Report of the 'Life in United Kingdom' Advisory Group* (Home Office, 2003). The report recommended that an adult citizenship curriculum, rather than dealing with the broad social and political themes recommended for schools, should focus on specific practical topics: British national institutions in a recent historical context, Britain as a multicultural society, knowing the law, employment, sources of help and information, everyday needs. Sir Bernard was then appointed chair of the Advisory Board for Naturalisation and Integration (ABNI), which had a wide membership including ESOL experts.[11]

ESOL teachers in general, and NATECLA in particular, welcomed some of these developments, but were exercised about the direction that some others were taking. These were summed up by Pauline Moon in *Language Issues* (vol. 16.1, pp. 25–9), in which she covered the Cantle Report, David Blunkett's *Secure Borders, Safe Haven*, the 2002 Immigration and Asylum Act, *The New and the Old* (Home Office,

2003), a number of David Blunkett's other statements, and responses by the CRE and the National Association of Teachers in Further and Higher Education (NATFHE).

Moon welcomed the recognition in *The New and the Old* that competence in language was essential for access to work and education and noted that this had already been recognised in the Home Office report by Griffiths (2003; see p. 197, earlier). However, speaking on behalf of herself and the ESOL students she had discussed this with, Moon rejected any idea that governments should determine which language was spoken in the home. She also found it was both insulting and unrealistic to suggest that 'the schizophrenia that bedevils inter-generational relationships' applied only in the families of ESOL speakers.

In criticising the government's hasty response to the civil unrest in 2001, Moon made the point that, as in 1981, the cause of unrest was not nationality or race, but social exclusion, unemployment, discrimination and poverty.

Moon was generally positive about the new citizenship arrange-ments that had been announced and about the fact that applicants for citizenship would not have to take an English test. Those with sufficient English (Entry Level 3 and above) would take the online test for citizen-ship, which was written in English. She welcomed the fact that applicants with English below Entry Level 3 would be able to combine learning about the UK with their ESOL studies. They would have to demonstrate that they had attended classes and had made progress from one Skills for Life level to the next, and that the classes had included citizenship in the curriculum. She noted that there had been some reservations about making any form of adult education compulsory, even that requiring applicants for citizenship to attend English classes, but that there was no general opposition to the language requirement.

Moon welcomed the new curriculum, believing it would broaden and deepen ESOL learning. She noted, however, that it would be impossible to teach about society in the UK by concentrating only on its strengths and advantages, and ignoring issues with which the learners were familiar, such as unemployment and racism. She believed that, although a Handbook on Life in the United Kingdom was to be produced, ESOL teachers would need further materials and some training. There was, however, a shortage of ESOL teachers, and this would be bound to have an effect on the programmes. Finally, Moon noted that learning English was no guarantee of good citizenship, and that, while ESOL might not impact on citizenship, citizenship would certainly impact on ESOL.

The first citizenship materials for ESOL learners were developed by NIACE and LLU+ in conjunction with the DfES and the Home Office, funded by the Home Office but managed by the Skills for Life Strategy Unit. They were published in September 2005 (NIACE and LLU+, 2005) after an extensive national trial and consultation process. The various sections built on and developed the broad recommendations in the Crick Report (Home Office, 2003). Training was carried out throughout the UK, and there was evidence that the general response from students and teachers was very positive.[12] Versions for the other nations of the UK were developed later (see p. 256).

Postscript

An original title of this history suggested that the account should end with 2005. However, some events occurred after that date which were so important for their effect on ESOL across the UK that they cannot be ignored. They were influenced by three factors.

The first was the mounting evidence of the under-achievement of adults in some of the settled minority ethnic communities, and particularly the disadvantage faced by those not seen to be competent in the English language. The second factor was the government's continuing concern, reinforced by the Leitch Report (see p. 253), to increase the overall level of skills in the UK. The third factor was the rising demand for ESOL tuition, influenced to some extent by the arrival after 2004 of migrant workers from the new EU Accession countries. This meant that, despite the availability of considerable funding in England and Wales under the Skills for Life initiative, there were still too many potential learners, and there was insufficient provision to meet that demand, particularly in London and the South-East.

However, responsibility for these three areas of concern fell to different departments of government: to the Department for Work and Pensions, the Cabinet Office, the Treasury, the departments of education in the four countries, as well as the Welsh Assembly and the Scottish Parliament. The Home Office had responsibility for citizenship, settlement, refuge and dispersal across the whole of the UK.

A brief evaluation of some of the major policy documents which were issued by these various departments of government illustrates some of the often mutually incompatible positions being held. It also shows how, in the case of ESOL, some of the evidence could be shaky and the understanding of what was involved very limited.

Evidence of the need for ESOL provision and how it should be provided

Between 2000 and 2006 there was growing and compelling evidence of the disadvantages faced by ESOL speakers, the increasing need for ESOL tuition and the inadequacy of the current provision. This evidence came from a number of sources and from different departments of government. Some related to the whole of the UK, but many were confined to the situation in England.

From the Department for Education and Skills (England) came Schellekens's well-grounded *English Language as a Barrier to Employment and Training: A Research Report* (Schellekens, 2001) and the more limited *Skills for Life Survey: A National Needs and Impact Survey of Literacy, Numeracy and ICT Skills* (DfES, 2003b).

Ethnic Minorities and the Labour Market

In 2003 the Cabinet Office published *Ethnic Minorities and the Labour Market* (Cabinet Office Strategy Unit, 2003). This dealt with settled communities – Indian, Pakistani, Bangladeshi and Chinese – and did not include other groups or migrant workers and refugees. It was a quite reflective exercise. It looked back at government policy over the previous 40 years to the departments of education reports for England and Wales 1963, 1965 and 1971 (above, Chapter 3) and expressed the belief that there had been a policy shift, at least with regard to schoolchildren, away from 'viewing them as a "problem" to be dealt with, to the con-temporary multi-cultural view of diversity being an asset to the school environment' (p. 51) (although, as has been seen, this view of the value of a multi-cultural approach was being contested). The disadvantage of being an adult who was not fluent in English was incontrovertible and could actually be quantified: 'immigrants who are fluent in English have, on average, wages about 20 per cent higher than non-fluent individuals' (p. 29); and research evidence for this was cited (Shields and Wheatley-Price, 2002). The report noted in particular that 'three quarters of Bangladeshi women over the age of 25 do not speak fluent English'

(Cabinet Office Strategy Unit, 2003, p. 55). The evidence for this was taken from the influential Fourth National Survey of Ethnic Minorities (FNSEM), carried out in 1993–4 and first published in 1997 (Modood, Berthoud *et al.*, 1997).

The FNSEM survey's evidence for the language levels of respondents came from the judgements of the interviewers themselves. At the end of each interview, which might have been conducted entirely in the respondent's mother tongue, the interviewer was asked to say whether respondent '[s]peak[s] English fluently, fairly well, slightly or not al all'. The justification for this approach was that, '[s]ince the respondent was not asked to provide his or her own assessment of fluency, unlike many other surveys, there was no chance of self-reported measurement error' (Leslie and Lindley, 2001, p. 592). However, an examination of the instructions to interviewers and the end-of-project report (P. Smith, 1996; Berthoud, 1997) shows that they were not told how to carry out this assessment or given level descriptors for levels of English; the only guidance given was that, at the end of an interview conducted in the respondent's mother tongue, the interviewer should switch language and initiate a conversation in English. This tactic alone could have disconcerted the respondent and led to a mis-reporting of the actual level of his or her English. However, the survey's findings reiterated judgements on the language levels of women from the sub-continent which were similar to those that had prompted the CRC language schemes in the 1960s and the BBC *Parosi* project in the middle 1970s, and as was noted in the Kennedy Report in 1997.

From the time of their publication in 1997, these FNSEM findings on language levels were drawn on heavily in government policy documents, but the data was used in a very generalised and summative way. (However, one academic study did provide a more thoughtful analysis of the relationship between fluency in English and age, gender, exposure to the language and length of time in the country: that by Modood (1997, pp. 60–63.)

Ethnic Minority Employment Task Force
One outcome of the Cabinet Office's *Ethnic Minorities and the Labour Market* report was the establishment of the cross-departmental Ethnic Minority Employment Task Force. This was chaired by the Minister of State for Work and Pensions and had representatives from most government departments – including the DfES, the DTI and the Treasury – as

well as from the CBI, the TUC and the CRE. It is surprising, therefore, that, although the Ethnic Minority Employment Task Force had been given a clear cross-departmental role in relation to ethnic minorities, it was not formally consulted in 2007 for the Race Equality Impact Survey of the proposal to end automatic remission for ESOL learners in England (below), even though individual organisations represented on the Task Force were consulted.

In the autumn of 2004 the Ethnic Minority Employment Task Force published its *Year One Progress Report* (Department for Work and Pensions (DWP), 2004). In describing the levels of English it cited the Strategy Unit report which in turn drew on the FNSEM report:

> *Lack of fluency in English is a major barrier to employment and it is one that affects several ethnic minority groups. For example, the Strategy Unit report found that over three quarters of Bangladeshi women over the age of 25 do not speak fluent English. The Strategy Unit therefore recommended research to develop a better understanding of the demand for provision for training in English for Speakers of Other Languages.* (DWP, 2004, p. 27)

KPMG Review

Concern over the need for ESOL provision began to be matched by anxiety over its cost. In 2005 the *KPMG Review of English for Speakers of Other Language* (KPMG, 2005) was published. This had been undertaken for the DfES, the Skills for Life Strategy Unit and the Learning and Skills Council. It noted that London accounted for 50 per cent of the ESOL provision in England, that the demand was increasing, and that there was a need to manage and quantify this situation. It suggested the removal of automatic fee remission. The report itself demonstrated far less understanding of ESOL learners, and the curriculum and qualifications appropriate to their needs, than the London Strategy Plan did (below)

A Profile of Londoners by Language

In September 2006 *A Profile of Londoners by Language* was produced for the Greater London Authority (GLA 2006), focusing on the labour market and dealing with ESOL learners from all backgrounds. This demonstrated how many 'ESL' speakers lived and worked in the GLA area, and that they accounted for 20 per cent of the total population of working age. The *Profile* demonstrated again the disadvantage they faced in the labour market, especially if they were not fluent in English (pp. 19, 22 and *passim*).

London Skills for Life Strategy

Further evidence of the growth in the numbers of ESOL speakers in London – long-term residents, migrant workers, refugees – came with the research for the London Skills Commission's *London Skills for Life Strategy*, published in November 2006. This was a thorough review. It included a 'The Three Year Action Plan for ESOL in London', which reported that:

> *Conservative estimates indicate 600,000 people of working age with a range of ESOL needs, probably around two thirds of these are economically inactive or unemployed. In addition, there are 35,000 EU economic migrants, many from the Accession States.* (London Skills Commission, 2006, p. 13)

The ESOL Action Plan reported that London delivered half of England's ESOL at a cost of £180 million a year, but only around 125,000 people were currently accessing ESOL learning and only a third achieved full Skills for Life qualifications (p. 12). It accepted the diversity of ESOL learners and attempted to deal with this by grouping them by a mixture of status and intent – home-makers, the employed, the unemployed, 14–19-year-olds, parents. This was one way of tackling the diversity, but practitioners were concerned that it might mask the fact that real people could fit into several groups at once, and that in any case people's situations changed and they moved from one group to another.

The *Summary of Evidence and Recommendations for ESOL*, which was published by the London Skills Commission in November 2005, gave a more detailed picture of ESOL provision in London. In its summary of findings and recommendation (London Skills Commission, 2005, pp. 2–3) it acknowledged the role of language learning in personal development and social inclusion and cohesion, as well as its role for those seeking citizenship; but the emphasis was on employment. It alluded to the unwillingness of employers to contribute towards essential training. The need to provide basic provision for learners at Entry Levels was accepted, but difficulties in progression were also described. A depressing picture of an underpaid, under-qualified teaching force was painted. (The sterling efforts of teacher trainers since 2000 had clearly reached only a few new entrants to the profession.) The cost of London ESOL was contrasted with unmet demand. In considering where the money should best be spent, the universal provision of free tuition was challenged. There was also a hint that EU learners should pay for EFL courses, so resuscitating the canard that speakers of European languages needed, and would pay for, overseas qualifications.

Practitioners continued to be concerned about the segmentation of the ESOL community – better in oranges than in groups of adult learners. They also challenged the assumptions about migrant workers; these were in fact usually in very low-paid jobs, and in any case needed the same information and social and work-related language as immigrants. And the segmentation of learners led back to the old EFL/ESL divide which many thought had long outlived its usefulness.

Barriers to Employment for Pakistanis and Bangladeshis in Britain
In 2006 a Department for Work and Pensions report, *Barriers to Employment for Pakistanis and Bangladeshis in Britain* (DWP, 2006), was published. This had been carried out by the Institute for Employment Studies. Again, the disadvantage in the employment market faced by this group was identified especially for those with 'poor English'. This time the statistics quoted (again from the Fourth National Survey of Ethnic Minorities, now 13 years old) were that 'only four per cent of Bangladeshi and 28 per cent of Pakistani women aged 45–64 years spoke English fluently or well' (p. 2).

The Leitch Report
Then, also in 2006, the Treasury's prestigious – and by no means uncontroversial – Leitch Report, *Prosperity for All in the Global Economy*, appeared (HM Treasury, 2006). This covered the skills needed by the whole UK economy but omitted migrant workers and refugees. The Leitch Report noted the disadvantage in the labour market faced by those with difficulties with English (p. 55) (and also that graduates from minority ethnic communities did less well than their 'White' counterparts) (p. 55). Once more, the 75 per cent of Bangladeshi women over the age of 25 who 'do not speak fluent English' was quoted (p. 55), citing the DWP Ethnic Minority Employment Task Force (see p. 250), which in its turn went back again to the 1993–4 Fourth National Survey of Ethnic Minorities.

The NIACE report, 'More than a Language...?'
The most detailed and, from the point of view of ESOL practitioners, best informed, account came in October 2006, with the NIACE report *'More than a Language...?' NIACE Committee of Inquiry on English for Speakers of Other Languages: Final Report* (NIACE 2006a), dealing with the situation in England. The report based its finding on sound research and a well-organised programme of consultation. It accepted the 'hyper-diversity' of the ESOL community. It recognised that actual and potential ESOL learners were not only members of the workforce – or attempting to enter the labour market – but also citizens, members of family groups, members of their local community and individuals with personal aspirations. Once again, the point was made that the provision was insufficient – this time across the whole of England – and the teaching force inadequately trained.

A strength of the report was its call for a cross-departmental govern-ment approach to the needs of ESOL learners and that 'A ministerial lead on ESOL should be identified with a specific brief to address ESOL issues across the full range of government policies and to ensure imple-mentation across government of the Comprehensive Spending Review Study' (p. 11).

More than a Language made a number of further recommendations, which can be summed up as ensuring that learners should have the maximum entitlement to good-quality provision up to and including Level 1, and including work-related courses, and that this should be run by properly trained staff. Employers should be encouraged to contribute to the costs of training their workers. The report also recommended that spouses should not have to wait a year before being entitled to free tuition and that asylum-seekers should be entitled to language tuition after eight weeks in the country.

The report was launched 3 October 2006. Its findings were warmly welcomed by the Minister of State for Adult, Further and Higher Education, and most of the recommendations were either accepted or considered worthy of consideration.[13] However, several recommenda-tions were rejected. Fundamental to the provision of ESOL in England was the rejection of the recommendation that all ESOL learners should be entitled to free ESOL provision up to Level 1. Also rejected were the recommendations that there should be a 'ministerial lead' for ESOL and that the 'gang masters' involved in bringing over migrant workers should be required 'at their expense to ensure their workers are enabled to secure adequate English language skills'. The recommendation that there should be 'regulatory measures' to ensure that employers did not transfer the costs of ESOL provision onto employees was side-stepped. The recommendation that spouses and family members should be entitled to ESOL tuition immediately upon arrival in the UK was put on hold. The recommendation that asylum-seekers should 'have the same entitlement as home learners when the target period for decision on their application has expired' was met with only a commitment to monitor with the Home Office 'the impact of withdrawal of entitlement from asylum seekers with a view to remedial action if necessary'.

A number of the NIACE recommendations aimed to pre-empt suggestions that were already circulating that the government in England was considering ending automatic fee remission for ESOL learners and removing all entitlement of asylum-seekers to education provision. These fears were confirmed when, at the end of October 2006, the Learning and Skills Council announced its proposal to withdraw automatic fee remission for ESOL tuition in England and replace it with a means-tested system. Asylum-seekers lost the absolute right to any educational provision. The announcement affirmed that there would be no reduction in the current levels of investment in ESOL provision, but that would obviously do nothing to reduce the shortfall in provision.

Aspects of this decision to re-focus resources on to priority areas caused considerable disquiet to ESOL practitioners and providers. They were worried in particular about the impact on the recently-arrived, on low-income families not on benefit (and it was the women in these groups whom the government wanted to encourage into classes), on migrant workers and on asylum-seekers waiting long periods for a decision on their applications. It was also clear that ESOL learners would be confused by the continuing availability of free tuition for adult literacy and numeracy learners. The trade unions were anxious about the implications for work-based training, communication among colleagues and health and safety in the workplace.

A major campaign was mounted in the early months of 2007, involving lecturers, voluntary organisations, community groups, the TUC and learners themselves. The Minister was urged to reconsider these proposals. At the time of writing this history there had been the Race Equality Impact Assessment, which had brought some concessions. Notably, asylum-seekers would be entitled to education provision if there had been no decision on their application after six months of their being in the country; a Learner Support Hardship Fund of £4.6 million for one year would support 'vulnerable learners, including spouses and low-paid workers'; and alternative means of proving inability to pay fees would be sought. The main difficulty, however – too many learners and too little provision – remained, and this would be exacerbated by the requirement on those applying for *settlement* (indefinite leave to remain) to demonstrate the same levels of language competence and knowledge of life in the United Kingdom as those applying for *citizenship*.

In May 2007 the Mayor of London negotiated an allocation of £15 million for one year towards paying for ESOL provision in the capital. This was jointly funded by the Learning and Skills Council and the London Development Agency. Announcing this, the Mayor showed his support for ESOL: 'Being supported in English language skills is vital to ensure that those who choose to come to London can make their contribution to the workplace and play an active role in the community.'

The other nations

Similar problems were facing ESOL practitioners and their governments/administrations in Scotland, Wales and Northern Ireland. One UK-wide initiative was the development of the ESOL citizenship materials, specially adapted versions of which were published in 2006 for Northern Ireland (NIACE, 2006c) and for Scotland (NIACE, 2006b), with contributions from the Scottish Qualifications Authority and on behalf of the Scottish Executive as well as for the Home Office and DfES. The version for Wales appeared in 2007 (NIACE, 2007).

However, in most other ways the systems for providing ESOL nations continued to differ from that in England, with more significant developments in Wales and Scotland. A further caveat has to be entered in that at the time of going to press the effects of the May 2007 elections and the changes in the administrations in Cardiff and Edinburgh had still to be felt.

Scotland

In March 2007 the Scottish Executive published its final strategy for ESOL (Scottish Executive, 2007), which reiterated the vision set out in the consultation paper:

> ... *that all Scottish residents for whom English is not a first language have the opportunity to access high-quality English language provision so that they*

can acquire the language skills to enable them to participate in Scottish life: in the workplace, through further study, within the family, the local community, Scottish society and the economy. These language skills are central to giving people a democratic voice and supporting them to contribute to the society in which they live. (Scottish Executive, 2007, p. 4)

The publication of the strategy was accompanied by the announcement that an extra £5 million had been allocated to support ESOL, amounting to an extra 4,000 classroom places. The announcement was prefaced by statements from the First Minister and Deputy First Minister on the importance of ESOL: 'Those who come to Scotland to work or study should be given every opportunity to participate fully in Scottish life.'

Practitioners welcomed this, but at the time of writing they were still evaluating the full implications of this decision, and trying to determine whether it was only a short-term measure. ESOL learners in Scotland were still able to access provision without fulfilling rigid residence requirements, and this included spouses and asylum-seekers. However, defining who was a 'Scottish resident' continued to be complex (Scottish Executive, 2007, p. 4). Fees were still waived for asylum-seekers; for other ESOL students the system was quite complex, though in general they still had to prove inability to pay if they were to receive any remission of fees.

Wales

In Wales there were still waiting lists of learners in some areas; there were also too few qualified teachers and a challenge of dealing with new learners from different backgrounds – migrant workers, refugees and asylum-seekers, as well as longer-established ESOL communities; but again, the response was different from that in England.

The second phase of the Basic Skills Strategy was launched in 2005 with *Words Talk: Numbers Count* (Welsh Assembly Government, 2005) This highlighted ESOL learners as being in one of ten priority groups, with a pledge of enhanced support. However, Strategy funding supported only development programmes, and not core basic provision. On the other hand, ESOL also featured in other priority areas, notably developing skills in the workplace.

At the time of writing, there was a continuing commitment from the Welsh Assembly Government and the BSA to maintain fee remission for ESOL tuition (alongside other basic skills) for EU and EEA citizens, and for residents of three years' standing with indefinite leave to remain, and this applied to spouses too. There were further commitments to maintain favourable staff–learner ratios, which was a requirement for the achievement of the Basic Skills Agency's Quality Mark and to fulfilling the recommendation in the Moser Report to support the establishment of workplace provision skills and to engage employers in this.[14]

Northern Ireland

The decision to develop a Skills Strategy for Northern Ireland led to a widespread programme of consultation. The report on this process, published in August 2005, revealed growing concern over the increasing numbers of migrant workers coming to the province, but also a worry about how to provide for young people for whom the main language of education had been Irish (Northern Ireland Government 2005, p. 12). The province continued to allow asylum-seekers immediate access to classes.

The situation in 2007

So by 2007 ESOL learners found themselves in a no-man's land between government departments. The competing claims of equality of opportunity, social cohesion and the demands of the economy came up against the restrictions imposed by the Treasury. There was no overall or coherent view of the needs of ESOL communities, and different departments pursued different and often contradictory policies. The differences in residence eligibility and requirement to pay fees in different parts of UK, as well as the wide differences in provision, could seriously affect learners' access to tuition.

In England, with by far the largest ESOL population, the government was particularly concerned about the cost of ESOL provision, and in particular worried that learners from the EU were taking up places in Skills for Life provision which it felt should be available to hard-to-reach groups such as Bangladeshi women. The government response to this challenge was to revert to a rough compartmentalising of the learners, and their learning aims, into non-residents requiring EFL courses and relying on the private sector, and residents drawing on means-tested LSC funded provision. Migrant workers and other employees were to be offered work-focused qualifications, though it was hard to see how these might meet the complex needs of such learners; migrant workers needed the same social language and information about the UK as immigrants and refugees. Many were already settled in the community and their families were beginning to join them. Polish children were enrolling in UK schools just as the Pakistani, Indian and Cypriot children had done in the 1960s. In May 2007, the Minister of State for Adult, Further and Higher Education was unable to offer any view on what the unintended consequences of these new rulings might be.

English as a lingua franca

In all the fragmented debates on what to do about ESOL, one factor was never seriously confronted: the place of the English language as a lingua franca. We had moved on from the ambitions of Winston Churchill in the 1940s to use Basic English to establish English as the international language. By 2007 English *had* become the world language, at least for the time being. The British Council now had to take account of the fact that there were many 'Englishes',[15] and many groups and many countries teaching it.[16]

It was recognised in some quarters that the language itself could be a pull factor for those seeking to come to the UK, but there was no equal realisation that this had its advantages. The UK tended to attract migrant workers and refugees who were relatively well educated and qualified (Kirk, 2004) and who chose the UK, rather than say Holland or Germany, precisely because they had studied some English as the main foreign language offered in the secondary school and college systems in their home countries.

Conclusion

At the end of this history of ESOL in the UK, and looking back over the 137 years covered, it is important first of all to pay tribute to the energy and commitment of practitioners and voluntary organisations, the goodwill of institutions like the BBC and the contribution by governments to fighting racism and ameliorating the condition of settlers already in the UK. In England and Wales the government had also allocated substantial funds in the later period to support ESOL. In demonstrating that learning the language of the county of settlement is almost never a neutral act, it is also important to report that very little evidence of opposition to learning English was found. It is also important to recognise the resilience and contribution of ESOL communities across the generations.[17] Over the period as a whole, an improved ESOL pedagogy was developed and refined to meet the needs of a heterogeneous group of learners, although that development was often fitful, with lessons being learned and then lost.

However, by 2007 the fact remained there was still too little provision and too many learners seeking to access it, and many of the problems that had long confronted communities, practitioners and governments remained largely unresolved. The global movements of peoples, whether refugees fleeing war or persecution or the arrival of legal and illegal economic migrants seeking work, had intensified and accelerated in the final decades of the twentieth and early years of the twenty-first centuries. This affected the UK, along with all other countries of the 'developed' world. However, apart from further legislation to restrict immigration from countries outside the EU, government responses to this new world were still often fitful, uncoordinated and uncertain.

At the same time, and perhaps paradoxically, the concern of the UK government to develop and sustain a skilled workforce turned attention to under-performing and under-achieving groups. These included ESOL speakers in long-settled communities, for whom there had never been systematic and ongoing provision to meet their needs.

The legacy of Empire had accustomed the UK to taking the English language *out* to others, or providing for visiting students, and many early developments in the pedagogy drew on this experience. But for nearly all the periods covered by the present history, there was little acceptance by governments that the UK was also a country of immigrants who required regular and continuing programmes for settlement. This view of the incomers led to a series of short-term measures to meet immediate needs, which were probably appropriate for the Belgian refugees in 1915, or the Allied service personnel in the 1940s, whom it was assumed would go 'home'. However – as the chequered history of Section 11 demonstrated – it became increasingly clear that such an approach was inadequate to meet the needs of arrivals from the New Commonwealth; while other groups, such as the Vietnamese, were still being offered the same short-term programmes as the Belgians in the First World War or the Poles after the end of the Second World War.

ESOL had always had a political dimension, and governments, sensitive to domestic prejudice, had often chosen to channel their support through the voluntary sector – often, as one commentator on

Section 11 noted, preferring to do 'good by stealth'. The moves to align ESOL with adult literacy, and to bring it under the umbrella of adult basic education, or basic skills, or Skills for Life, sometimes betrayed the same unease about highlighting the needs of immigrants. In the 1980s it also accompanied a wish to avoid the financial costs involved in making separate provision. All this had serious implications for ESOL, both for developing the pedagogy and for providing tuition.

From 2000 onwards, however, ESOL *was* thrust into the limelight. It was positioned at the centre of government concern over social cohesion, identity and national security. It was given further importance by the legislation stipulating that those applying for citizenship, or for permission to stay in the United Kingdom, must demonstrate a knowledge of life in the UK and some level of English, or evidence that they were attending ESOL classes to acquire these. The onus was now on the learner to fulfil the requirements of the state, but there was still too little provision by the state to help them to do this.

As to the future? An optimist might forecast that there would be a re-evaluation of ESOL that would take into account the views of all departments of government across the UK. This re-evaluation might calculate that the benefits to the individual, to the economy and to society of making adequate ESOL provision would outweigh the immediate costs involved. A pessimist might predict further unco-ordinated and under-funded measures which would continue to fail the economy, society as a whole, minority communities and many individual learners.

What was clear was that the challenge of funding and providing ESOL would continue for the foreseeable future.

Notes

Introduction

[1] When he became a citizen in 1727, he had to swear oaths of supremacy and allegiance and to produce a certificate testifying that Holy Communion according to Anglican rites had been received. Yet there was no language test. However, Handel was clearly familiar enough with the cadences of English to set verses from the Authorised Version of the Bible for the *Messiah*.

Chapter One

[1] The Alien Registration Act of 1914 gave the Secretary of State the power to regulate aliens during war, including internment. The Alien Act of 1919 placed controls on the entry, employment and deportation of aliens. The Alien Act of 1920 imposed further restrictions, including the need to possess a work permit and to show evidence of the ability to support one's self and one's dependants. A further Act in 1925 applied to alien seamen.

[2] Gregory and Williams (2000), in *City Literacies*, define this as 'complex heterogeneity of traditions, whereby reading practices from different domains are blended in a form of reinterpretation which is both new and dynamic' (p. 13).

[3] The work itself could well have been used by learners planning to emigrate to Palestine.

[4] Jacob Mazin wrote the *Elementary Manual of the Yiddish Language with Exercises and Conversations* (published by R Mazin), the third revised edition of which appeared in 1913. This is interesting to those concerned with the issues and problems involved with all mother-tongue maintenance. Mazin's elementary manual assumes that the intended readers had to be taught the Hebrew alphabet, and this occurred on a page that read from left to right, while the book as a whole read from right to left. Readers were also given a pronunciation

guide. The Hebrew characters were then transliterated throughout into English characters, e.g. 'Ich ken ir man'. There was also an informed account of the three varieties of Yiddish – Lithuanian, Polish and south Russian – with the Lithuanian version seen as the leading one.

5 This is the only edition I have been able to locate.

6 I am indebted to Mr Benny Scheiner for this translation.

7 Gartner (2001, p. 239) says 1893–4 and I say 1892, based on the Board of Deputies Annual Report 1892.

8 However, if they were using the Jacobs and Landauer *Yiddish–English Manual* it would have been difficult to avoid being exposed to models of spoken English.

9 Board of Deputies of British Jews, Annual Report 1892 (Archives of the Board of Deputies of British Jews Acc 312/G1/1/3 London Metropolitan Archives).

10 The date often given is 1894, but the British Library copy is dated 1893.

11 By the 1902–3 session, out of total of 777,945 students, 27,969 were over the age of 21 and 19,274 were over the age of 18. *(Final Report of the School Board for London 1904*, p. 280).

12 Nesfield produced a Catalogue of Sanskrit MS in Oudh, and rewrote Eastern folk tales and tales from the *Mahabharata*. He also wrote on the caste system in the North-West Provinces. As a linguistician, he wrote on diglottism in Tamil and English, and produced a bilingual English–Nepali grammar. A posthumous edition in 1961 of his *Errors in English Composition* includes a section by C A Shepherd (himself a professor of English at St Berchman's College, Changanacherry) on 'Indian Errors in English' in which he gives as an example: 'I have an idea to be an engineer when I leave school' (p. 120).

13 This provoked some eminent scholars of the day, including Henry Skeat, to a rebuttal in the *Times Literary Supplement* (6 January 1914).

14 'The Tables on pages 299–301 show that 12,473 pupils have been taught in language classes during the Session 1902–3. All the languages named in the table except Russian were taught prior to 1898, but not to the same extent. Russian was first of all taught voluntarily in one school, but latterly the Board have defrayed the cost of the two classes which are now in existence. Special efforts have been made to improve the teaching of French. An organising teacher was appointed on October 4, 1900 to look after these classes. Only those teachers are allowed to teach the subject who have obtained a First Class Certificate at the Board's French examination which was first held in 1900. This examination is oral as well as written, and much attention is given in the schools to pronunciation. Classes

suitable for teachers have been taught on the Gouin system in two or three schools, and a similar number of special classes have been taught on the system of Phonetics. In other schools special courses of lecture, or causeries, have been given by some of the best qualified teachers, the lectures being delivered in French and followed by conversation between the students and the lecturer on the topic of the evening' (School Board for London, 1904, pp. 292–3).

[15] 'The syllabus is very comprehensive, dealing with Representative government, Empire, and Industrial and Social Life and Duties. In some preliminary notes to the syllabus it is suggested that '[t]he object of the teacher should be to proceed from the known and familiar, such as the policeman, the rate collector, the board of guardians, and the town council, to the history of, and reasons for, our local and national institutions, and our responsibilities in connection with them' (School Board for London, 1904 p. 289).

[16] Pembrokeshire County Records (PCC/ED/10/2).

[17] *Ibid.*, 2 December.

[18] Pembrokeshire County Records (PCC/ED/10/2)

[19] It is a matter of interest for this account that a number of Belgian families who had come to Milford Haven in 1914–15 returned again in 1940! (*Western Telegraph*, 23 May 1940).

[20] Palmer himself is seen as bringing together 'the linguistic rigour of the Reform Movement with the serious examination of the psychological roots of the Direct Methods' (Howatt and Widdowson, 2004, p. 235).

[21] Howatt and Widdowson (2004); quote from the 8th impression in 1934 (p. 237 and fn. 2).

[22] E Schaap was still credited on the title page with the joint authorship of the 1914 manual.

[23] For France, see e.g. Hospitalier (1900); Camerlynck and Beltette (1921).

[24] E.g. Bradley, *The Making of English*. Revised by Simeon Petter 1968.

[25] *English Language Teaching* II, p. 84.

[26] See Winder (2004) for chillingly detailed accounts covering this period.

Chapter Two

[1] The extent to which UK funding was supplemented by any resources the Allied government in exile had been able to bring with them out of Nazi Occupied Europe has still to be explored.

[2] Palmer and Hornby (1937).

[3] The British Library copy, donated by Carlisle Public Library, shows it was taken out as late as November 1973.

[4] Costing 5/– as opposed to 1/6.

[5] Eckersley's *England and the English,* first published by Longman in 1932, went through a series of editions. The 1946 edition was reproduced in 1995.

[6] The *Times Educational Supplement* for January 1944 contains a series of articles on army education, including language instruction for service personnel from the Middle East.

[7] This commitment is echoed in Fred Pelican's memories (see p. 54) as the recruits anglicised their names, in his case from Pelikan to Pelican, and joined the conflict. He himself left with the British Expeditionary Force in 1940 and was evacuated from Dunkirk.

[8] Two letters: 29 August to F R Wood and 2 September to John Chancellor.

[9] Parkinson's office handled the budgets for the overall programme, whether it was the money directly allocated to the Council, or the invoicing of the three armed service departments for services and goods supplied. She was also responsible for the maintenance of all the national houses and, through the Institut Français, received a direct grant from Parliament (Donaldson, 1984, p. 117). It was administered by the British Council. These all placed a heavy burden on the administration. There were also problems in cash flow. One invoice was too late to present to the War Office, so she asked if it could be charged to 'Contingencies' or, alternatively, 'to the Books and Periodicals Committee's grant for Resident Foreigners' (BW 2/55).

[10] The University of Cambridge Local Examinations Syndicate – with which the British Council had close ties – recommended the use of Basic English for the Lower Certificate in English (Gordon, 1990, p. 36).

[11] Ogden was paid £23,000. This figure was precisely chosen to echo the amount paid to Jeremy Bentham by the government of the day for his *Panopticon* on prison reform. In this way Ogden was paying tribute to Bentham, the philosopher he admired and from whose ideas about language Basic English had been developed. The copyright was then assigned to the Trustees of the Basic English Foundation in June 1948. This was finally relinquished in 1953.

[12] Other groups too stayed, including German prisoners of war who had married local girls. But there was no programme for them.

[13] 'Poles Go Home': see Henderson (2001, p. 60).

Chapter Three

[1] By 1970 the estimated Greek population was 120,000 (Butterworth and Kinnibrugh, 1970, p. 69).

[2] There is insufficient space here to discuss the linguistic distinctions between dialect variations of English and Patois/Creole as distinct and separate languages; see e.g. the ILEA Afro-Caribbean Language and Literacy Project, *Language and Power* (ILEA, 1990, pp. iv and 345).

[3] This in turn replaced the National Advisory Committee for Commonwealth Immigrants (1963–5).

[4] DES (1971, pp. 53–4).

[5] See Eckersley's *England and the English*, first printed 1938, and the British Council's work with Allied personnel during the Second World War. The early English language teaching materials followed the same pattern of teaching learners about the host community, from Jacobs and Landau's *Yiddish/English Manual* in 1893 through Michael West's *New Method Readers* in the 1920s and 1930s to Constance Ripman's *Let's Talk English* in 1938 and Eckersley's *English for the Allies* in 1942 and 1943. The works of Alexander and Hornby were less didactic about England and Englishness, but their course books were still set in very specific social, national and cultural contexts.

[6] LEAs adopted radically different positions on this (DES, 1971, pp. 16–21).

[7] The ILEA grouped the boroughs into divisions: Hammersmith and Fulham, Kensington and Chelsea (Division 1), Westminster and Camden (Division 2), Islington (Division 3), Hackney (Division 4), City of London and Tower Hamlets (Division 5), Greenwich (Division 6), Lewisham (Division 7), Southwark (Division 8), Lambeth (Division 9), Wandsworth (Division 10).

[8] His *Essential English* (1938) and *English for the Allies* (1943) have already been described. Longman continued to publish Eckersley's works until 1984, long after his death in 1967.

[9] It has been impossible to find a complete set of the Scope books and materials in one place. While it might indicate that this innovative project was overtaken by new developments in ESOL teaching and learning among teachers, it is more likely that it is because there were no subsequent government-funded initiatives to build on its work.

[10] See p. 117, 152, for a discussion of the functional approach to language teaching and learning.

[11] See Chapter 2, pp. 44–5, for a consideration of vocabulary selection.

[12] Gordon Ward's *Deciding What to Teach in English* (1977) was listed in the 1979 and 1981 NATESLA catalogues. In 1979 the NATESLA reviewer's

judgement was that this was '[a] succinct account of the problems of syllabus planning with the present state of ideas on language teaching. But not so good on the solutions to the problems' (NATESLA, 1979, p. 54).

[13] Devereux (1982, p. 118) and personal knowledge.

[14] Roberts (1988, p. 20).

[15] Flint (1969, pp. 17–18).

Chapter Four

[1] *Five Views of Multi-Racial Britain* (CRE, 1978b). John Twitchen's introduction refers to worsening race relations: 'The authors of these talks are among the many well-informed specialists who are worried that such events are signalling an overall worsening of race relations – despite the anti-discrimination legislation and the efforts so far of agencies like the CRE. Stuart Hall and Bikhu Parekh are particularly concerned, too, to note the slippage since the early 1960s, in the language of public debate and opinion towards racist assumptions ... all the authors point to a need for further changes in public policies – at parliamentary level and local authority level – together with changes in priorities and training needs at workplaces, in schools, in public community services and, not least, in the media, if the direction of these trends is to be reversed' (p. 5). The programmes were: Professor John Rex, 'Race in the Inner City', a public talk given at the University of Warwick on 8 June 1978; Dr Stuart Hall, 'Racism and Reaction', a public talk arranged by the British Sociological Association and given in London on 2 May 1978; Dr Bikhu Parekh, 'Problem or Opportunity', a lecture arranged by the Adult Education Department of Hull University on 12 June 1978; Professor Alan Little, 'Schools and Race', talk given to an audience of teachers and parents at Southlands College, Wimbledon, on 20 June 1978; Bishop Trevor Huddleston, 'Third World perspective', the 1978 Runnymede Lecture, delivered at the Commonwealth Institute on 21 March 1978. Thames Television's *Our People*, Programme 1: *Immigrants*, looked at who immigrants were, and the working of the immigration laws. Programme 2, *Facts?* combated stereotypical prejudices by examining the lives of immigrants in Britain in relation to jobs, housing and the law. Programme 3, *Empire*, looked at the long history of the British Empire which had brought about the multi-racial Britain of the day. Programme 4, *A Long Way to Work*, compared the role of immigrants in Britain with migrant workers in Europe, with examples from Germany, France and Sweden. Programme 5, *Law and Order*, examined the recent increase in racist tension. Programme 6, *Carnival*, looked at some

of the work being done on a local level to combat racism. The accompanying illustrated booklet (Thames Television, 1979), which was to be used as a discussion document, covered the history of groups coming to the UK.

[2] Arthur Jones, principal of the City Literary Institute, was on the Russell Committee and influenced the debate and wrote much of the report. The ILEA's own submission is with the ILEA records in the London Metropolitan Archives.

[3] William Devereux went on to make a major national contribution through his subsequent appointment as head of the Adult Literacy Resource Agency (ALRA).

[4] Eric Bourne, for his championship of the development of Appendix II work in the colleges, and Sydney Heaven, for his work with literacy and ESOL.

[5] In 1977 the first borough language co-ordinator (BLC) was appointed, working across all the adult education providers in the borough of Lambeth. Two borough-wide co-ordinators in Wandsworth and Greenwich, who had been operating under the auspices of their CRCs, were taken into the ILEA, and co-ordinators were soon appointed for all the other Inner London boroughs. Classes in Camden and Islington, which had been established under Ruth Hayman's Neighbourhood English Classes, were later also taken over by the ILEA. Although two Industrial Language Training Units (ILTUs) separately funded by the Manpower Services Commission (MSC) were set up, north and south of the river. The general principle was to provide a unified service for the whole ILEA community.

[6] The *Newspaper Pack* supported the developments of ESOL students' literacy skills and aimed to give them the confidence to tackle the different visual and graphical conventions used in newspapers. This was followed by the *Telephone Pack*, intended to develop the skills that students needed to operate successfully on the phone in a number of everyday situations, and then by the *At Work* pack.

[7] There were other projects, for example a Brick Lane project to up-skill clothing workers.

[8] With representatives from the British Council for Aid to Refugees (BCAR), the Ockenden Venture, the World University Service (WUS), Christian Aid and the Standing Conference on Refuges (Kushner and Knox, 2001, p. 297).

[9] For the different uses of the terms 'functions' and 'notions', see Howatt and Widdowson (2004, p. 339).

[10] In 1975, J A van Ek produced *Systems Development in Adult Language Learning: The Threshold Level as a European unit/credit system for modern language learning by adults* (van Ek, 1976). This was further developed in the report by Rene

Richterich and Jean-Louis Chancerel (1977); and then in 1978 by Trim's *Some Possible Lines of Development for an Overall Structure for a European Unit/Credit Scheme for Foreign Language Learning by Adults*.

[11] Howatt and Widdowson (2004, p. 326). The opening section of Chapter 20, pp. 326–40, is also a detailed account of the communicative approach.

[12] See glossary for the use of EFL, ESL, ESOL.

[13] ESOL teachers in the UK have always been able to share their experience with their counterparts in other countries, for example over making provision for Vietnamese refugees (Rosenberg *et al.*, 1982). And these international contacts would continue. NATECLA was represented at a European Commission Task Force conference in Berlin in 1999 on the integration of refugees, and ESOL teachers have attended and given papers at conferences of the International Association of Teachers of English as a Foreign Language (IATEFL) and International Association of Teaching English to Speakers of English as a Second or Other Language (IATESOL).

[14] The isolation of the mother who arrives in the labour ward knowing no English is well described.

[15] See p. 96 for a comparison between *Senior Scope* and L Alexander's *First Things First* (Alexander, 1967).

[16] The Longman 'Nucleus' series for English for science and engineering is a good example.

[17] However, as will be seen in Chapter 5, the availability of courses varied widely from area to area.

[18] For example, the work of Jean McAllister and Margaret Robson at Shipley College, which led to *Building a Framework* (McAllister and Robson, 1984).

[19] On the other hand, even in 2007 there were home-bound students – mothers with young children who could not get into scarce nursery provision; the elderly and disabled – for whom home tuition remains the only option.

[20] It was first broadcast on BBC1 at 10 am on 2 October 1977 and repeated on BBC2.

[21] PEP *Racial Disadvantage in Employment*. Runnymede Trust, 1975.

[22] The Springboard scheme involved the Camden Council for Community Relations, the ILEA Language and Literacy Unit, North London College and the MSC, with money from the Urban Programme, and supported by employers like Rank Xerox. Together, they set up a programme for school-leavers who spoke English as a second or other language and who had few or no formal qualifications. The ILEA paid the teachers, the MSC provided the trainees' allowances, and the programme was developed by all the agencies working together, with the CRC supporting the outreach. The scheme was

judged to be a success and was followed by two more programmes before it was taken over by North London College itself.

[23] See Chapter 5 for a more detailed account.

[24] The NCILT published C Roberts (1977a); C Roberts (1977b); Bonamy (1978); Ladbury (1980).

[25] NCILT Catalogue, 1984–5.

[26] For a critical account by the TSA itself of such provision, see Chapter 6, p. 218.

[27] From my personal papers.

[28] For much of its history NATECLA has been funded largely through modest membership fees, and has rarely had more than one full-time-equivalent paid officer. It has never been a large organisation, and there was no official funding at all until its contract to manage some areas for development under the Skills for Life initiative. The membership has remained surprisingly constant, with older members retiring and newer ones joining.

[29] I am indebted to Mary Hamilton and Yvonne Hillier's *Changing Faces* (University of Lancaster) timeline, www.lancs.ac.uk/fss/projects/edres/changingfaces

[30] It also recommended that 'considerations should be given by the Secretary of State for Wales to the possibility of establishing a Welsh sub-committee of the Development Board to address adult basic education in Wales'.

Chapter Five

[1] There was already a large Turkish-speaking immigrant population in the UK, and the immigration authorities could not distinguish between Kurds who spoke Turkish and Turks who spoke Turkish (Kushner and Knox, 2001, p. 341). So it was often hard to convince them that an applicant for asylum was in fact a Kurd who faced persecution if returned to Turkey.

[2] This Project employed a multi-disciplinary team whose work cut across age groups and institutional boundaries and looked at bilingual communities as a whole. It aimed 'to develop research methods which were community based, and which had some immediate application, as well as making longer-term contributions to the academic fields of education and ethnic relations' (inside cover). Much of the Project's work had a school dimension, built on the ethnic and language monitoring undertaken by LEAs in different areas of immigration. Euan Reid's 'Minority Languages in England: A Neglected Resource?' in Nicholls and Hoadley-Maidment's *Current Issues in Teaching English as a Second Language* (1988, pp. 10–20), argued in favour of building

on, and using, people's mother tongues, and many LEAs did this.

[3] These were made easier with the establishment in 1987 of a national administrative centre in South Birmingham and the appointment of its first part-time administrator. For other explorations by the author of the history of NATECLA, see Rosenberg and Hallgarten (1985) and Rosenberg (2006).

[4] This was the aim of a day conference in May 1993 at the University of Sheffield, addressed by HMI Inder Geera and representatives from LEAs, and followed by workshops. Participants spoke of their feelings of isolation and the sense that they lacked political and professional direction. They generally welcomed the opportunity to meet to discuss issues and plan a policy document. (*NATECLA News*, vol. 42, p. 1).

[5] There was also an article on working with training and funding organisations. The section dealing with developing effective provision included how to use the students' own language and experience in the classroom. Other sections examined how to choose and use effective systems for assessment and record-keeping and appropriate systems for the accreditation of students' learning. The last section dealt with teacher training and staff development.

[6] He responded to the portmanteau question: 'What does a body of linguistic theory which emphasises the interrelationship of form and function, the semantic choices open to each speaker, the grounding of language in social processes, have to offer the ESL practitioner?'

[7] See Council of Europe report (1983a).

[8] The Bangladesh Associations of Glasgow and North East Scotland; the Central Scotland Chinese Association; the Chilean Language Class Glasgow; the Urdu Club Glasgow; Community Language Teaching Organisation Glasgow; the Neighbourhood English Teaching Project, the Roundabout Centre YWCA Edinburgh.

[9] See also ALBSU, 1987, p. 5.

[10] Advisory Council on the Supply and Training of Teachers.

[11] The importance of language teaching in further education was further underlined in a 1986 FEU report, *Language for All: An Analysis of the Importance of Language in Post-16 Education*. The sweep of this report was broad and took in modern foreign language and ESOL teaching and learning, referred to the Threshold Levels (p. 7) and noted the bilingual skills already possessed by many students. It identified the language skills needed in the classroom and the narrow and often conflicting requirements of examination systems. It cited the Bullock Report for the concept of language across the curriculum (p. 2) and the Swann Report for its celebrations of the 'linguistic repertoire of young people in Britain today' (p 5). *Language for All* 'urged the validation

of language knowledge beyond sixteen' (p. 28) and looked forward to the development of a 'common communicative core' for language learning (pp. 31–2). It cited the work of Jean McAllister and Margaret Robson in their *Building Framework* (1984, p. 3) for language across the curriculum, argued for college language policies, and urged the development of negotiated a curriculum along the lines already used by ESL and communications teachers (p. 42).

Chapter Six

[1] That being said, Kushner and Knox (2001) cite evidence that in the 1990s only five per cent of those applying for refugee status as individuals were successful, and refusal rates for applicants from Africa were almost 100 per cent (pp. 375, 378–9).

[2] All quotations are taken from fliers for the programme.

[3] Robson had been involved in developing materials for supporting the language across the curriculum at Shipley College and had written *Language Learning and Race* for the FEU (see Chapter 5).

[4] This project was funded by the Paul Hamlyn Foundation. After receiving a grant from the London Docklands Development Corporation for computing hardware, a survey was carried out in conjunction with NATECLA and its network of teachers.

[5] This had been created in 1991 as the Basic Skills Agency, a company limited by guarantee and a registered charity.

[6] 'City Guilds Initial Certificate in Teaching Basic Skills (9284) ESOL' (*Language Issues*, vol. 6.1, pp. 13–15).

[7] The company limited by guarantee and a registered charity.

[8] The evidence for these interchanges is in the NATECLA archives.

[9] These letters are in the NATECLA archives.

[10] The *Report on the Survey of English for Speakers of Other Languages in Occupational Training Provided in London through Youth Training and Employment Training Programmes*, by C Carr, V Coffie, D Rush and R Thomas, is an unpublished report produced in 1991. I am indebted to Ann Janssen (1992) for information.

Chapter Seven

[1] CELTA (Certificate in English Language Teaching to Adults) and DELTA (Diploma in English Language Teaching to Adults).

[2] The Department for Education and Skills' *Delivering Skills for Life: The National Strategy for Improving Adult Literacy and Numeracy Skills*, diagnostic materials, ESOL (no date), is a pack containing guidance for the tutors on the Skills for Life levels, and resources, including visual prompts and a tape, to help them in the assessment of learners' skills in reading, writing and listening/speaking,

[3] The Common European Framework identified five levels of language learning from level A1, 'Breakthrough', to levels C, 'Operational Proficiency' and C2, 'Mastery'. The Cambridge Certificate in Advanced English was assessed as level C1, which was seen as equivalent to Level 2 in the NQF.

[4] 'The Three Year Strategic Action Plan for ESOL in London' (London Skills Commission 2006) found that '[t]he London region continues to make the greatest progress towards achieving the Government Skills for Life ESOL targets, but still only around one third of learners gain qualifications' (p. 12). One experienced head of department of Literacy, Numeracy, ESOL Key Skills and Learning Support pointed out the consequence of ESOL students' having to pass three modes, compared with literacy students' having to pass just one, by taking two hypothetical classes – one literacy and one ESOL. If 85 per cent of the literacy class passed the single mode required, the pass rate would be 85 per cent with 15 per cent failing. In the equivalent ESOL class, if 15 per cent of the students failed all three modes and the rest passed all three modes, the pass rate would be 85 per cent too; but if a different 15 per cent failed each of the three modes, the pass rate could fall to 61 per cent, which would affect the college's overall targets and under-represent the real achievement of the students.

[5] For example the UCLES 'main suite of qualifications' Key Test in English (KET), Preliminary Test in English (PET) and First Certificate in English (FCE).

[6] LLU+, 'Teaching Basic Literacy to ESOL Learners', Videos 1 (2001), and 2, (2002), and *Teaching Literacy to ESOL Learners: Course Materials 2001*.

[7] Undertaken by Lancaster University.

[8] An adult ESOL literacy learner, funded under adult literacy and numeracy streams, was defined as '[a] person who has little or no literacy in his/her own mother-tongue and who has little or no literacy in English and whose spoken

English may range from basic to fluent' (Scottish Executive, *Adult ESOL Strategy for Scotland,* 2005, p. 1).

9 Schellekens (2001). An account of the barriers in employment – 'the glass ceiling' – faced by ethnic minorities in general, was given by Saggar (2002, pp. 78–90).

10 Regulations were to come into force in September 2007 requiring that those applying for indefinite leave to remain fulfil the same requirements as those applying for citizenship.

11 'Membership of the board was drawn from leading public figures and experts from the fields of English for Speakers of Other Languages (ESOL), citizenship training, employment of migrants and community development and integration' (press release, 12 May 2005. These members included the principal of Tower Hamlets College (an experienced ESOL practitioner herself) and representatives from LLU+.

12 I am indebted to Helen Sunderland for a copy of an unpublished briefing paper.

13 Letter to Alan Tuckett, Director of NIACE, 18 October 2006. NIACE website.

14 'A key element of the national strategy and the Assembly's Skills Concordat was the Employers' Pledge award, an approach recommended in the Moser Report to engage employers and support the establishment of workplace provision. A National Support Project (NSP) worked with public and private sector employers who signed a pledge to produce and implement Basic Skills Action Plans. Another NSP provided resources and training for employers, a union learning representative and providers. As a result, many participating employers established workplace ESOL courses for the increasing number of migrant worker employees.' I am indebted to Celine Castelino for this information.

15 Graddol (2006) and Howatt and Widdowson (2004, p. 362).

16 There was already evidence that Australia had moved its thinking from providing English for its immigrants to teaching its neighbours on the shores of the Pacific.

17 The massive evidence for this ranges from an exhibition at the National Archives to research projects at the Institute for Public Policy Research (IPPR) with Sriskandarajah *et al.* (2005). Other individual publications include works such as the Refugee Council's *Credit to the Nation*, published in 2002, and Malet and Grenville (2002).

Appendix: Selective timeline

Chapter 1

1870	Elementary Education Act
1878	First Berlitz School opens
1881	Elementary Education Act
1890	Elementary Education Act
1891	Code for Evening Continuation Schools
1894	Joseph Jacobs and Herman Landau, *Yiddish-English* Manual
1902	Education Act: abolishes School Boards and gives responsibility for education to local boroughs and county councils
1904	Abolition of the School Board for London and creation of London County Council
1905	Aliens Act
1910	Wilfrid C. Thorley, *A Primer of English for Foreign Students*
1913	First Cambridge Certificate of Proficiency in English (CPE) – only taken in the UK
1914	E. C. Marshall and E. Schaap, *A Manual of English for Foreign Students*
1914	Aliens Restriction Act and Aliens Registration Order
1914–18	First World War
1915	Programme for Belgian refugees
1917	Russian Revolution
1921	Henry Palmer, *The Oral Method of Language Teaching*

Chapter 2

1930	C. K. Ogden, *Basic English*
1931	Cambridge Certificate of Proficiency in English held overseas for first time

1933	Laurence Faucett, *Oxford English Course* begins
1934	Founding of the British Council
1936–9	Spanish Civil War; 4,000 Basque children are admitted to the UK
1938	C. E. Eckersley, *Essential English* begun
	Harold Palmer, *A New Method Grammar*
1938–9	10,000 *Kindertransport* children are admitted to the UK
1939–45	Second World War
1942/3	C. E. Eckersley, *English for the Allies*
1947	Polish Resettlement Act

Chapter 3

1948	The *Windrush* arrives: the beginning of migration of labour from the Commonwealth
	British Nationality Act
1951	Foundation of UNHCR; internationally agreed definition of refugee
1962	Commonwealth Immigrants Act
1963	Ministry of Education, *English for Immigrants*
	Local Government Act: abolition of the London County Council and creation of the GLC and ILEA
1964	Industrial Training Act
1965	DES *The Education of Immigrants*
1966	Local Government Act (Section 11 provided opportunities for some ESOL funding)
1966	June Derrick, *Teaching English to Immigrants*
1967	Schools Council Overseas Pupils Project in English for Immigrant Children (Scope) begins
	Scope, *English for the Children of Immigrants*
	Louis Alexander, *New Concept English*
	BBC TV, *Look, Listen and Speak*
	RSA Certificate in the Teaching of English as a Second or Foreign Language
1968	Beginning of the Urban Programme
	Enoch Powell's 'Rivers of blood' speech
	Commonwealth Immigrants Act
	Race Relations Act: creation of the Community Relations Commission (CRC)

1969	E. J. B. Rose, *Colour and Citizenship*
1971	DES, *The Education of Immigrants*

Chapter 4

1971	Immigration Act (the 'Grandfather Act')
1972	1 January, Immigration Act comes into force
	Uganda Resettlement Board (Ugandan Asians)
1973	Russell Report on adult education
	On the Move adult literacy campaign
	Military junta under General Pinochet takes power in Chile
	Establishment of the Manpower Services Commission (MSC)
1974	Establishment of National Centre for Industrial Language Training (NCILT)
	CRC, *Language Teaching Schemes in England and Scotland*
1975	Pol Pot and Khmer Rouge take power in Cambodia
	T. C. Jupp and S. Hodlin, *Industrial English*
	J. A. van Ek, *Systems Development in Adult Language Learning*
	The Threshold Level in a European Unit / Credit System for Modern Language Learning by Adults, Strasbourg
	Fall of Saigon: Boat People begin to flee
	First ESOL teachers' course at Westminster College (leading to TESLFACE)
	A Language for Life (the Bullock Report)
	Adult Literacy Resource Agency (ALRA) set up
1976	Race Relations Act: the Commission for Racial Equality (CRE) is set up
	D. A. Wilkins, *Notional Syllabuses*
	CRC, *Language Teaching Schemes in Britain*
	CRC, *A Second Chance, Further Education in Multi-Racial Areas*
1977	David C. Smith, *Racial Disadvantage in Britain, the PEP Report*
	Michael Mobbs, *Meeting Their Needs: An Account of Language Tuition Schemes for Ethnic Minority Women*, CRC
	CRE, *Home Tutor Kit*
	BBC, *'Parosi' Tutors' Handbook: An Introduction to Teaching English at Home*
1978	ALRA is replaced by the Adult Literacy Unit (ALU)
	ILEA accepts first Boat People, housed in former Kensington Barracks

Establishment of National Association for Teaching English as a Second Language to Adults (NATESLA)

BBC, *Five Views of Multi-racial Britain*

1979   BBC, *Cross Talk*

A Strategy for the Basic Education of Adults (the ACACE Report)

International convention in Geneva on the refugees from Vietnam

Mrs Thatcher agreed to accept 10,000 refugees from Hong Kong; leads to establishment of Joint Committee for Refugees from Vietnam (JCRV)

BBC Radio, *Teaching English as a Second Language*

NATESLA, first *Catalogue of Resources*

Thames Television, *Our People*

'Save Adult Education' campaign

Chapter 5

1979   ILEA, *At Home in Britain*

NEC, with the Home Office, *Lessons from the Vietnamese*

ALRA replaced by the Adult Literacy and Basic Skills Unit (ALBSU)

BBC, *Speak for Yourself*

1981   British Nationality Act

S. Nicholls and J. Naish, *Teaching English as a Second Language*, BBC

The Brixton Disorders (the Scarman Report)

NATESLA, *Survey Report: English as a Second Language Teaching for Adults from Ethnic Minorities*

RSA Certificate in Initial Training in the Teaching of English as a Second Language to Adults

Pilot of RSA ESOL Profile Certificate (for learners)

1982   CRE, *Further Education in a multi-racial society A policy report*

NATESLA Occasional Paper 2, *ESL Provision for the 16–19(+) Age Group in Further and Adult/Community Education* (submission to the Swann Committee)

1984   Jean Macallister and Margaret Robson, *Building a Framework*

1985   *Education for All* (the Swann Report)

The Other Languages of England (Linguistic Minorities Project Report)

NATESLA, *Research Project into Training of Teachers of English as a Second Language in the Post-16 Sector*

C. J. Brumfitt, Rodd Ellis and Josie Levine (eds), *English as a Second Language in the United Kingdom*

1986 CRE, *Teaching English as a Second Language* (the Calderdale Report)

First issue of *Language Issues* (NATECLA)

J. Eggleston, *Education for Some*

1987 ALBSU, *English as a Second Language: Provision for Adults in England and Wales*

Abolition of National Centre for Industrial Language Training

1988 Immigration Act

S. Nicholls and E Hoadly-Maidment, *Current Issues in Teaching English as a Second Language to Adults*

Home Office, *A Scrutiny of Grants under Section 11 of the Local Government Act 1966: Final Report*

1989 ALBSU, *A Nation's Neglect: Research into the Need for English amongst Speakers of Other Languages*

ALBSU, *English for Speakers of Other Languages: A programme for Action*

End of funding for Industrial Language Training

Matheson and Weir, *Language Matters?* NATECLA Scotland

Chapter 6

1989 Education Reform Act (introduces the National Curriculum and leads to abolition of the ILEA)

1991 Civil war in Somalia begins

1991–5 Break-up of Yugoslavia

1992 Further and Higher Education Act (leading to funding for ESOL)

C. Roberts, E. Davies and T. Jupp, *Language and Discrimination*

1993 Asylum and Immigration Appeals Act

Section 11: definition widened to cover all ethnic minorities

1996 Asylum and Immigration Act

R Carr-Hill et al., *Lost Opportunities*

1997 *Learning Works: Widening participation in Further Education* (the Kennedy Report)

Literacy Skills for the Knowledge Society (the OECD Report)
1998   Abolition of Section 11
Education for Citizenship and the Teaching of Democracy in Schools
Scotland Act (leads to establishment of Scottish Parliament)
Rebellion in Kosovo against Serbian rule
Khanna et al., *Adult ESOL Learners in Britain: a cross-cultural study*
1999   Immigration and Asylum Act
The Stephen Lawrence Inquiry published (tackling racism in educational institutions)
Improving literacy and numeracy (the Moser Report)
Scottish Parliament and National Assembly for Wales established

Chapter 7
2000   DfEE *Breaking the Language Barriers*
Race Relations (Amendment) Act
2001   Skills for Life Strategy: Adult ESOL Core Curriculum in England (and equivalent in Wales)
Riots in northern towns, leading to Home Office *Community Cohesion* (the Cantle Report)
Attack on the Twin Towers (9 September)
National Basic Skills Strategy for Wales
2002   D. Blunkett 'Integration with Diversity', in *Reclaiming Britishness: Living Together After 11 September*
Home Office, *Secure Borders, Safe Havens; Integration with Diversity in Modern Britain*
Nationality, Immigration and Asylum Act
Subject Specifications for Teachers of ESOL
Establishment of the National Research and Development Centre (NRDC)
2003   *The New and the Old: The Report of the United Kingdom Advisory Group* (the Crick Report on Citizenship)
2004   Enlargement of the European Union
London bombings, 7 July
Citizenship Materials for ESOL learners (first version)
2006   Racial and Religious Hatred Act
NIACE, *More than a language?* (the NIACE ESOL Report)

HM Treasury *Prosperity for All in the Global Economy* (the Leitch Report)

Proposal to end automatic fee remission for ESOL in England

Proposal that applicants for settlement fulfil requirements similar to those applying for citizenship

Proposals for a revised Adult ESOL Strategy for Scotland

Glossary and acronyms

ABE	Adult basic education
ACACE	Advisory Council for Adult and Continuing Education
Accession States	The ten new countries which joined the European Union in May 2004
ACSTT	Advisory Council on the Supply and Training of Teachers (later the Advisory Committee on the Supply and Education of Teachers, ACSET)
AE	Adult education
ALBSU	Adult Literacy and Basic Skills Unit
ALI	Adult Learning Inspectorate
ALRA	Adult Literacy Resource Agency
ALU	Adult Literacy Unit
ATTI	Association for Teachers in Technical Institutions (then NATFHE, now UCU)
BBC	British Broadcasting Corporation
BC	British Council
BE	Basic English (C K Ogden)
BL	British Library
BSA	Basic Skills Agency
CBI	Confederation of British Industry
CEF	Common European Framework (for the mutual recognition of language qualifications)
CGLI	City and Guilds of London Institute
CILT	Centre for Information on Language Teaching and Research
CPE	Cambridge Certificate of Proficiency in English

CRC	Community Relations Commission
CRE	Commission for Racial Equality
DES	Department of Education and Science
DfEE	Department for Education and Employment
DfES	Department for Education and Skills
DWP	Department for Work and Pensions
EAL	English as an Additional Language (used to describe provision to support bilingual pupils in schools in the UK)
EAP	English for Academic Purposes
EFL	English as a Foreign Language. The term is used in this account to refer to English language teaching for learners whose main purpose is to acquire the language per se, and not because they are settlers in the UK
ESF	European Social Fund
ESL	English as a Second Language. In this account the term is used to refer to English for adult speakers of other languages who are resident in the UK and need the language to in order to live, work, study and bring up their families here. However this term has a number of other associations and has, for instance, been applied to English language teaching and learning in countries in which the citizens speak a different, or many different languages, but where English is the official language of administration (see Howatt and Widdowson, 2004, pp. xv–xvii for the history of this and other terms)
ESOL	English for Speakers of Other Languages is now the generally preferred term because it makes no assumptions about the intentions of the learners
ESP	English for Specific Purposes
ESRC	Economic and Social Research Council
ESWC	Education Service for the Whole Community (ILEA)
EU	European Union
FE	Further education
FEDA	see FEU
FEFC	Further Education Funding Council

FEU	Further Education Unit (later FEDA, Further Education Development Agency and then LSDA, Learning and Skills Development Agency)
GCSE	General Certificate of Secondary Education
GLA	Greater London Authority
GLC	Greater London Council
HE	Higher education
HMI	Her Majesty's Inspectorate
HMSO	Her Majesty's Stationery Office
HO	Home Office
IELTS	International English Language Testing System
ILEA	Inner London Education Authority
ILT	Industrial Language Training
ILTU	Industrial Language Training Unit
IPA	International Phonetic Alphabet
ITB	Industrial Training Board
JCRV	Joint Committee for Refugees from Vietnam
LCC	London County Council
LDA	London Development Agency
LEA	Local Education Authority
LI	*Language Issues*
LLU	Language and Literacy Unit (now LLU+)
LSC	Learning and Skills Council
MSC	Manpower Services Commission (succeeded by TC, Training Commission, TA, Training Agency, and TEED, Training Education and Employment Directive)
NATECLA	National Association for Teaching English and other Community Languages to Adults (see NATESLA)
NATESLA	National Association for Teaching English as a Second Language to Adults (later NATECLA)
NCCI	National Council for Commonwealth Immigrants
NCILT	National Centre for Industrial Language Training

NEC	National Extension College
NFER	National Foundation for Educational Research
NIACE	National Institute of Adult and Continuing Education (England and Wales)
NN	*NATECLA News*
NRDC	National Research and Development Centre for Adult Literacy and Numeracy
NUT	National Union of Teachers
NVQ	National Vocational Qualification
OECD	Organisation for Economic Co-operation and Development
Ofsted	Office for Standards in Education
PEP	Political and Economic Planning 1925–78. Merged with the Centre for the Study of Social Policy in 1978 to become the Policy Studies Institute (PSI)
QCA	Qualifications and Curriculum Authority
RAC	Regional Advisory Council (for Further Education)
RSA	Royal Society of Arts
SBL	School Board for London
Scope	Schools Council Project in English for Immigrant Children
Section 11	Section 11 of the Local Government Act 1966
SFEFC	Scottish Further Education Funding Council
TEC	Training and Enterprise Council
TESLA	Teaching English as a Second Language
TOP	Training Opportunities Programme
TSA	Training Services Agency
UCLES	University of Cambridge Local Examinations Syndicate
YOP	Youth Opportunity Programme

Bibliography

This bibliography lists all the documents, works and publications cited in the text. With the exception of Jane Ward's ESOL: The Context for the UK Today *(in preparation), which I am grateful to have had sight of, no other bibliographies or background material on the economic, political or social history of the period, or general works on language and language teaching, have been included; the bibliography would have been too long, and decisions on what to include too arbitrary. In order to indicate the paucity of material produced by mainstream publishers, and the energy and commitment of practitioners, it has been important to include some materials that were locally produced by language schemes. However, such materials were frequently not dated, and a full bibliographic description has often been impossible. In describing on-line publications, where it has been possible to do so the general source (e.g. Home Office) has been cited along with the number of the document, but not the full website address.*

Abbey, W, Brinson, C, Dove, R, Malet, M and Taylor, J (eds) (1995) *Between Two Languages: German Speaking Exiles in Great Britain 1933–1945*. Verlag Hans-Dieter Heinz, Stuttgart.

Advisory Council for Continuing and Adult Education (ACACE) (1979) *A Strategy for the Basic Education of Adults: A Report Commissioned by the Secretary of State for Education and Science*. ACACE, London.

ALBSU (1983) *Special Development Projects Report no 3*. ALBSU, London.

ALBSU (1987) *English as a Second Language: Provision for Adults in England and Wales*. ALBSU, London.

ALBSU (1989a) *A Nation's Neglect: Research into the Need for English amongst Speakers of Other Languages'. A Summary Report*. ALBSU, London.

ALBSU (1989b) *English for Speakers of Other Languages: A Programme for Action*. ALBSU, London.

ALBSU (1991) *Annual Report, 1990–1991*. ALBSU, London.

ALBSU (1992) *The ALBSU Standards for Basic Skills Teachers*. ALBSU, London.

Alexander, L G (1967) *New Concept English*, Book I: *First Things First*. Longmans, London.

Anders, A (1981) *An Army in Exile*. Battery Press, Nashville, Tenn.

Anon. (1967) *Situational English*. Longmans, London.

Bagley, C A (1992) *Back to the Future: Section 11 of the Local Government Act 1966, Local Authorities and Multicultural/Antiracist Education*. NFER, London.

Bandali, S (1979) 'Small Accidents', in *Our Lives: Young People's Autobiographies*. ILEA English Centre, London.

Barr, V and Fletcher, C (1983a) *English for Driving*. NEC, Cambridge.

Barr, V and Fletcher, C (1983b) *Topics and Skills in English*. Hodder & Stoughton, London.

Barton, D and Pitt, K (2003) *Adult ESOL Pedagogy: A Review of Research, an annotated bibliography and recommendations for future research*. NRDC, London.

Barton, P (ed) (2000) *White Eagle: A Collection of Memories from the Nottinghamshire Polish Air Force Community*. Nottinghamshire Living History Archive Millennium Award Scheme.

Baynham, M, Roberts, C, Cooke, M, Simpson, J, Ananiadou, K, Callaghan, J, McGoldrick, J and Wallace, C (2007) *Effective Teaching and Learning: ESOL*. NRDC, London.

BBC (1967) *Look, Listen and Speak: English for Immigrants by Television*. BBC Publications, London.

BBC (1977) *Parosi Students' Book*. BBC Publications, London.

BBC (1981) *Speak for Yourself: The BBC Project on English as a Second Language*. BBC Publications, London.

Bedford Language Scheme (BLS) (1970s – n.d.) *Living in England*. BLS, Bedford.

Beech, B, Brierley, C and Moselle, M (1981) *Use Your English: A Course in English as a Second Language for Adults*. Hodder & Stoughton, London.

Belgian Refugees in Bristol (1915) *Report of the Executive Committee for the Year 1914–15*; reprinted from the *Bristol Times and Mirror*, 9 October.

Bentwich, N (1956) *They Found Refuge*. Cresset Press, London.

Benz, W *et al.* (2003) *Die Kindertransporte, 1938–9*. Fischer Taschenbuch Verlag, Frankfurt-am-Maine.

Bermant, C (1969) *Troubled Eden.* Vallentine Mitchell, London.

Berthoud, R G (1997) *The Fourth National Survey of Ethnic Minorities: End of Award Report.* Economic and Social Science Research Council, London.

Bird, B and Brierely, C (1985) *Switch on to English: A Handbook for Developing Reading and Writing.* BBC Publications, London.

Blackburn Language Scheme (BLS) (n.d.) *Neighbourhood Book of Asian Cookery.* BLS, Blackburn.

Blackman, P (1915) *A Textbook of the English Language for Yiddish Students,* 2nd rev. edn. R Mazin, London.

Blackman, P (1919) *English in Yiddish.* E. Marlborough & Co, London.

Blackman, P (1924) *Hebrew Self-taught: A Manual of Conversation.* R Mazin & Co, London.

Blackman, P (1935) *The Beginner's Hebrew Self-taught.* R Mazin & Co, London.

Blunkett, D (2002) 'Integration with diversity in modern Britain: globalisation and the renewal of democracy', in P Griffiths and M Leonard (eds), *Reclaiming Britishness: Living Together after 11 September and the Rise of the Right.* Foreign Policy Centre, London, pp 65–77.

Bolton Language Scheme (BLS) (n.d.) *Readers.* BLS, Bolton.

Bolton Language Scheme (BLS) (n.d.) *Speak/Teach Project Readers.* Bolton.

Bonamy, D (1978) *Immigrants from Bangladesh.* NCILT, London.

Booker, J, Graham, F, Jackson, P, Joshi, R, Piotrowska, E and Turner, M (1985) *ESL/Literacy: An Introductory Handbook for Tutors.* ALBSU, London.

Bradford Language Scheme (BLS) (1970s onwards) *Asmat Readers.* BLS, Bradford.

Bradley, H (1968) *The Making of English,* rev. by Simeon Potter. Macmillan.

Bray, S E (1900) 'The Evening Continuation School', in T A Spalding, *The Work of the London School Board.* P S King & Son, London, pp 257–67.

Brereton, C (1938) *Modern Language Teaching in Day and Evening Institute with Special Reference to London.* University of London Press.

Briggs, A (1984) *Toynbee Hall: The First Hundred Years.* Routledge & Kegan Paul, London.

Brumfitt, C, Ellis, R and Levine, J (eds) (1985) *English as a Second*

Language in the United Kingdom, ELT Document no 121. Pergamon Press, Oxford.

Butterworth, E and Kinnibrugh, D (1970) *The Social Background of Immigrant Children from India, Pakistan and Cyprus, Scope Handbook 1.* Schools Council Project, London.

Cabinet Office Strategy Unit (2003) *Ethnic Minorities and the Labour Market: Final Report.* Cabinet Office, London.

Cahalan, P (1982) *Belgian Refugee Relief in England during the Great War.* Garland, London.

Camerlynck, G and Beltette, E (1921) *Handbook of Commercial English.* Didier, Paris.

Carey-Wood, J (1995) *The Settlement of Refugees in Britain*, Home Office Research Study no 141. HMSO, London.

Carey-Wood, J (1997) *Meeting Refugees' Needs in Britain: The Role of Refugee-Specific Initiatives.* Home Office, London.

Carr-Hill, R, Passingham, S, Wolf, A and Kent, N (1996) *Lost Opportunities: The Language Skills of Linguistic Minorities in England and Wales.* Basic Skills Agency, London.

Clyne, P (2006) *Russell and After: The Politics of Adult Learning, 1969–97.* NIACE, Leicester.

Cogill, S (1980) *Writing Business Letters and Memos.* NCILT, London.

Cogill, S (1982) *Personal Business Letters.* NCILT, London.

Cogill, S and Gubbay, D (1978) *Materials and Lesson Plans for an Advanced Intensive English Language Course for Women in the Community.* NCILT, London.

Commission for Racial Equality (CRE) (1977) (1981) *Home Tutor Kit.* CRE, London.

Commission for Racial Equality (CRE) (1978a) *Between Two Cultures: A Study of Relationships between Generations in the Asian Community in Britain.* CRE, London.

Commission for Racial Equality (CRE) (1978b) *Five Views of Multi-Racial Britain.* BBC Publications, London.

Commission for Racial Equality (CRE) (1980) *Youth in Multi-racial Society: The Urgent Need for New Policies. 'The Fire Next Time'.* CRE, London.

Commission for Racial Equality (CRE) (1982) *Further Education in a Multi-Racial Society: A Policy Report.* CRE, London.

Commission for Racial Equality (CRE) (1986) *Teaching English as a Second Language: Report of a Formal Investigation by the Commission* for Racial Equality into the Teaching of English as a Second Language in Calderdale Local Education Authority. CRE, London.

Community Relations Commission (CRC) (1974) *Language Teaching Schemes in England and Scotland*. CRC, London.

Community Relations Commission (CRC) (1976a) *Language Teaching Schemes in Britain*. CRC, London.

Community Relations Commission (CRC) (1976b) *A Second Chance. Further Education in Multi-Racial Areas*. CRC, London.

Community Relations Commission (CRC) (1977) *Industrial Training Boards and Race Relations: A Discussion Paper*. CRC, London.

Cooke, A (2006) *From Popular Enlightenment to Lifelong Learning: A History of Adult Education in Scotland, 1707–2005*. NIACE, Leicester.

Council of Europe (1983a) *The Coventry Community Education Project* (CDCC Project no 7): *The Education and Cultural Development of Migrants*. Council for Cultural Co-operation, Strasburg.

Council of Europe (1983b) *Adult Education in the Inner London Education Authority*, a case study. Council for Cultural Co-operation, Strasbourg.

Craigie, W A (1917) *The Pronunciation of English reduced to Rules by Means of a System of Marks applied to the Ordinary Spelling*. Clarendon Press, Oxford.

Crispin, A and Hibberd, P (1987) *Education Funding for Ethnic Minorities: A Case Study of Section 11 of 1966 Local Government Act*. University of London Institute of Education /Economic and Social Science Research Council, London.

Croydon English Language Scheme (1987–) *Our Lives*. Croydon English Language Scheme.

de Chaumont, M (1941) *I Want to Learn English*. Hachette, London.

de la Motte, F, Fraser, H, Greatbanks, M, Rees, S and Slater, A (1980) *Lessons from the Vietnamese*. NEC, Cambridge.

Deakin, N (1970) *Colour, Class and British Citizenship. An abridged and updated version of the report by E J B Rose*, 1969. Panther, London.

Department for Education and Employment (DfEE) (1998) *Education for Citizenship and the Teaching of Democracy in Schools* DfEE/ Qualifications and Curriculum Authority, London.

Department for Education and Employment (DfEE) (1999) *Improving Literacy and Numeracy: A Fresh Start. The report of the Working Group chaired by Sir Claus Moser*. DfEE, London.

Department for Education and Employment (DfEE) (2000) *Breaking the Language Barriers. The report of the Working Group on English for Speakers of Other Languages (ESOL).* DfEE, London.

Department for Education and Employment (DfEE) (2001) *Skills for Life: The National Strategy for improving Adult Literacy and Numeracy Skills.* DfEE, London.

Department for Education and Science (DES) (1965) *Circular 7/65: The Education of Immigrants.* DES, London.

Department for Education and Science (DES) (1971) *The Education of Immigrants. Education Survey no 13.* HMSO, London.

Department for Education and Science (DES) (1973) *Adult Education: A Plan for Development. Report by a Committee of Inquiry appointed by the Secretary of State for Education and Science under the chairmanship of Sir Lionel Russell.* HMSO, London.

Department for Education and Science (DfES) (1975) *A Language for Life. Report of the Committee of Inquiry appointed by the Secretary of State for Education and Science under the chairmanship of Sir Alan Bullock.* HMSO, London.

Department for Education and Skills (DfES) (2001a) *Adult Literacy Core Curriculum.* DfES, London.

Department for Education and Skills (DfES) (2001b) *Adult ESOL Core Curriculum.* DfES, London.

Department for Education and Skills (DfES) (2002) *Subject Specifications for Teachers of English for Speakers of Other Languages (ESOL).* DfES and FENTO, London.

Department for Education and Skills (DfES) (2003a) *Pathways to Proficiency: The Alignment of Language Proficiency Scales for Assessing Competence in English Language.* DfES, London.

Department for Education and Skills (DfES) (2003b) *The Skills for Life Survey: A National Needs and Impact Survey of Literacy, Numeracy and ICT Skills.* DfES, London.

Department for Education and Skills (DfES) (2004) *Skills for Life: ESOL Exemplars.* DfES, London.

Department for Work and Pensions (DWP) (2004) *Equality, Opportunity, Success: Year 1 Progress Report.* Ethnic Minority Employment Task Force, DWP, London.

Department for Work and Pensions (2006) *Barriers to Employment for Pakistanis and Bangladeshis in Britain*, Research Report no 360. Corporate Document Services, London.

Derrick, J (1966) *Teaching English to Immigrants*. Longmans, London.

Devereux, W (1982) *Adult Education in Inner London, 1870–1980*. Shepheard-Walwyn/Inner London Education Authority.

Donaldson, F (1984) *The British Council: The First Fifty Years*. Jonathan Cape, London.

Douglas, R W (1920) *English for Foreigners: An Elementary Manual*. Hachette, London.

Dove, R (1995) 'The Gift of Tongues: German-Speaking Novelists writing in English', in W Abbey *et al.* (eds), *Between Two Languages*. Verlag Hans-Dieter Heinz, Stuttgart pp 95–115.

Dummett, A (1973) *A Portrait of English Racism*. Penguin Books, Harmondsworth.

Eckersely, C E (1938–42) *Essential English: A Progressive Course for Foreign Students*, 4 books. Longmans & Co, London.

Eckersely, C E (1942) *English for the Allies*, Book 1. Longmans & Co, London.

Eckersely, C E (1943) *English for the Allies*, Book 2. Longmans & Co, London.

Eggleston, J (1986) *Education for Some: the Educational and Vocational Experiences of 15–18 year old Members of Minority Ethnic Groups. Report on a research project for the Department of Education and Science directed by Professor John Eggleston*. Trentham Press, Stoke on Trent.

Elsdon, K *et al.* (2001) *An Education for the People? A History of HMI and Lifelong Learning, 1944–1992*. NIACE, Leicester.

Faucett, L W (1933–39) *The Oxford English Course*. Oxford University Press.

Further Education Unit (FEU) (1986) *Language for All: An Analysis of the Importance of Language in Post-16 Education*. FEU, London.

Further Education Unit (FEU) (1987) *FE in Black and White: Staff Development Needs in a Multi-Cultural Society*. FEU/Longman, London.

Further Education Unit (FEU)/NATECLA (1989) *Language in Education: Guidelines and Checklists for Institutional and Curricular Development in English for Speakers of Other Languages and Language Support*. NATECLA/FEU, London.

Flint, G (1969) 'Immigrant Teenagers in Further Education'. *Technical Journal* [organ of the Association of Teachers in Technical Institutions], June, pp 17–18.

Freeman, W (1939) *English for Foreigners*. J M Dent & Sons, London.

Furnborough, P, Cogill, S, Greaves, H and Sapin, K (1980) *A New Start.* Heinemann, London.

Further Education Funding Council (FEFC) (1995) *Annual Report for 1994–5.* FEFC, Coventry.

Further Education Funding Council (FEFC) (1996) *Annual Report for 1995–6.* FEFC, Coventry.

Further Education Funding Council (FEFC) (1998) *Curriculum Area Survey Report: Basic Education.* FEFC, Coventry.

Further Education Funding Council (FEFC) (1999) *Basic Education: Report from the Inspectorate 1998–99.* FEFC, Coventry.

Gartner Lloyd, P (2001) *The Jewish Immigrant in England, 1870–1914.* Vallentine Mitchell, London.

Gershon, K (ed) (1989) *We Came as Children: A Collective Autobiography.* Macmillan, London.

Goldwasser, I E and Jablonower, J (1916) *Yiddish–English Lessons.* D. C. Heath & Co, Lexington, Mass.

Gordon, W T (1990) *C K Ogden: A Bio-bibliographic Study.* Scarecrow Press, London.

Graddol, D (2006) *English Next.* British Council, London.

Grant, R and Self, E (eds) (1984) *'Can You Speak English?' A History of Neighbourhood English Classes.* Neighbourhood English Classes, London.

Greater London Authority (GLA) (2006) *A Profile of Londoners by Language: An Analysis of Labour Force Survey Data on First Language.* GLA, London.

Gregory, E and Williams, A (2000) *City Literacies: Learning to Read across Generations and Cultures.* Routledge, London.

Grief, S, Murphy, H, Nijjar, B and Taylor, C (2002) *Opening up a New World: A Good Practice Guide for Delivering Basic Skills and ESOL in the Local Community.* NIACE, Leicester.

Griffiths D (2003) *English Language Training for Refugees in London and the Regions,* Online Report 14/03. Home Office, London.

Griffiths, P and Leonard, M (eds) (2002) *Reclaiming Britishness: Living Together after 11 September and the Rise of the Right.* Foreign Policy Centre, London.

Gubbay, D (1977) *Teaching English at Home: A 'Worktalk' Film. Discussion notes for tutors and organisers of language teaching schemes.* BBC Publications, London.

Gubbay, D (1978/79) *The Teaching of Communication Skills through the Use of*

Role Play to Speakers of English as a Second Language. NCILT, London.

Gubbay, D (1980) *Role-play: The Theory and Practice of a Method for Increasing Language Awareness.* NCILT, London.

Gubbay D and Cogill, S (1980) *Speak for Yourself.* BBC Publications, London.

Gumperz, J J, Jupp, T C and Robert, C (1979) *Crosstalk: A Study of Cross-Cultural Communication. Background materials and notes to accompany the BBC film.* NCILT, London.

Hamilton, M and Hillier, Y (2006) *Changing Faces of Adult Literacy, Language and Numeracy: A Critical History.* Trentham Press, Stoke on Trent.

Harefields English Language Project (n.d.) *HELP Maternity Language Course.* HELP, Leeds.

Hawkins, T H and Brimble, L J F (1947) *Adult Education: The Record of the British Army.* Macmillan, London.

Hayes, S (1984) *Drama as a Second Language.* NEC, Cambridge.

Henderson, D (ed) (2001) *The Lion and the Eagle: Reminiscences of Polish Second World War Veterans in Scotland.* Cualann Press, Dunfermline.

Henley, A (1979) *Asian Patients in Hospitals and at Home.* King Edward's Hospital Fund for London.

HM Treasury (2006) *Prosperity for All in the Global Economy: World Class Skills* (Leitch Report). HMSO, London.

HMI (1990) *Education Provision for Ethnic Minority Adults in the London Borough of Croydon.* DES, London.

HMI (1991) *Bilingual Adults in Education and Training, September 1990–April 1991,* Ref 7/92/NS. DES, London.

Hodlin, S, Jupp, T C and Laird, H M R (1974) *English in the Laundry.* Kings Fund Centre, London.

Home Office (1988) *A Scrutiny of Grants under Section 11 of the Local Government Act 1966: Final Report.* Home Office, London

Home Office (2001) *Community Cohesion: A Report of the Independent Review Team Chaired by Ted Cantle* (Cantle Report). Home Office, London.

Home Office (2002) *Secure Borders, Safe Havens: Integration with Diversity, presented to Parliament by the Secretary of State for the Home Department,* White Paper. Home Office, London.

Home Office (2003) *The New and the Old: The Report of the 'Life in the United Kingdom' Advisory Group* (Crick Report). Home Office, London.

Hospitalier, E (1900) *Technical, Industrial, Commercial English, French and German Vocabulary*. L'Industrie electrique (Paris).

Hornby, A S (1954–6) *Oxford Progressive English for Adult Learners*, vols 1–3. Oxford University Press, London.

Hornby, A S (1964) *Oxford Progressive English: Alternative Course*. Oxford University Press, London.

Howatt, A P R and Widdowson, H G (2004) *A History of English Language Teaching*. Oxford University Press.

ILEA (1973a) *Review of Vocational, Further and Higher Education: Report by the Education Officer*. ILEA, London, May.

ILEA (1973b) *An Education Service for the Whole Community*. ILEA, London, November.

ILEA (1978–9) *At Work, Telephone and Newspaper Packs*. ILEA, London.

ILEA (1980a) *At Home in Britain* (4 packs) NEC, London.

ILEA(1980b) *Training the Trainers: Ideas for Training Volunteers in English as a Second Language*. ESL Publishing Group, London.

ILEA (1982) *Mother Tongue and ESL*. ESL Publishing Group, London.

ILEA (1983) *Linked Skills: A Handbook for Skills and ESL Tutors*. ILEA Language and Literacy Unit/NEC, London.

ILEA (1984–86) Collections of student writing all published by the ILEA ESL Publishing Group: (1984) Vol 1, *Festivals, Folktales and Stories*; (1985) Vol 2, *Family and Friends*; (1985) Vol 3, *Changes*; (1986) Vol 4, *More Festivals and Folk Tales*; (n.d.) Vol. 5, *Refugee Writings*.

ILEA (1986) *ESL and Unemployment*. ESL Publishing Group, London.

ILEA (1990) *Language and Power*, Afro-Caribbean Language and Literacy Project. Harcourt Brace Jovanovich, London.

Jacobs, J and Landau, H (1893) *Yiddish–English Manual Compiled for the English Evening Classes Committee in Connection with the Russo-Jewish Community*. E W Rabbinowitz, London.

Janssen, A (1992) *A Study of the Education and Training Opportunities Available to Bilingual Learners in the Post-16 Sector*. MA thesis, Kings College London.

Jaworzyn, J F (1984) *No Place to Land*. Kimber, London.

Johnson, J (1989) *Help Yourself to English*. NEC, Cambridge.

Jordanhill College (1979) *English as a Second Language for Adults in the Glasgow Area*. Jordanhill College of Education with the Co-operation of Strathclyde Community Relations Council, Glasgow.

Jubelin, A (1953) *Flying Sailor*, trans. J Cleugh. Hurst & Blackett, London.

Jupp, T (1981) *Language Disadvantage and Ethnic Minorities*, Occasional Paper. NCILT, London.

Jupp, T and Davies, E (1974) *The Background and Employment of Asian Immigrants*. Runnymede Trust, London.

Jupp, T and Hodlin, S (1975) *Industrial English: An Example of Theory and Practice in Functional Language Teaching*. Heinemann, London.

Kennedy, H (1997) *Learning Works. Widening Participation in Further Education* Further Education Funding Council, Coventry.

Khan, S and Pearn, M (1977) *Worktalk Manual*. Runnymede Trust, London.

Khanna, A L, Verma, M K, Agnihotri, R K and Sinha, S K (1998) *Adult ESOL Learners in Britain: A Cross-Cultural Study*. Multilingual Matters, Clevedon.

Kirk, R (2004) *Skills Audit of Refugees*. Online Report 37/04, Home Office, London.

KPMG (2005) *KPMG Review of English for Speakers of Other Languages for the Department of Education and Skills for Life Strategy Unit and the Learning and Skills Council*. DfES/LSC, London.

Kuepper, G, Lackey, G L and Swinnerton, E N (1975) *Ugandan Asians in Great Britain: Forced Migration and Social Absorption*. Croom Helm, London.

Kundnani, A (2002) 'The Death of Multiculturalism', *Independent Race and Refugee News Network* (online): http://.www.irr.org .uk/2002/april/ak000001.html

Kushner, T (1999) 'Local Heroes: Belgian Refugees in Britain during the First World War'. *Immigrants and Minorities*, 18.1. Frank Cass, London, pp 1–28.

Kushner, T (2000) 'Do Not Give Flowers to Me: Refugees, Language and Power in the Twentieth Century', in A Kershen (ed), *Language: Labour and Migration*. Ashgate Press, Ashford, Kent, pp 39–56.

Kushner, T and Knox, K (2001) *Refugees in an Age of Genocide*. Frank Cass, London (first published 1999).

Ladbury, S (1980) *Cypriots in Britain*. NCILT, London.

Laird, E (1977) *English for Catering Staff*, parts 1 and 2. Pathway Centre and Kings Fund Centre, London.

Lambermont, P (1956) *Lorraine Squadron*, trans. A Pirie. Cassell & Co, London.

Language and Literacy Unit (LLU) (1995) *Working with the Criteria for the Assessment of English Language Skills: Examples of Current Practice.* LLU, London.

Leach, R (1980) *Coping with the System* NEC, Cambridge .

Leach, R (1983) *Communicating with the System.* NEC, Cambridge.

Leach, R (1985,1992) *Making, Using and Adapting Materials.* NEC, Cambridge.

Legarrata, D (1984) *The Guernica Generation: Basque Refugee Children of the Spanish Civil War* University of Nevada Press, Reno.

Leslie, D and Lindley, J (2001) 'The Impact of Language Ability on Employment and Earnings of Britain's Ethnic Minority Communities', *Economica*, vol 68, pp 587–606.

Lewis, C, Love, D and Sidhu, J (1981) *First Language Support in an ESL Classroom.* NCILT, London.

Linguistic Minorities Project (1985) *The Other Languages of England.* Routledge & Kegan Paul, London.

Lipman, V D (1954) *A Social History of the Jews in England, 1850–1950.* Watts & Co, London.

Littlewood, W (1881) *Communicative Language Teaching: An Introduction.* Cambridge University Press.

Livshin, R (1989) 'The Acculturation of the Children of Immigrant Jews in Manchester, 1890–1930', in D Cesarani (ed), *The Making of Modern Jewry.* Basil Blackwell, Oxford, pp 79–96.

London County Council (LCC) (1912) *Eight Years of Technical Education and Continuation Schools.* LCC, London.

London Skills Commission (2005) *Developing a Three Year Strategic Action Plan for Skills for Life in London: Summary of Evidence and Recommendations for ESOL.* JH Consulting, London.

London Skills Commission (2006) 'The Three Year Strategic Action Plan for ESOL in London', in *The London Skills for Life Strategy.* JH Consulting, London.

Looms, S (1986a) *English for Business.* NEC, Cambridge.

Looms, S (1986b) *You and Your Business.* NEC, Cambridge.

Malet, M and Grenville, A (eds) (2002) *Changing Countries: The Experience and Achievement of German-speaking Exiles from Hitler in Britain from 1933 to Today.* Libris, London.

Mallows, D (2007) *Insights: What Research Can Tell us about ESOL: Review of NRDC Studies on English for Speakers of Other Languages.* NRDC, London; 2nd edn forthcoming.

Mares, P (1982) *The Vietnamese in Britain: A Handbook for Health Workers.* Health Education Council/NEC, Cambridge.

Marshall, E C and Schaap, E (1914) *A Manual of English for Foreign Students.* Hachette, London.

Marshall, E C and Schaap, E (1955) *A Concise Manual of English for Foreign Students,* [revised and condensed version of their 1914 work]. Hachette, London.

Matheson, P and Weir, J (1989) *Language Matters? Teaching English as a Second Language ands Other Community Languages to Adults. Provision in Scotland: An Initial Survey.* NATECLA, Scotland, Edinburgh.

McAllister, J and Robson, M (1984) *Building a Framework: Developing Communication Skills with ESL Students.* NEC, Cambridge.

Milton Keynes Language Scheme (n.d.) *The New Baby.* Milton Keynes Language Scheme.

Ministry of Education (1963) *English for Immigrants,* Pamphlet 43. Ministry of Education, London.

Ministry of Health (1920) *Report on the Work Undertaken by the British Government in the Reception and Care of the Belgian Refugees.* HMSO, London.

Mobbs, M (1977) *Meeting their Needs: An Account of Language Tuition Schemes for Ethnic Minority Women.* Community Relations Commission, London.

Modood, T (1997) 'Qualifications and English Language', in T Modood and R Berthoud (eds), *Ethnic Minorities in Britain: Diversity and Disadvantage.* Policy Studies Institute, London, pp 60–82.

Modood, T, Berthoud, R *et al.* (1997) *Ethnic Minorities in Britain: Diversity and Disadvantage, Fourth National Survey of Ethnic Minorities.* Policy Studies Institute, London.

Morpeth, R and Lo, J (1985) 'English for Driving', *Programmed Learning and Educational Technology,* 22.4, pp 334–42.

Moss, M and Southwood, S (2006) *E-Learning for Teaching English for Speakers of Other Languages.* NIACE, Leicester.

Myers, S and Ramsay, E (1936) *London Men and Women: An Account of Men's and Women's Institutes.* British Institute of Adult Education, London.

NATESLA (1979) *Catalogue of Resources.* NATESLA, London.

NATESLA (1981a) *Catalogue of Resources* and *Supplement.* NATESLA, London.

NATESLA (1981b) *English as a Second Language: Teaching for Adults from*

Ethnic Minorities. Report of a NATESLA survey carried out between January 1980 and January 1981. NATESLA, London.

NATESLA (1982) *ESL Provision for the 16–19(+) Age Group in Further Education and Adult/Community Education,* submission to the Swann Committee of Inquiry. Occasional Paper no 2. NATESLA, London.

NATESLA (1985) *Research Project into Training of Teachers of English as a Second Language in the Post-16 Sector: Report.* NATESLA, London.

National Foundation for Education Research (NFER) (1992) *Go to Work on Your English.* NEC, Cambridge.

National Institute of Adult Continuing Education (NIACE) (2006a) *'More than a Language…'? NIACE Committee of Inquiry on English for Speakers of Other Languages, Final Report.* NIACE, Leicester.

National Institute of Adult Continuing Education (NIACE) (2006b) *Citizenship Materials for ESOL Learners in Northern Ireland.* NIACE, Leicester, for the DfES and Home Office.

National Institute of Adult Continuing Education (NIACE) (2007) *Citizenship Materials for ESOL Learners in Wales.* NIACE, Leicester, and NIACE dysgu cymru for the DfES and Home Office.

National Institute of Adult Continuing Education (NIACE) and LLU+ (2005) *Citizenship Materials for ESOL Learners.* NIACE, Leicester, for DfES and Home Office.

National Institute of Adult Continuing Education (NIACE) and LLU+ (2006) *Citizenship Materials for ESOL Learners in Scotland, with contributions from the Scottish Qualifications Authority.* NIACE, Leicester, for DfES, Home Office and Scottish Executive.

National Research and Development Centre (NRDC) (2007) *Effective Teaching and Learning: ESOL. Summary Report.* NRDC, London.

National Union of Teachers (NUT) (1978) *Section 11: An NUT Report.* NUT, London.

Nesfield, J C (1898) *Manual of English Grammar and Composition.* Macmillan, London.

Nicholls, S and Arora, R (1977) *The Parosi Tutor's Handbook: An Introduction to Teaching English at Home.* BBC Publications, London.

Nicholls, S and Hoadley-Maidment, E (eds) (1988) *Current Issues in Teaching English as a Second Language.* Edward Arnold, London.

Nicholls, S and Naish, J (1981) *Teaching English as a Second Language.* BBC Publications, London.

Noblet, A (1943) *French–English, English–French Dictionary of Technical Military Terms.* Crosby, Lockwood & Son, London.

Northern Ireland Government (2005) *A Skills Strategy for Northern Ireland: Summary of Consultation Responses.* Department for Employment and Learning, Belfast.

Nottingham Language Scheme (NLS) (n.d.) *The Forest Readers.* NLS, Nottingham.

Ofsted (1993) *Section 11 and Further Education for Adults.* Ofsted, London.

Ofsted (1994) *Educational Support for Minority Ethnic Communities.* Ofsted, London.

Ofsted (2000) *Hackney and Islington 16–19 Area-Wide Inspection,* HMR 129/00/AW. Ofsted, London.

Ofsted (2003) *Literacy, Numeracy and English for Speakers of Other Languages: A Survey of Current Practice in post-16 and Adult Provision,* Joint OFSTED and ALI Report HMI 1367. Ofsted, London.

Ofsted (2005) *Skills for Life in Colleges: One Year On.* Ofsted, London.

Ogden, C K (1932) *Basic English,* 3rd edn. Kegan Paul, London.

Ogden, C K (1935) *Basic Step by Step.* Kegan Paul, Trench & Trubner, London.

Ogden, C K (1939) *Le Basic English en 30 leçons graduées.* Basic English Publishing Co, Cambridge.

Ogden, C K (1941a) *Basic English for Norwegian Students.* Evans Brothers, London.

Ogden, C K (1941b) *Basic English for Dutch Students.* Evans Brothers, London.

Ogden, C K (1941c) *Basic English for Polish Students.* Evans Brothers, London.

Ogden, C K (1942a) *Basic English for Dutch and Flemish Students.* Evans Brothers, London.

Ogden, C K (1942b) *Basic English for Czecho-Slovak Students* Evans Brothers, London.

Opienski, J (1973) *English Language Assessment Interviews for Hospital Ancillary Staff.* Kings Fund Centre, London.

Organisation for Economic Co-operation and Development (OECD) (1997) *Literacy Skills for the Knowledge Society: Further Results from the International Adult Literacy Survey.* OECD, Paris.

Palmer, H E (1921) *The Oral Method of Language Teaching.* W. Heffer & Sons, Cambridge.

Palmer, H E (1922) *Everyday Sentences in Spoken English.* W. Heffer & Sons, Cambridge.

300

Palmer, H E (1924) *A Grammar of Spoken English on a Strictly Phonetic Basis*. W. Heffer & Sons, Cambridge.

Palmer, H E (1938) A *New Method Grammar* Longmans Green & Co, London.

Palmer, H E, with Harman, H A (1940) *Teaching English to Soldiers.* Longmans & Co, London.

Palmer, H E, with Hornby, A S (1937) *One Thousand Word English.* George Harrap & Co, London.

Pelican, F (1993) *From Dachau to Dunkirk.* Vallentine Mitchell, London.

Potter, F F (1918) *English for Technical Students.* Isaac Pitman & Sons, London.

Potter, S (1927) *Everyday English for Foreign Students.* Isaac Pitman & Sons, London.

Potter, S (1930) *An English Vocabulary for Foreign Students.* Isaac Pitman & Sons, London.

Potter, S (1932) *An English Grammar for Foreign Students.* Isaac Pitman & Sons, London.

Proudfoot, M J (1957) *European Refugees 1939–52.* Faber & Faber, London.

Quinault, R J (1947) 'English by Radio', *English Language Teaching*: I.5, March 1947, pp 119–25; III. 2, October 1948, pp 47–52.

Rees, S and Sunderland, H (1990) *Not Meeting the Demand? A Report of Research into Waiting Lists, Fees and Provision in ESOL in London.* Language and Literacy Unit, London.

Refugee Council (2002) *Credit to the Nation Refugee Council*, London.

Rhodes-Wood, E H (1960) *A War History of the Royal Pioneer Corps.* Gale & Polden, Aldershot, Hants.

Rice, C, McGregor, N, Thomson, H and Udagawa, H (2005) *National 'English for Speakers of Other Languages' Strategy [ESOL]: Mapping Exercise and Scoping Study.* Scottish Executive, Edinburgh.

Richards, J C and Rodgers, T S (2001) *Approaches and Methods in Language Teaching.* Cambridge University Press.

Richterich, R and Chancerel, J-L (1977) *Identifying the Needs of Adults Learning a Foreign Language.* Council of Europe, Strasbourg.

Ripman, C (1938) *Let's Talk English: Everyday Conversation for the Use of Foreigners.* J M Dent & Sons, London.

Ripman, W (1935) *An English Course for Adult Foreigners.* J M Dent & Sons, London.

Roberts, C (1977a) *Notes on the Sending Areas of Immigrants from Hong Kong.* NCILT, London.

Roberts, C (1977b) *Asians in Kenya and Tanzania, with Reference to Immigration in Britain.* NCILT, London.

Roberts, C (1988) 'Maps of Interaction for the Language Traveller', in S Nicholls and E Hoadley-Maidment (eds), *Current Issues in Teaching English as a Second Language to Adults*, pp 20–33. Edward Arnold, London.

Roberts, C, Baynham, M, Shrubshall, P, Barton, D, Chopra, P, Cooke, M, Hodge, R, Pitt, K, Schellekens, P, Wallace, C and Whitfield, S (2004) *English for Speakers of Other Languages [ESOL]: Case Studies of Provision, Learners' Needs and Resources.* NRDC, London.

Roberts, C, Davies, E and Jupp, T (1992) *Language and Discrimination: A Study of Communication in Multi-ethnic Workplaces.* Pearson Education, London.

Roberts, J T (*c* 1999) 'Two French Language Teaching Reformers Reassessed: Claude Marcel and Francois Gouin', *Studies in Linguistics and Semiotics,* vol 2. E Mellen, Lampeter/Lewiston, NY.

Robson, M (1987) *Language, Learning and Race: Developing Communication Skills for a Multi-cultural Society.* FEU/Longman, London.

Romijn, J (1976) *Ugandan Asians: The Old, the Weak, the Vulnerable.* London Council of Social Services.

Rose, E J B and associates (1969) *Colour and Citizenship: A Report on British Race Relations.* Institute of Race Relations/Oxford University Press.

Rosenberg, S *et al.* (1982) *Joint Committee for Refugees from Vietnam: English Language for Adults' Tutor Training Scheme April 1981–March 1982: Final Report.* Home Office, London.

Rosenberg, S (1988) 'Measuring Student Achievement: National Examination and Profile Assessment Schemes', in S Nicholls and E Hoadley-Maidment (eds), *Current Issues in Teaching English as a Second Language to Adults*, pp 137–46. Edward Arnold, London.

Rosenberg, S and Hallgarten, K (1985) 'The National Association for Teaching English as a Second Language to Adults (NATESLA): Its History and Its Work', in C Brumfitt (ed), *English as a Second Language in the United Kingdom*, ELT Document no 121, pp 131–9. Pergamon Press, Oxford.

Rosenberg, S (2006) 'NATECLA's Role in the History of ESOL', *Language Issues,* 18.1, pp 2–9.

Rudd, E (1971) *Pronunciation for Immigrant Children from India, Pakistan and Cyprus and Italy*, Scope Handbook 2. Schools Council, London.

Saggar, S (2002) 'Ethnic Minorities in the Labour Market', in P Griffiths and M Leonard (eds), *Reclaiming Britishness: Living Together after 11 September and the Rise of the Right*. Foreign Policy Centre, London, pp 78–90.

Sargant, F P and Anderson, J R L (1977) *C K Ogden: A Collective Memoir*. Elek Pemberton, London.

Sayers, P, George, T, Greenwood, S and Peterson, R (1979) *Signing Off: English for Adult Immigrants Seeking Work*. NCILT, London.

Scarman (Lord) (1981) *The Brixton Disorders, 10–12 April 1981: Report of an Inquiry by the Rt Hon the Lord Scarman OBE* (Scarman Report). HMSO, London.

Schaap, E and Paul, E L (1935) *A Modern English Reader*. Macmillan, London.

Schellekens, P (1996) *TEC Provision for English as a Second Language: Guidelines for Effective Practice*. DfEE, London.

Schellekens, P (2001) *English Language as a Barrier to Employment and Training: A Research Report*. DfES, London.

School Board for London (SBL) (1904) *Final Report of the School Board for London 1870–1904*. P S King & Son, London.

Schools Council Project in English for Immigrant Children: (Scope).
(1967a) *English for the Children of Immigrants*, Working Paper no 13. HMSO, London.
(1967b) *Scope 1*. Schools Council, London.
(1972) *Scope Senior Course*. Schools Council, London.
(1976) *Scope 2*. Schools Council, London.
(*See also* Butterworth and Kinnibrugh (1970); Rudd (1971).)

Schwab, I and Stone, J (1986) *Language Writing and Publishing Work with Afro-Caribbean Students*. ILEA Afro-Caribbean Language and Literacy Project in Adult and Further Education.

Scotland's Debt to Belgium: Belgian Refugees (1915) Meeting held in the City Chambers, Edinburgh (in BL).

Scottish Education Department (1975) *Adult Education: The Challenge of Change in Scotland* (Alexander Report). HMSO, London.

Scottish Executive (2005) *Adult ESOL Strategy for Scotland: Consultation Paper*. Enterprise, Transport and Lifelong Learning Department of the Scottish Executive, Edinburgh.

Scottish Executive (2006) *A Consultation on an Adult ESOL Strategy for*

Scotland: Analysis of Response. Enterprise, Transport and Lifelong Learning Department of the Scottish Executive, Edinburgh.

Scottish Executive (2007) *The Adult ESOL Strategy for Scotland.* Scottish Executive Enterprise, Transport and Lifelong Learning Department, Edinburgh.

Scottish Further Education Funding Council (SFEFC) (2001) Circular Letter no FE/51/2001. SFEFC, Edinburgh.

Shields, M and Wheatley Price, S (2002) 'The English Language Fluency and Occupational Success of Ethnic Minority Immigrant Men Living in English Metropolitan Areas', *Journal of Population Economics,* vol 15, pp 137–60.

Smith, D (1977) *Racial Disadvantage in Britain* (PEP Report). Penguin, Harmondsworth, Middx.

Smith, P (1996) *The Fourth National Survey of Ethnic Minorities: Technical Report.* Social and Community Planning Research Publications, London.

Spalding, T A (1900) *The Work of the London School Board.* P S King & Son, London.

Spiegel M and Sunderland H (2006) *Teaching Basic Literacy to Adult Learners.* LLU+, London.

Squire, L (1969) 'Training Immigrants within Industry', *Race Today,* vol 1, June, pp 39–40.

Sriskandarajah, D, Cooley, L and Reed, H (2005) *The Fiscal Contribution of Immigrants to the UK.* IPPR, London.

Stevens, A (1975) *The Dispossessed: German Refugees in Britain.* Barrie & Jenkins, London.

Sunderland, H (1991) *Still Not Meeting the Demand: Report of Research into ESOL and Language Support, Waiting Lists and Fees in FE and AE.* Language and Literacy Unit, London.

Sunderland, H (1992a) *ESOL Materials Database* Language and Literacy Unit, London.

Sunderland, H (1992b) *A Tutor's Guide to ESOL Materials for Adult Learners.* Language and Literacy Unit, London.

Swann (Lord) (1985). *Education for All: Report of the Committee of Inquiry into the Education of Children from Ethnic Minority Groups* (Swann Report). HMSO, London.

Taylor, A J P (1975) *English History 1914–1945.* Oxford University Press (first published 1965).

Thames Television (1979) *Our People.* Thames Television, London.

Thorley, W C (1910) *A Primer of English for Foreign Students*. Macmillan & Co, London.

Thorley, W C (1912) *Examples and Exercise in English for Foreign Students: Supplement to a Primer of English for Foreign Students*. Macmillan & Co, London.

Thorley, W C and Lewis, R T (1921) *Colloquial and Business English for Foreign Students*. Macmillan & Co, London.

Trim, J L (1978) *Some Possible Lines of Development for an Overall Structure for a European Unit/Credit Scheme for Foreign Language Learning by Adults*. Council of Europe, Strasburg.

Turner, M (1985) *Literacy Work with Bilingual Students: A Resource for Tutors*. ALBSU, London.

van Ek, J A (1975) *Systems Development in Adult Language Learning: The Threshold Level*. Council of Europe, Strasbourg.

Varlez, A (1917) *Les Belges en Exil*. Librairie Moderne, London.

Vincent, W O (1936) *A Textbook of English for Foreign Students*. Isaac Pitman & Sons, London.

Wales National Assembly (2001) *The National Basic Skills Strategy for Wales* BSA, London, for the National Assembly for Wales.

War Refugee Committee (1915) *Information of Interest for Belgian Refugees* (also in French and Flemish). WRC, London.

Ward Gordon, W S (1977) *Deciding What to Teach in English as a Second Language Lesson*. National Association for Multi-racial Education, Derby.

Ward, J (2007) *ESOL: The Context for the UK Today*. To be published by NIACE, Leicester.

Weir, C and Milanovic, M (2003) *Continuity and Innovation: Revising the Cambridge Proficiency in English Examination 1913–2002*, 'Studies in Language Testing' series, no 15. Cambridge University Press.

Welsh Assembly Government (2005) *Words Talk – Numbers Count: The Welsh Assembly Government's Strategy to Improve Basic Literacy and Numeracy in Wales*; replaces the *National Basic Skills Strategy for Wales*. National Assembly for Wales Circular 15/2005, Cardiff.

West, M (1926) *Bilingualism (with special reference to Bengal)*. Bureau of Education India, Calcutta.

West, M (1953) *A General Service List of English Words* (rev. and enlarged edn). Longmans, Green & Co, London.

White, J (2003) *Rothschild Buildings: Life in an East End Tenement Block, 1887–1920*. Pimlico Press, London.

Whitworth, W (ed) (2003) *Survival: Holocaust Survivors Tell their Story.* Quill/Aegis, Retford.

Wilkins, D A (1976) *National Syllabuses*, Oxford University Press.

Williams, R C (1969) 'The Training of Immigrant Workers', *Race Today*, vol 1, June, pp 41–3.

Wilson, A (1978) *Finding a Voice: Asian Women in Britain.* Virago Press, London.

Wilson, A and Naish, J (1979) *Asian Women Speak Out: A Reader.* NEC, Cambridge.

Winder, R (2004) *Bloody Foreigners: The Story of Immigration to Britain.* Abacus, London.

Windsor, V and Healey, C (2006) *Developing ESOL: Supporting Achievement.* NIACE, Leicester.

Wyatt, T and Roach, J (1947) 'The Examinations in English of the Cambridge University Local Examinations Syndicate', *English Language Teaching* I.5, March 1947, pp 125–6.

Youett, M (n.d.) *Keep My Name a Secret.* Coventry and Warwickshire Industrial Language Service, Coventry.

Zubrycki, J (1956) *Polish Immigrants in Britain: A Study of Adjustment.* Martinus Nijhoff, The Hague.

Unpublished material and sources

The National Archive for the British Council papers (cited in the text as BW)

The London Metropolitan Archive for the records of
> The School Board for London
> The London County Council
> The papers of the Board of Deputies of British Jews

The archives of the National Association of Teachers of English and other Community Languages (NATECLA) (not yet formally collected together and accessible)

Personal collection

Interviews

Index

Note: The titles of publications are given in *italics*. These are listed under the author(s) name, e.g. Barton, P, and Pitt, K, *Adult ESOL Pedagogy*, and by title followed by the author(s)' name(s) in brackets, e.g. *Adult ESOL Pedagogy* (Barton and Pitt)